The New York Times Correspondents' Choice

RESTAURANTS AND RECIPES FROM AROUND THE WORLD

Contributors

Raymond H. Anderson, David Binder, William Borders, Moshe Brilliant,
Stanley Carr, Peggy Durdin, Clyde H. Farnsworth, James Feron, Henry
Giniger, Steffen Gram, Richard Halloran, John L. Hess, Paul Hofmann,
Marvine Howe, Stephen Hughes, Thomas A. Johnson, Brendan Jones,
Jonathan Kandell, Paul D. Kemezis, Samuel Kim, M. A. Kislali, Ellen
Lentz, Anthony Lewis, Flora Lewis, Richard J. Litell, Victor Lusinchi,
Olav Maaland, H. J. Maidenberg, Wim Van Der Meulen, Mario S. Modiano,
Harrison E. Salisbury, Harold C. Schonberg, Richard Severo, Donald
H. Shapiro, Alvin Shuster, Hugh G. Smith, Raymond A. Sokolov, James P.
Sterba, Henry Tanner, Robert Trumbull, Alice Villadolid, Jay Walz,
Judith Weinraub, Alden Whitman

The New York Times Correspondents' Choice

RESTAURANTS AND RECIPES FROM AROUND THE WORLD

Edited by Lee Foster

Quadrangle / The New York Times Book Co.

Illustrations courtesy of The Picture Collection,
The New York Public Library

Book design by Rita Naughton

LIBRARY OF CONGRESS CATALOGING IN PUBLICATION DATA

The New York times correspondents' choice: restaurants
and recipes from around the world.

    1.   Restaurants, lunch rooms, etc.—Directories.
2. Cookery, International. I. Anderson, Raymond H.
II. Foster, Lee, 1922–   ed.
TX907.N46 1974   641.5'9   73–79911
ISBN 0–8129–0406–0

For Leslie and Laurie

CONTENTS

Acknowledgments

For their encouragement, kindness and help with this book, I am indebted to a number of people. Two who showed enthusiasm from the very outset and lent assistance at critical points are Max Frankel, Sunday Editor of *The New York Times*, and Al Marlens, formerly Travel Editor and now Week in Review Editor. They have my thanks. I also want to express my gratitude to Judy Miceli of *The Times*'s Travel Section for her invaluable aid in keeping tabs on and corresponding with contributors around the world. Among others to whom I am grateful are Herb Nagourney, Roger Jellinek, Zinaïda Alexi, Rebecca Sacks, and Alfred Imhoff of Quadrangle/The New York Times Book Company, Phyllis Goldblatt and Marie Courtney of *The Times*, Susan Friedland, Didi Ziffren, Adnan Ozaktas, and Linda Stewart. My special thanks to Mollie Webster, May Wong Trent and my wife, Leslie Foster, for their zeal and expertise in testing the recipes in this book. And, above all, my gratitude to those people without whom there could never have been a book at all—the restaurant owners, chefs, and correspondents whose contributions grace these pages.

—*Lee Foster*

A Word of Caution

As Abraham Cowley, the metaphysical poet, wrote in 1647, "The world's a scene of changes, and to be/Constant, in Nature were inconstancy." Or to put it in the plainer tongue of our day, everything is subject to change in the course of time, including restaurant prices. Moreover, kitchen personnel can change, and so can managements, and restaurants have occasionally been known to change their days and hours of operation, or to move to new locations, or even to go out of business altogether. So while great care has been exercised to assure the accuracy of all the information in this book, the wise diner-out abroad will still call ahead to make certain of a restaurant's address and hours and, if need be, its menu and price level. Phone numbers are given for each restaurant, and if it seems there may be a language problem, a hotel concierge or other native speaker can usually be found to make the call.

L. F.

Introduction

This book offers good dining abroad and good eating at home.

To begin with, it addresses itself to a question repeatedly asked by people traveling to unfamiliar foreign cities for business or pleasure: "What's a good restaurant to try?" The answers are supplied by *New York Times* correspondents and contributors, newsmen and women who really know their way around foreign lands. They recommend restaurants and tell why in reviews that are full of practical information, rich detail, revealing anecdote, and fascinating snippets of history and sociology.

What's more, in almost all cases the reviewers have been able to obtain one or more recipes from the recommended restaurants, which means that readers of this book do not have to travel abroad to partake of a global feast. They can savor chefs' specialties from around the world right in their own homes. Every recipe has been thoroughly tested and adapted, where necessary, to the American kitchen.

A small portion of the material in these pages—24 restaurant reviews, most in somewhat shorter form and all without recipes—previously appeared in the Travel Section of *The New York Times*, which comes out every Sunday under the watchful eye of *The Times*'s Sunday Editor, Max Frankel. He was quick to see the possibilities in this feature of a book that would combine restaurant write-ups by *Times* correspondents with recipes supplied by the restaurant owners and chefs. The original 24 reviews were updated and expanded; new reviews were ordered expressly for this book, and recipes were requested and obtained. Almost 100 restaurants are now discussed and nearly 150 recipes are provided.

You can start at the front of the book with Argentina, read about the Chaleco Colorado Restaurant in Buenos Aires and cook one of that establishment's specialties, *carbonada criolla*, a mélange of steak, vegetables, and (yes) peaches. Then proceed all the way through the alphabet to Yugoslavia, investigate the Riblji Restoran in Dubrovnik and learn how to prepare its cold lobster salad with cucumber pickles. In between, make the acquaintance of restaurants in Quito, Kyoto, Katmandu and Quebec, Lisbon, Leningrad, Lagos and London, Marrakesh and Mexico City, Paris and Peking, Palermo and Prague.

Not every city in the world is covered, nor even every country, for no news-gathering organization, not even *The New York Times*, has someone everywhere. And since everyone concerned with this book wanted it to be solely a *New York Times* book, because of the expertise of those who write for it and the paper's reputation for credibility, it was decided to limit its restaurant recommendations to localities where *The Times* had correspondents or with which *Times* people were intimately familiar. It was decided, too, right at the outset, that the book would have a strictly foreign flavor. In other words, there would be—and there are—no restaurants or recipes from the United States.

Naturally, then, the overwhelming majority of the restaurant reviews in these pages are by foreign correspondents of *The Times*, most by full-time correspondents, with a smaller number by part-timers. These latter are journalists working for papers or other news organizations abroad who cover stories for *The Times* or file memorandums when called upon by the home office or one of its bureaus. The relatively few reviews not by full- or part-time correspondents are by *Times* reporters, editors, and a *Times* columnist, all with expertise in various parts of the world, and even three correspondents' wives who are contributors to the paper in their own right.

All were given the same instructions for selecting a restaurant. Basically, it was to be a place they ate in themselves, liked, and would recommend to a friend. Hopefully, it would be the kind of place where local people ate, a restaurant which, if it catered to tourists, would not be completely overrun by them. What was sought was not necessarily the "best" restaurant in town in a standard guidebook sense, but rather a place that readers would do well to try because it promised authentic ambience, or haute cuisine, or typical peasant fare, or regional specialties, or one-of-a-kind dishes, or an unusual setting, or whatever, even in a few cases—too few, alas—the lure of ridiculously low prices. And each correspondent was asked to limit himself to one or two restaurants in each city, because it was his first choices that were wanted, not a grab bag of a dozen places.

The restaurant recommendations that came back were truly marvelous in their diversity, as each correspondent selected a place that he felt had something special about it, regardless of its fame or obscurity, the type of food it served, or the people who patronized it. Sometimes the restaurant chosen was indeed the "best" in town; sometimes it was offbeat and a bit out of the way. The choices range from temples of gastronomy in France where a couple can spend the better part of $50 for a lunch with appropriate wines to inns in Munich and Frankfurt that offer filling meals for a song. Such world-renowned eating places as the Hotel Sacher in Vienna are included, but in Jakarta the choice is that city's first buffet-style restaurant, a place with the wildly un-Indonesian name of Vic's Viking, and in Singapore the "restaurant" is no restaurant at all but a parking lot in the daytime and a collection of street stalls at night where a Westerner, wonderful to relate, can eat cheaply, deliciously, and—most important—safely. In Amsterdam one selection is a restaurant that specializes in traditional Dutch food, which seems to be increasingly hard to get in the Netherlands, but in Mexico City the choice is a place where the correspondent recommends, of all things, not *tacos* and *chiles rellenos* but pasta and pizza. Don't laugh, you'll find out why. If you do want sensational *chiles rellenos*, go to Cuernavaca.

Just as the restaurants chosen by the correspondents are often intriguing and sometimes surprising, so are the recipes. First of all, they do not necessarily reflect the cuisine of the country in which a restaurant is located although often, of course, they do. Furthermore, they do not necessarily reflect the classic way of making a particular dish, but rather the way a chef at a certain restaurant makes it, a dish he or the correspondent or both feel is noteworthy. Because the recipes were supplied by the chefs and restaurant owners themselves, they are not equally balanced between appetizers, soups, seafood, poultry, meats, and desserts, although each category is represented. The range is from the hautest of haute cuisine, with stock and sauce, wine and cream, down to a recipe for *Frankfurter Rippchen* that, aside from water, has but two ingredients—pork and butcher's brine, both of which you buy from the butcher. Finally, in the small number of instances where we could not obtain a recipe from a particular restaurant, or one that would work in the American kitchen, we simply let the restaurant review stand without a recipe. The sole exception is Singapore because it is a special case, its recommended "restaurant" being street stalls, so in Singapore three recipes have been given for typical street-stall dishes. By the same token, where we could get more than one recipe from a single restaurant, we did not hesitate to include more than one.

As noted earlier, all the recipes have been tested and adapted, where necessary, to the American kitchen. Hence the line in each to the effect that it is "based on" the recipe of a particular restaurant. Testing and adaptation were necessary for a number of reasons. First, even similar ingredients differ in different parts of the world. Cream and flour, for example, are often of a different consistency abroad than they are here, and adjustments have to be made. Second, restaurant equipment is different from home equipment—there are specialized utensils, broilers are much hotter, and so on—and consequently procedures and cooking times have to be adjusted. In addition, skilled chefs sometimes use less-than-precise terminology—"a fist-sized piece," for instance—and frequently they will say to make a fish fumet, or a veal stock, or a demiglace, or a mousseline sauce, or other more-or-less standard components of a dish without bothering to specify exactly how they themselves make it. Lastly, of course, cooking is an art rather than a mechanical procedure, and subject to all sorts of variables, so the same dish cooked from the same recipe with the same ingredients by the same methods will vary in appearance at home and in a restaurant. All the recipes in this book, however, were adapted with the utmost possible fidelity to the originals. Whenever it was felt that a deviation would have to be substantial, the recipe in question was simply omitted.

So now, spread before you on the pages of this book is a feast—one you can enjoy in the restaurants around the world to which the correspondents call your attention, or cook yourself and eat at home. Either way, and I hope it's both, the appropriate words seem to be be, "Bon appétit!"

—*Lee Foster*

The New York Times Correspondents' Choice

RESTAURANTS AND RECIPES FROM AROUND THE WORLD

Argentina

BUENOS AIRES

CHALECO COLORADO. In the oldest section of Buenos Aires, along the cobblestone alleyways and colonial buildings collectively called San Telmo, are some of this city's most interesting, colorful, and overlooked restaurants. Among them is the Chaleco Colorado. Its ambience recalls the 1840s, a period of Argentine history dominated by Juan Manuel de Rosas, the great caudillo and tyrannical president. The name *Chaleco Colorado*— it means "red vest"—was taken from the mode of dress affected by Rosas's followers. Banners, paintings, and other paraphernalia of the period form the restaurant's decor.

The food, typically Argentine, includes such dishes as *locro* (a stew made with ears of corn), *carbonada criolla* (a meat, vegetable, and fruit stew), *pollo con cebolla de verdeo al jerez* (chicken with scallions and sherry sauce) and, of course, when available, fine beef.

The entertainment is also first rate, featuring performances of melancholy nineteenth-century Argentine music, tangos, and boisterous and often humorous ballads inspired by Rosas's followers. The patrons are almost exclusively Argentine and their rapport and repartee with the singers adds to the warm atmosphere.

The Chaleco Colorado is at Cochabamba 267, a stone's throw from the old port section. For reservations phone 88-39-12. Dinner only is served, from 8 P.M. to 2 A.M., but the best time to arrive is about 10 P.M. Prices are in the $5 to $7 range, including a bottle from the well-stocked wine cellar.

—Jonathan Kandell

CARBONADA CRIOLLA

Based on the recipe of Chaleco Colorado, Buenos Aires

cooking oil
1 tomato, diced
½ green pepper, sliced
1 medium onion, coarsely chopped
black pepper
1 pound steak, cut into ½-inch cubes
1 pound potatoes, cooked and sliced
1 cup canned corn kernels, drained
1 ear of corn, cooked and cut into 4 pieces
3 peaches, peeled and sliced, or 1½ cups canned peach slices, drained
1 tablespoon or more sugar
1 pound sweet potatoes, cooked and sliced
1 cup pumpkin, or acorn, Hubbard, or other winter squash, cooked and cut
      into pieces
salt

1. Liberally cover the bottom of a large, heavy pot with oil and sauté the tomato, green pepper, and onion over low heat, stirring, until the onion is translucent.
2. Grind black pepper generously over the sautéed vegetables. Add the steak cubes and cook them until they are medium rare or medium.
3. Add the potatoes, corn kernels, corn on the cob, peaches, and a tablespoon or more of sugar according to the degree of sweetness desired. Stir gently and cook over a low flame until the vegetables and peaches are heated through.
4. Add the sweet potatoes and pumpkin or squash. Stir thoroughly but gently. Cook until heated through. Add salt and pepper to taste. Stir again and serve.

Yield: 4 servings

Australia

CANBERRA

BACCHUS TAVERN. For a capital with a sizable cosmopolitan community of diplomats and international journalists and a steady flow of official and unofficial visitors, Canberra is singularly short of distinguished eating places. Small wonder, then, that the Bacchus Tavern, a top-quality restaurant, was an immediate success when Theo Moulis and a now-deceased partner opened it in 1965 in the basement of an office building. On the stairs leading down to the dimly lit restaurant, which seats about 100 diners, one may rub elbows with an ambassador or two, several Australian cabinet ministers, or even the prime minister himself, a regular patron.

High-grade beef is featured, and there is also a wide selection of other meat dishes, chicken, and seafood. Standard favorites from the menu include *filet de boeuf medaillon,* with the host's special red wine sauce, and carpetbag steak (a tenderloin stuffed with oysters), which Australians love. Knowledgeable patrons may ask for specialties not on the daily menu, such as beef Westerman (marinated filet mignon with wine sauce in a pastry crust) or chicken Marie-Louise (chicken breast dipped in a crushed almond and bread crumb mixture and fried), both inventions of Mr. Moulis, who is head chef as well as proprietor.

The Bacchus is known for its extensive selection of Australian and European wines, displayed in a huge rack at the front of the restaurant. Patrons select from the rack instead of ordering from a wine list. Mr. Moulis also has a private cellar of vintage wines for the connoisseur. Diners less serious about their wines can skip both rack and cellar and simply order a house white or red by the glass or the carafe.

The Bacchus Tavern is on the "lower ground floor"—that is, the basement—of the City Mutual Building, Hobart Place, in the middle of Canberra's shopping section. It is handy to government buildings, the embassy neighborhood, Lake Burley Griffin, and such must-sees as the War Memorial Museum with its relics and dioramas depicting Australia's martial past. Lunch is served at the Bacchus Tavern from noon to 3 P.M. Monday through Friday, dinner from 6 P.M. to midnight Monday through Saturday. Reservations are advisable and can be made by calling 48-7939. Men are required to wear a coat and tie. Main course prices run about $6 for a porterhouse or New York cut steak. The average expenditure per person for food and wine is about $12 to $15. Tipping is light in Australia compared to American standards; 10 percent, rounded off upwards, is adequate.

—*Robert Trumbull*

BEEF WESTERMAN
Based on the recipe of the Bacchus Tavern, Canberra

Theo Moulis of the Bacchus Tavern created this dish for Sir Alan Westerman, head of the Australian Industry Development Corporation.

2 ½-pound filets mignon, about 1½ inches thick
½ cup red burgundy wine
½ teaspoon dried tarragon
1 tablespoon vegetable oil
2 tablespoons butter
salt
black pepper

SHORT PASTRY

1 cup all-purpose flour
¼ teaspoon salt
4 tablespoons butter
3 tablespoons water

SAUCE

1 teaspoon chopped shallots
1 tablespoon chopped parsley

1 clove garlic, minced
½ cup chopped mushrooms
2 tablespoons butter
1 tablespoon arrowroot or flour
½ cup beef stock (see page 95) or canned beef bouillon
1 teaspoon tomato paste
1 teaspoon dry sherry
dash of red burgundy wine

1. Marinate the meat for 2 hours in the burgundy, tarragon, and oil.
2. About an hour before assembling and cooking the dish, make the short pastry: Sift the flour and salt into a bowl. Add the butter and rub it with the flour between your fingers until the mixture resembles coarse bread crumbs. Add the water and blend quickly, knead, and press the dough firmly into a fairly smooth ball. Wrap and chill for about 1 hour.
3. Remove the meat from the marinade, pat it dry, and brown in a skillet in 2 tablespoons butter to desired degree of doneness. Remove the meat from the skillet and set aside.
4. Using the same skillet, make the sauce by sautéing the shallots, parsley, garlic, and mushrooms in 2 tablespoons butter until limp. Dissolve the arrowroot or flour in the stock and add to the skillet, along with the tomato paste, sherry, and a dash of burgundy. Simmer, stirring, until liquid has reduced and thickened. Place the meat in the sauce and simmer briefly to reduce further. Correct the seasoning.
5. Preheat oven to 425 degrees.
6. Divide the short pastry in half and roll out each piece to double the size of each filet. Place a filet mignon on each pastry round and top with half the sauce. Seal the filet and the sauce within the pastry; make sure it is sealed tightly so the sauce cannot escape. Place in a baking pan, seam side down. Prick the crust once on top. Bake until golden brown, about 15 minutes. Serve at once.

Yield: 2 servings

CHICKEN MARIE-LOUISE
Based on the recipe of the Bacchus Tavern, Canberra

When Theo Moulis, proprietor and head chef of the Bacchus Tavern, created this dish, his secretary jokingly suggested that he name it after her. Much to her delight, he did.

½ cup toasted fine bread crumbs
¼ cup crushed almonds
2 whole chicken breasts, skinned, boned, and lightly pounded
salt
black pepper
flour
2 eggs, beaten
1 banana, halved lengthwise, then halved again
2 slices pineapple
3 tablespoons butter
¼ cup vegetable oil

1. Combine the bread crumbs and almonds.
2. Sprinkle both side of the chicken breasts with salt and pepper, dredge with flour, dip in the beaten eggs, then coat with the bread crumb and almond mixture.
3. Dip the banana and pineapple in the beaten eggs, then roll in flour to coat.
4. In a skillet heat the butter and oil. When hot, add the chicken and fry slowly to light golden brown. Remove and keep warm. Then fry the banana and pineapple to a golden brown.
5. Serve the chicken garnished with banana and pineapple.

Yield: 2 servings

SYDNEY

DOYLE'S ON THE BEACH, WATSON'S BAY. Getting to this famous seafood restaurant on the beach is part of the fun. The trip by car or bus to Watson's Bay, seven miles from the heart of Sydney, passes through the posh "eastern suburbs" with one superb marine view after another. Best of all is the view from the restaurant itself, looking down the harbor to the city's towering skyline.

Doyle's at Watson's Bay has been on "the same spot since 1885," as the sign on the old frame building says. An overpowering Australian presence totally submerges the tourists on hand, who usually include a smattering of the celebrities in town.

When the weather is favorable, which is more often than not in sunny Sydney, a table outside on the terrace is recommended. Any evening, and all day on weekends, an engaging cross section of trendy Australian youth promenades to and from the popular bar of the adjacent Watson's Bay Hotel. Inside Doyle's old main building, where the decor recalls colonial Sydney of the 1880s, window tables are in demand. An adjunct of recent vintage is a beach pavilion, called Doyle's Fisherman's Wharf, with tables right over the water.

I prefer Doyle's at Watson's Bay to a sister restaurant at nearer Rose Bay because of the famous mussels in wine, a dish to begin with, listed on the menu as mussels à la Portuguese. Other favorites are Queensland mud crab, jewfish, and John Dory. All fish, served grilled or fried only, is caught the day you eat it. A couple of the young waitresses represent the fifth generation of the Doyle family in the seafood business.

Doyle's is at 11 Marine Parade, Watson's Bay. The phone number is 937-2007. The place is open from noon to 3 P.M. and 5:30 to 9:30 P.M. every · day except Christmas. Most main courses run from about $3.50 to $5.50. No bar, but patrons may bring their own wine or order through the waiter from the hotel next door, also a Doyle property. Australian wines are so popular that one seldom sees an imported brand being poured in the best Sydney restaurants. The waiter will suggest an appropriate "drop," or try the Australian beer, considered among the best—and strongest—in the world and preferred ice-cold by the Australians.

—*Robert Trumbull*

MUSSELS IN WINE

Based on the recipe of Doyle's on the Beach, Watson's Bay

3 dozen mussels in the shell
2 tablespoons butter
1 teaspoon chopped shallots
2 cloves garlic, minced
¼ cup chopped onions
1 bay leaf
2 cups dry white wine
1 cup water
½ cup heavy cream
salt

1. Scrub mussels well and remove beards.
2. Heat the butter in a medium-size heavy pot. Sauté the shallots, garlic, and onions until they are limp. Add the mussels, bay leaf, wine, and water and bring to a boil. Simmer for about 5 minutes or until all the mussels open. Discard any that do not open.
3. Add the cream, bring just to a boil, season with salt, and serve in soup bowls at once.

Yield: 2 to 4 servings

Austria

VIENNA

HOTEL SACHER RESTAURANT. This is a place that takes you back in time—back to when the Danube was really blue and Franz Josef was monarch of the Austro-Hungarian Empire. The Sacher epitomizes the phrase "elegant dining," for there are fresh flowers on every table, the napery gleams in its whiteness, and the cutlery and glassware are sparkling. And the chairs are plush and comfortable—to contain the serious eater who has obviously misplaced his calorie chart, if he ever had one.

Because the Sacher caters to a world clientele, the kitchen can meet a variety of national demands, even to bacon and eggs and steak and potatoes for the unadventuresome. But the kitchen's glories are its Austrian dishes and sauces. I recommend the schnitzels, delicate veal thinly sliced and breaded; the lean porks, roasted or in chops; the wursts; and the chicken dishes. The portions are copious and the prices tend to be large, too. Lunch costs about $10 a person, dinner rises to $15, and you can spend more if you have a French wine. Austrian wines tend to be sweet. The service is leisurely but efficient.

Any meal at the Sacher, as at most Viennese restaurants, is ritually topped with a torte or a pastry. At the Sacher, of course, it must be Sacher Torte, an incredibly rich chocolate cake with apricot jelly filling, the whole crowned *mit Schlag*. The *Schlag*, or whipped cream, is genuine cream and gorgeously whipped. Who can resist?

Lunch or dinner at the Sacher is best followed by a walk through down-

9

town Vienna. The walk will settle your meal while sharpening your appetite for yet another piece of Sacher Torte. The hotel is at 4 Philharmonikerstrasse, just across from the State Opera, a location so central that many of Vienna's most famous landmarks are less than a mile away. The phone number of the Sacher is 52-55-75, and in the busy season one is well advised to book a table.

—Alden Whitman

WIENER SCHNITZEL
Based on the recipe of the Hotel Sacher Restaurant, Vienna

4 veal scallops
4 tablespoons flour
1 egg, beaten
1 cup fresh bread crumbs
salt
black pepper
3 tablespoons lard or oil
parsley
lemon slices

1. Trim the veal scallops neatly, making a few incisions all around the edges. Pound well with a mallet or rolling pin until very thin.
2. Dip the veal first in the flour, shaking off the excess, then into the beaten egg, and finally into the bread crumbs. Do not press the crumbs down; just shake off the excess. Season with salt and pepper.
3. Fry the veal slices in hot lard or oil until golden brown on one side. Turn carefully and fry the other side.
4. Serve immediately, garnished with parsley and lemon slices.

Yield: 4 servings

RAHMSCHNITZEL
Based on the recipe of the Hotel Sacher Restaurant, Vienna

4 veal scallops
salt

½ cup flour
4 tablespoons butter
½ cup water
1 teaspoon chopped capers
1 teaspoon Dijon-type prepared mustard
paprika
black pepper
½ cup heavy cream
a few drops lemon juice

1. Trim the veal scallops neatly, making a few incisions all around the edges. Pound well with a mallet or rolling pin until very thin.
2. Rub the veal with salt and dust with flour. Fry in the butter until just golden brown. Lift out carefully and keep hot.
3. Scrape the pan, pour in the water, stir to mix with the scrapings, and add the chopped capers, mustard, paprika, and pepper. Bring to a boil.
4. Turn heat down and simmer for 3 minutes.
5. Stir in the cream and lemon juice.
6. Pour the sauce over the veal slices and serve immediately.

Yield: 4 servings

PAPRIKA BEEF
Based on the recipe of the Hotel Sacher Restaurant, Vienna

4 ½-pound top round steaks
salt
black pepper
2 tablespoons butter or shortening
1 cup chopped onion
1 cup water
1 tablespoon paprika
1 tablespoon flour
1 tablespoon tomato paste
1½ pounds potatoes, sliced
½ cup sour cream

1. Trim the beef and flatten slightly with a mallet or rolling pin. Rub with salt and pepper.
2. Melt the butter and fry the beef lightly on both sides. Remove the beef and place in an ovenproof dish or casserole.

3. Sauté the onions until brown in the same pan in which the beef was fried. Stir in the water. Add the paprika, flour, and tomato paste. Simmer for a few minutes, stirring constantly.
4. Pour the mixture over the beef and cover. Either simmer gently on top of the stove or braise in 325-degree oven for about 1 hour, or until the beef is tender.
5. Add potatoes to meat about 30 minutes before serving.
6. When ready to serve, stir in the sour cream; heat but do not bring to a boil. Season to taste.

Yield: 4 servings

ESTERHAZY ROAST
Based on the recipe of the Hotel Sacher Restaurant, Vienna

2 ½-pound top round steaks
salt
black pepper
paprika
2 tablespoons flour
4 slices bacon
1 tomato, quartered
1 onion, sliced
1 large carrot, sliced in strips
1 rib celery, sliced in strips
½ green pepper, sliced in strips
1 bay leaf
pinch each of dried thyme and marjoram
1 teaspoon sugar
water
sour cream

1. Trim the beef and flatten with a mallet or a rolling pin.
2. Sprinkle the meat with salt, pepper, and paprika. Dust lightly with flour.
3. Cover the bottom of a heavy saucepan with the bacon. Fry gently until melted fat covers the bottom of the pan. Then add the tomato, onion, carrot, celery, green pepper, bay leaf, thyme, and marjoram. Sprinkle with sugar and again with salt and pepper.
4. Cover and simmer gently without stirring until vegetables have softened a little, about 5 to 6 minutes. Remove the lid and cook the vegetables, still without stirring. Add a little water from time to time if the vegetables stick to the pan.

5. When the vegetables are nicely browned (about 10 minutes), put in the steaks and toss lightly with the vegetables. Cover again and simmer at a very low heat until both the meat and vegetables are tender, about 15 to 20 minutes, adding water again as necessary.

6. Arrange the steaks on a hot dish, dab a little sour cream on the vegetables, remove the bay leaf, stir well, and pour over the steaks. Serve piping hot.

Yield: 2 servings

Belgium

BRUSSELS

THE OGENBLIK. With utter precision restaurant after restaurant in Brussels turns out steak, mussels, and golden fried potatoes. The Ogenblik breaks the pattern and offers excellent food of a more challenging nature at moderate cost. The atmosphere is that of a Paris bistro—young, casually dressed waiters, marble-topped tables with low green-shaded lamps, high windows, and theater posters. The small two-level room is usually noisy and crowded, with local people far outnumbering tourists. Reservations are not accepted and a wait can be expected (go to the cafe across the street for a drink and place your order from there). The Ogenblik is in the famous Ilôt Sacré eating district which, besides wall to wall restaurants, offers the unique Toone puppets and open-air art and handicrafts dealers. The breathtaking Grand' Place is two blocks away.

The menu is handwritten and mimeographed in two colors every day. Purple for the permanent dishes and either green or red for the day's specialties (which depend on what looks good at the market). Most first courses—cheese soufflé, anchovies, snails in casserole—are always available. Among the permanent main courses is the house specialty, sole à l'Ogenblik (sole in a sauce of cream and herbs). There is also sole garnished with purslane, and there are steak dishes, including an outstanding roquefort steak.

Fish dishes dominate the day's specialties too—perhaps something in a creamed mushroom sauce, or fillet of St. Pierre (a delicately flavored fish also known as John Dory) in a cheese sauce on a bed of spinach. The specialty meats, leg of lamb and Flemish rabbit among them, are also well worth trying. The house moselle wine, served cold, is excellent with the fish, and there is a fine house beaujolais, too. The moselle runs about $3.50 a bottle, the beaujolais about $5, but for the house wines the policy is to pay not per bottle but for as much as you drink.

The Ogenblik is at 7 Galerie des Princes (facing Rue des Dominicains). The phone number is 11-61-51. A meal should cost around $6.50 to $8.50 a person with wine and service charge. You need not tip. The place is open every day but Sunday from 11:30 A.M. to 2:30 P.M. and 6 P.M. to 12:30 A.M.

—Paul D. Kemezis

FISH FILLETS WITH SPINACH AND CHEESE
Based on the recipe of the Ogenblik, Brussels

At the Ogenblik this dish is made with fillets of St. Pierre, but Chef Marc Leroy says the recipe can be used with sole, turbot, or almost any other white-fleshed fish.

COURT BOUILLON

fish heads and bones
1 cup dry white wine
4 cups water
1 sprig parsley
1 onion, quartered
1 teaspoon salt
pinch of sugar
6 peppercorns
1 bay leaf
pinch of dried thyme
1 slice of lemon

Combine all the ingredients in a saucepan. Bring to a boil, lower the heat, and simmer for 20 to 30 minutes. Strain.

NOTE: As a quick substitute for the court bouillon, combine ¾ cup dry white wine with enough water to barely cover the fillets; sharpen with a few drops of lemon juice.

SAUCE MORNAY

4 tablespoons butter
6 tablespoons flour
2 cups milk

(CONTINUED)

5 tablespoons grated gruyère cheese
2 tablespoons heavy cream
salt
black pepper
good pinch of freshly grated nutmeg

1. Melt the butter and blend in the flour. Remove from heat.
2. Slowly add the milk, blending until smooth.
3 Add the grated cheese and heavy cream.
4. Return to the heat and cook slowly, stirring constantly, until the sauce is thickened and smooth. Season with salt, pepper, and nutmeg.

FISH FILLETS AND ASSEMBLING

3 pounds spinach
2 pounds sole fillets or other white-fleshed fish
court bouillon
butter
sauce mornay
grated gruyère cheese to sprinkle atop fish

1. Preheat the oven to 350 degrees.
2. Prepare the spinach by removing the stems at the base of the leaves and discarding any wilted or yellow leaves. Plunge the spinach into a large bowl of cold water and wash well. Lift out into a colander, leaving any sand at the bottom of the bowl. Repeat the procedure until there is no sand left at the bottom of the bowl. Drain.
3. Fold the fillets in half lengthwise and lay them in a buttered baking dish. Barely cover with hot court bouillon. Place in the oven for about 3 minutes, or until fillets barely turn white. Keep the fillets warm in the broth out of the oven until needed.
4. Preheat the broiler.
5. Drop the spinach, a handful at a time, into boiling salted water. Bring quickly back to the boil and boil gently for 5 minutes. Pour the spinach into a colander and refresh under cold water for several minutes, to preserve color and texture. Squeeze the spinach in your hands, a small amount at a time, to extract as much water as possible.
6. Arrange the spinach as a bed on a buttered ovenproof serving dish.
7. Gently place the fish on the spinach. Cover with the sauce mornay, sprinkle cheese on top, and place under broiler until nicely brown.

Yield: 4 servings

Brazil

RIO DE JANEIRO

CHALÉ. Probably the most authentically indigenous eating places around Rio de Janeiro are the rowdy *churrascarias*, restaurants specializing in beef, but for a relaxed evening with colonial charm, there is the Chalé. Its specialty is Afro-Brazilian dishes from Bahia, the region that produces this vast country's best cuisine.

My personal preference is for the Chalé's exotic seafood concoctions— baked crab soufflé with coconut milk; *muqueca*, the Bahian bouillabaisse; and the very subtle *vatapá*, a creamy fish and shrimp dish served with a mush made of rice flour and coconut milk. Tasty meat dishes are also available. Everything should be washed down with white wine from Rio Grande do Sul or a *batida*, which is sugar cane brandy mixed with lemon, coconut, cashews, passion fruit, or just about anything.

The Chalé, in a handsome colonial home built in 1884, was formerly an antique shop and is still tastefully decorated with antiques and paintings by local artists. The waitresses are Bahian and wear what is called "sophisticated slave dresses"—in reality mini-midriffs. Jodiamar, known as Black John, strums a guitar and sings old Bahian classics and the latest sambas.

The Chalé is in the Botafogo district, a quiet part of town. The address is 54 Rua da Matriz. The telephone number is 246-4856. The cost of an average meal, including aperitif, wine, entree, and dessert, is about $7.50. The Chalé is open evenings from 7 P.M. to 1 A.M. or later. Brazilians generally amble in between 10 and 11, perhaps because earlier one risks running into a tour group.

—*Marvine Howe*

17

SHRIMP BAHIANA
Based on the recipe of Chalé, Rio de Janeiro

2 pounds unshelled shrimp
juice of 3 lemons
1 clove garlic, finely chopped
pinch of dried basil
1 tablespoon oil or lard
1 onion, chopped
3 tomatoes, peeled and chopped
2 tablespoons chopped parsley
1 teaspoon butter
1 teaspoon flour
½ cup coconut milk (if unavailable, substitute water)
salt
1 small hot pepper, finely sliced or 2 teaspoons hot pepper sauce

1. Marinate the shrimp for several hours in the lemon juice, garlic, and basil. Then shell them, devein, and drain.
2. Heat the oil or lard in a skillet and sauté the onion, tomatoes, and parsley for 2 minutes.
3. Add the marinated shrimp and cook for 3 minutes on a low fire until the shrimp are nearly done.
4. Heat the butter in a saucepan, add the flour and coconut milk or water. Simmer for a few minutes.
5. Pour this mixture over the shrimp and let simmer for a few more minutes, stirring all the time. Add salt and hot pepper. Serve with rice.

Yield: 6 to 8 servings

SÃO PAULO

CHURRASCARIA RUBAIYAT. In cosmopolitan São Paulo, Brazil's supermetropolis, the finest eating places are probably Italian, Japanese, or Lebanese. But you can be sure of authentic Brazilian atmosphere at one of the many *churrascarias*, or rotisseries. The best of these is the Churrascaria Rubaiyat.

The Rubaiyat is rustic in tone and supposed to be a vast hacienda, but various partitions skillfully laid out prevent the place from looking like a barn. Like any self-respecting *churrascaria*, the Rubaiyat is full of noise and movement, but its cowhide furniture is comfortable and its service excellent.

The barbecued beef is superb, which is not surprising since all the meat served at the restaurant comes from the Rubaiyat's own ranch, where the baby steers are ration-fed and pampered until they are 18 to 22 months old and ready for the table. But great as the beef is, the specialty of the house is something quite different—Brazil's incorrigable national dish, the *feijoada*, which is basically pork and beans with frills. At the Rubaiyat it is served Wednesday and Saturday only, and even then just at lunchtime because the chef himself admits it's too heavy for dinner. Brazilians, as a matter of fact, generally reserve *feijoada* for the weekend, when they can go home and collapse after eating. The ritual starts at about 2 o'clock and includes careful degustation of every part of the pig from ear to toe, the whole annointed with large swigs of the excellent local draft beer. Says Carlos Lorca, director of the Rubaiyat, "There's no better *feijoada* in the world than ours!"

The Churrascaria Rubaiyat is at 134 Avenida de Carvalho, near the Praça da Republica, one of the main squares and rare green spaces in downtown São Paulo, where every Sunday morning there is a hippie craft and art fair with a large variety of very good wares. Fairgoers often end up at the Rubaiyat. The restaurant is open every day from 11 A.M. to 1 A.M. The phone number is 37-43-48. Barbecued beef costs about $6, including a soft drink and dessert. A *feijoada* lunch, with beer and dessert, is about $4 and is usually plenty for two people.

—*Marvine Howe*

CHURRASCO RUBAIYAT
Based on the recipe of the Churrascaria Rubaiyat, São Paulo

*This is charcoal-grilled baby beef with a vinegar and oil
sauce. If you don't mind losing that charcoal taste, it can be
done in a regular broiler, but it must be one in which the
beef can be placed far enough from the flame so that it broils
slowly.*

**1 3–4 pound rack of prime ribs of baby beef
salt**

CHURRASCO SAUCE

**2 cups white vinegar
2 cloves garlic, finely minced
½ cup olive oil
1 teaspoon salt
2 medium onions, chopped
1 teaspoon dried oregano
1 teaspoon chopped parsley**

1. Rub the ribs well with salt.
2. Prepare the sauce by combining all the ingredients in a bowl and mixing them well. There will be about 2½ cups of sauce.
3. Brush the meat with the sauce and barbecue very slowly over a charcoal grill, turning frequently and basting with the sauce from time to time. Barbecue the beef for about 30 to 40 minutes, or to desired degree of doneness.
4. Serve the beef with the remaining sauce.

Yield: 4 servings

FEIJOADA RUBAIYAT
Based on the recipe of the Churrascaria Rubaiyat, São Paulo

*Here is Brazil's national dish of "pork and beans with frills."
The principal ingredients are available at grocers and
butchers specializing in Latin American products. In addition,
salted and smoked meats can be found at butcher shops in
German neighborhoods.*

2 pounds cured pork (a combination of salted or smoked loin, sausage, and chops)
2 pounds dried beef
1 pound seasoned Brazilian pork sausage (if unavailable, substitute Italian hot sausage)
2 pounds salted beef tongue (if unavailable use smoked tongue)
½ pound unsliced bacon
1 pound pigs' ears, feet, and tail (if unavailable, substitute head cheese)
4 cups black beans
juice of 1 lemon
2 cloves garlic, crushed
½ tablespoon prepared mustard
salt
4 tablespoons vegetable oil
1 onion, chopped
4 sprigs parsley, chopped
½ cup bread crumbs

ACCOMPANIMENTS

6–8 cups cooked rice
6–8 cups farofa (manioc flour fried slightly in butter)
1 orange, sliced
1 bunch Swiss chard, cooked
3 cups hot pepper sauce (recipe below)

1. The day before, put all the meat in a large bowl and cover with cold water. Let stand overnight.
2. Also the day before, pick over the beans, wash them well, and put them in another bowl. Cover them with cold water and let them stand overnight.
3. The next day, drain the meat and season it with the lemon, half the garlic, the mustard, and salt to taste. Put the meat into a large pot and add the beans. Cover with cold water. Bring to a boil and simmer 2 to 3 hours, or until the meat and beans are tender, adding water occasionally if necessary.
4. Heat the oil in a large skillet. Add the onion, parsley, the remainder of the garlic, and a little of the beans. Mash this mixture and sauté it for 5 to 7 minutes. Then add it to the pot of meat and beans. Cook until the sauce thickens, about 30 minutes.
5. To serve, remove meat, beans, and sauce from pot and place in a large earthenware or other suitable dish. Sprinkle with the bread crumbs. Accompany the meat and beans with the rice, farofa, hot pepper sauce, orange slices, and Swiss chard.

Yield: 12 servings

(CONTINUED)

HOT PEPPER SAUCE

2 large tomatoes, peeled, seeded, and chopped
4 hot peppers, seeded and minced, or 4 tablespoons Louisiana hot-pepper
sauce
2 cloves garlic, crushed
juice of 1 lemon
½ cup white vinegar
2 medium onions, finely chopped
4 scallions, minced
4 sprigs parsley, minced
¼ teaspoon white pepper
1 cup sauce from feijoada
salt
cayenne

Put the tomatoes, hot peppers and garlic in a blender container and puree.
Add the remaining ingredients and season with salt and cayenne to taste.
The sauce should be very hot and peppery.

Canada

MONTREAL

CHEZ LA MÈRE MICHEL. In France little girls named Micheline are apt to be called Mère Michel after a character in a popular nursery rhyme, and so it was with Micheline Delbuguet, who has given her childhood nickname to one of the most delightful restaurants in Montreal.

Mrs. Delbuguet learned about cooking in a restaurant that her parents operated on the French Riviera, and there is much of France in the brick town house that she and her husband, René, converted to an eating place in the mid-1960s. They live in an apartment above the restaurant, Mrs. Delbuguet supervising the food and often doing much of the cooking, and her husband, a commercial photographer, supervising everything else. He has kept the three small dining rooms pleasantly dark and decorated their whitewashed walls with his own photographs. Odd pieces of old crockery atop rough pine beams, a brass lantern here, a string of garlic cloves there, wooden floors, and simulated stained glass windows complete the decor.

The service is excellent and the menu, though short, is interesting, covering a broad range of French provincial cuisine and often including daily specialties that reflect Mrs. Delbuguet's early morning shopping tours. The delights of Chez la Mère Michel include an incredibly light lobster soufflé in the shell, *médaillon de la Mère Michel* made with tender fillet of beef, and *barquette alsacienne*, the last a delicate onion pie.

Including wine, a dinner for two might easily cost more than $30, but it will be money well spent. Because Chez la Mère Michel is small and its proprietors have not succumbed (as too many others in Montreal have) to the regrettable temptation to squeeze tables close together, reservations are essential.

Chez la Mère Michel is at 1209 Guy Street, just south of St. Catherine Street, a pleasant walk from the main hotels through a neighborhood that in summer is alive with outdoor cafes. Concentrated here are the discotheques, art galleries, and chic shops that give Montreal its justified reputation as the most cosmopolitan city in Canada. The phone number of Chez la Mère Michel is 934-0473. Most à la carte main dishes are in the $5 and up class. The restaurant is open from noon to 2 P.M. and 5:30 to 10:30 P.M. Monday through Friday. On Saturday it's open for dinner only, 5:30 to 10:30 P.M., and it's closed Sunday.

—William Borders

MÉDAILLON DE LA MÈRE MICHEL
Based on the recipe of Chez la Mère Michel, Montreal

This is fillet of beef with a sauce à médaillon, which is made by adding heavy cream and chopped mushrooms to a sauce provençale. The sauce provençale may be made ahead of time and can also be used over fish, chicken, pasta, rice, and omelets.

4 ½-pound fillets of beef
1 cup red burgundy wine
bouquet garni (1 bay leaf, 4 black peppercorns, and a sprig of fresh thyme or a
    pinch of dried tied in cheesecloth)

SAUCE PROVENÇALE (about 1 cup)

3 tablespoons olive oil
1 cup minced onion
2–3 sweet red peppers, diced
1 eggplant, peeled and cut into small cubes (about 5 to 6 cups)
4 small zucchinis, peeled and cubed (about 2 cups)
3 cloves garlic, crushed
bouquet garni (1 bay leaf and a sprig of fresh thyme or a pinch of
    dried tied in cheesecloth)
2 1-pound cans whole Italian tomatoes, or 6 very large ripe to-
    matoes, peeled and quartered
salt
black pepper

CONVERSION OF SAUCE AND SAUTÉING

3 tablespoons heavy cream
3 tablespoons chopped cooked mushrooms
2 tablespoons butter
1 tablespoon cooking oil

1. Place the beef in a nonmetallic dish, cover with the burgundy, and add the bouquet garni. Marinate for 4 to 5 hours.
2. Prepare the sauce provençale as follows: Heat the oil in an enamel saucepan and sauté the onion until limp and yellow. Add the peppers and cook, stirring, for about 5 minutes. Add the balance of the sauce provençale ingredients, season with salt and pepper, and simmer for 45 minutes to an hour. Put the sauce through a sieve and set aside until you are ready to cook the fillets. (The vegetables that have been removed from the sauce by straining can be chilled and eaten cold as an appetizer.)
3. When you are ready to cook the fillets, make a sauce à médaillon by putting 1 cup of the sauce provençale in an enamel pot; stir in the cream and the chopped mushrooms. Simmer the mixture for 10 minutes.
4. Remove the meat from the marinade, pat very dry, and trim off any fat. Heat the butter and oil in a heavy skillet and sauté the fillets to the desired degree of doneness (medium rare usually takes 8 to 10 minutes). Serve on hot plates, with the sauce poured over according to taste.

Yield: 4 servings

BARQUETTE ALSACIENNE
Based on the recipe of Chez la Mère Michel, Montreal

PASTRY

4 cups sifted all-purpose flour
1 teaspoon salt
1⅓ cups (21 tablespoons) shortening and/or butter
6–8 tablespoons ice water
1 egg white, beaten

1. Sift together the flour and salt.
2. Cut in the shortening or butter quickly, a little at a time, with 2 knives or a pastry blender until the mixture resembles coarse meal.
3. Add just enough water so the dough holds together and is neither crumbly nor sticky.

(CONTINUED)

4. Shape into a ball and chill in the refrigerator for at least 30 minutes. Add more water if necessary to roll.
5. Roll out the dough to make a thin pastry shell. Cut and line 12 4-inch ramekins or 15 3-inch ramekins, brush with egg white and let dry.

NOTE: For the pastry recipe above you may substitute your own favorite pastry crust, a packaged mix, or frozen shells, which must be re-rolled.

FILLING

2½ pounds large onions
8 tablespoons (1 stick) butter
½ cup heavy cream
5 eggs
1 cup sifted flour
salt
white pepper

1. Mince the onions finely. Melt the butter in a large saucepan, add the minced onions, and cook over low heat for about 20 minutes, or until the onions are soft and translucent.
2. Preheat the oven to 350 degrees.
3. Combine the cream and eggs and beat thoroughly.
4. Stir the flour into the onions, then stir in the cream and egg mixture.
5. Pour into the dough-lined ramekins and bake for 20 to 25 minutes, or until the barquettes are puffed and browned on top.

Yield: 12 to 15 servings

OTTAWA

L'OPÉRA. I like to take out-of-town visitors to this restaurant because it is actually in the handsomely designed National Arts Centre, which has given Canada's capital its greatest cultural lift in 100 years. In addition, it overlooks the Rideau Canal with its boats in summer and its skaters in winter. And most important, it makes a serious effort to overcome this city's most painful deficiency—a distinguished and distinctive restaurant.

L'Opéra has not yet altogether achieved its goal; the quality of both food and service is uneven and unpredictable, but both can be very good. At L'Opéra one can without too great risk explore what lies beyond the limits of the overpriced steakhouse cuisine that is the typical Ottawa restaurateur's mainstay. I usually choose from the fish and seafood offerings, especially when I am assured that one or more is fresh and from a local source. And according to the manager, James Pound, at least one is fresh and local when the season is right.

One dish that I have particularly enjoyed at L'Opéra is stuffed trout Kamouraska, a creation of Yannick Vincent, the restaurant's French chef. The fresh whole Quebec trout is filled with a thick sauce containing mushrooms, shallots, and wine that admirably complements the succulent, flaky flesh of the fish. With my trout came crisp glazed tiny carrots and buttered asparagus, the latter imported from France I was told. Both vegetables were canned, but it is difficult to complain of canned vegetables in the dead of a Canadian winter. And L'Opéra compensates by making available as varied a wine list as the unimaginative Liquor Control Board of Ontario makes possible. It also keeps a richly stocked pastry wagon. *Croquembouche*, little golden puffs filled with custard cream, piled up to form a cone and drizzled with a coating of crunchy caramelized sugar syrup, is irresistible.

L'Opéra, in the National Arts Centre, Confederation Square (telephone 232-5713), is open for lunch from noon to 2:30 P.M., Monday through Friday, and for dinner from 6 to 10 P.M., Monday through Saturday. On nights of theater performances light suppers are served from 10 P.M. to midnight. A full-course lunch can be had for around $5, a full-course dinner for under $10. There are also à la carte specialties, and the late-night supper is all à la carte.

—Jay Walz

STUFFED TROUT KAMOURASKA

Based on the recipe of L'Opéra, Ottawa

4 ½-pound trout, cleaned, gutted, and prepared as in step 1

STUFFING

2 tablespoons butter
2 tablespoons dry white wine
2 tablespoons lemon juice
salt
white pepper
1 pound mushrooms, finely chopped
1 shallot, chopped
1 tablespoon flour
½ cup warm milk

milk
flour
8 tablespoons (1 stick) butter
2 tablespoons lemon juice
2 lemons, halved

1. Ask your fish dealer to remove the backbone of the trout through the slit in the belly that was made when the fish was gutted. Or do it yourself. Leave the head and tail attached.
2. The stuffing should be prepared in advance and chilled in the refrigerator. To make the stuffing, melt 1 tablespoon butter in a large skillet, add the wine, lemon juice, and a pinch of salt and pepper. Stir in the mushrooms and shallot and cook slowly over low heat, stirring often, until all the liquid has evaporated. (The mushrooms will absorb all the wine and lemon juice but then make their own liquid, which must be evaporated by cooking.)
3. Over low heat, make a thick white sauce by melting 1 tablespoon butter, then blending in 1 tablespoon flour and slowly stirring in the warm milk. When the sauce is thick, season with salt and pepper, then measure out 6 tablespoons and mix it well with the cooked mushrooms. Refrigerate this mushroom mixture until cold.
4. Salt and pepper the inside of the trout and fill each with an equal portion of the chilled stuffing. Close up the slit in each fish with skewers or needle and heavy thread.
5. Dip the trout in milk, then in flour; shake off excess flour.

6. Melt the stick of butter in a large skillet until hot but not brown and sauté the trout over medium heat for about 5 minutes on each side, turning carefully.
7. Transfer the trout to a warm serving platter, remove the skewers or thread, pour 2 tablespoons of lemon juice over the fish, and serve garnished with the lemon halves.

Yield: 4 servings

QUEBEC CITY

AUX ANCIENS CANADIENS. As the citadel of French culture in North America, Quebec City has dozens of French restaurants, some of them quite good. But if, instead of having a meal that might be found in France, you would like to eat the way rural people in the Province of Quebec do, an excellent place to go is Aux Anciens Canadiens. French-Canadian cuisine is basically different from the classic French, and there is no better example of it than in this charming 300-year-old house in the center of the old city.

A meal might begin with *habitant* pea soup, a dish so typical of the *habitants*, or early settlers, of Quebec that people in other parts of Canada sometimes refer to their French-speaking countrymen as "peasoups." At Aux Anciens Canadiens it is a rich broth that also includes carrots and onions. A representative main dish, perfectly prepared here, is the *tourtière*, minced pork, veal, and onion in a pastry shell. And for dessert, the maple syrup pie is sinfully delicious.

Aux Anciens Canadiens also offers such conventional dishes as steak and fish, and a small but adequate range of French wines. Because it is heavily taxed, the wine is expensive, but even with it a dinner for two will probably not cost much more than $20. The service, like the blue checkered tablecloths, is friendly.

The restaurant is in the main tourist area of Quebec City, a few blocks from the historic fortress walls and from the Plains of Abraham, the battlefield on which the English won control of French Canada 200 years ago. With its steeply sloping red roof and whitewashed walls, the building the restaurant occupies looks like a farmhouse you might happen upon anywhere in the province. Inside, the rough pine furniture is authentically Quebecois, and so are the maple sugar molds and old earthenware jugs that decorate the walls.

Aux Anciens Canadiens is at 36 Rue St.-Louis. The phone number is 529-3443. It is open every day from 11 A.M. to 10 P.M., and most à la carte main dishes are around $5 or a little more.

—*William Borders*

HABITANT PEA SOUP
Based on the recipe of Aux Anciens Canadiens, Quebec City

2 cups dried yellow peas, washed, picked over, and soaked for 12 hours in enough cold water to cover
2 quarts cold water
½ pound salt pork
1 cup minced onion
1 tablespoon coarse (kosher) salt
1 teaspoon savory
1–2 carrots, diced

1. Remove the peas from the water in which they soaked and rinse and drain them.
2. In a large heavy pot combine the peas, the 2 quarts of water, and the salt pork. Bring to a boil. Skim off the scum that rises to the top and add all the other ingredients.
3. Lower the heat, partially cover the pot, and simmer, for 2½ to 3 hours, or until the peas are tender.

Yield: 8 servings

TOURTIÈRE
Based on the recipe of Aux Anciens Canadiens, Quebec City

½ pastry recipe (see page 25, steps 1 through 3)
½ pound ground lean pork
½ pound ground lean veal
1 cup minced onion
1 teaspoon salt
black pepper
½ cup water

1. Divide the dough into 2 balls and refrigerate for at least 30 minutes. When ready to use, roll out thin top and bottom crusts to fit 7–8-inch pie plates.
2. In a heavy saucepan, combine the pork, veal, onion, salt, pepper, and water. Bring to a boil and simmer, uncovered, for 20 minutes.
3. Remove from the heat, let cool, then place in the refrigerator to chill for an hour or more.
4. Preheat the oven to 425 degrees.

(CONTINUED)

5. Line your pie plate with unbaked pie crust. Brush with about half of the beaten egg and let dry. Then spoon in the chilled meat mixture. Put on a top crust, pressing the edges to seal, and cut several slits in the crust to allow steam to escape while the pie is baking. Brush the top crust with the remaining beaten egg to glaze. Let dry.

6. Bake the pie until the top crust is golden brown, about 45 minutes. Serve hot.

Yield: 2 servings

MAPLE SYRUP PIE
Based on the recipe of Aux Anciens Canadiens, Quebec City

⅓ pastry recipe (see pp. 25–26, steps 1 through 4)
1 cup brown sugar
1 cup pure maple syrup, preferably fresh
2 eggs, well beaten
½ cup heavy cream
heavy cream to serve with pie

1. Roll out the dough ⅛ inch thick. Fit into an 8-inch pie plate and trim. Brush with egg white and let dry.
2. Preheat the oven to 300 degrees.
3. Dissolve the brown sugar in the maple syrup. If necessary, let stand for a while, stirring occasionally, until well blended.
4. Combine the eggs and heavy cream and stir into the blended sugar and syrup.
5. Pour the mixture into the pie shell. Bake about 50 minutes, or until the top darkens and becomes bubbly and crinkly.
6. Chill and serve cold with heavy cream.

Yield: 6 to 8 servings

TORONTO

THREE SMALL ROOMS. The three rooms—the Grill (38 seats), the Wine Cellar (24), and the Restaurant (about 50)—are cosily fitted into the first floor of the Windsor Arms, a comfortable old (but fully renovated) hotel in the midtown University of Toronto area of this city. The prices may be a bit steep for neighborhood undergraduates, but the simple surroundings and absence of noisy entertainment attract many faculty members who plainly enjoy good talk along with elegantly presented food. Drawn, too, are many of the town's visiting actors and other celebrities who seem to be increasingly adopting the Windsor Arms as an Algonquin Hotel away from New York. One's table neighbor may be Rex Harrison, Christopher Plummer, or even Katharine Hepburn in Toronto for a pre-Broadway trial run.

The Swiss chef, Herbert Sonzagni, has built up a richly varied cuisine. But since he depends heavily on fresh Canadian meats, fowl, and fish, he changes the menu completely every week to take advantage of what he finds at the market. Thus his specialties are not always on the bill of fare. Since fresh Canadian lamb is a favorite of mine, I watch for it; if it's on the menu I know it is the home-grown product, not the commonly consumed frozen Australian or New Zealand import that to me has lost its taste and tenderness somewhere on the long Pacific voyage.

My idea of a delectable dinner begins with a plate of smoked Canadian sturgeon as a build-up for either the roast of lamb *Beaulieu* or the saddle of lamb *persillé*. If you'd prefer to try a main dish that is a favorite of Chef Sonzagni himself, order the three fillets Satchá, made with tender slices of beef, veal, and pork garnished with green and red peppers and chanterelle mushrooms. While certain items on the menu are for two, four, or more servings, Mr. Sonzagni says he can prepare an order for one, or for as many as one wishes, if he's given advance notice or if the guest isn't in too big a hurry.

Many good imported wines (on display in the Wine Cellar) are available, if a bit expensive because of the Ontario Liquor Control Board's stiff scale of mark-ups.

Three Small Rooms is at 22 St. Thomas Street, near Bloor Street. The phone number is 921-5141, and because space is limited, reservations are advisable any day or night of the week. Service in all three rooms is à la carte.

The Grill is open for breakfast from 7 A.M. to 11 A.M., for lunch from

33

noon to 3 P.M. and for dinner from 5 P.M. to 1 A.M. The limited menu is on a blackboard on a wall over the grill. A lunch should come to less than $5, a dinner to not more than $10, wine excluded.

The Wine Cellar is open for lunch (noon to 3 P.M.) and dinner (5:30 P.M. to 1 A.M.). A luncheon salad or sandwich and a glass of wine will come to under $5.

The Restaurant is open for lunch from noon to 3 P.M. and dinner from 6 to 10:30 P.M. Dinner for two with wine can run to around $40.

—Jay Walz

THREE FILLETS SATCHÁ
Based on the recipe of Three Small Rooms, Toronto

At the Three Small Rooms this dish is always made with those wonderfully meaty mushrooms known as chanterelles, which are available in cans in some shops carrying gourmet foods. If you can't get chanterelles, you could make a variation of the dish by substituting whole fresh mushrooms.

4 3-ounce fillets of veal, ½ inch thick
4 3-ounce fillets of pork, ½ inch thick
4 3-ounce fillets of beef, ¾ inch thick
8 tablespoons (1 stick) butter, clarified (see note)
1 large red pepper, cut into julienne
1 large green pepper, cut into julienne
14 ounces of canned chanterelle mushrooms, drained
¼ cup dry sherry
¾ cup beef stock (see page 95) or canned beef bouillon

1. Sauté the veal and pork fillets in 2 tablespoons clarified butter and remove when done. The pork fillets should be well cooked. Keep warm.
2. In the same pan and same butter in which the veal and pork were cooked, sauté the beef fillets to the desired degree of doneness, adding more clarified butter if necessary. Keep warm.
3. While the meat is being cooked, sauté the pepper strips in a separate pan in 2 tablespoons clarified butter. They should be slightly undercooked.
4. In a third pan sauté the chanterelles in an additional 2 tablespoons clarified butter. Then add the peppers to the chanterelles and keep warm.
5. Discard the fat from the pan in which the fillets were sautéed. To the

residue in the pan add the sherry and reduce over low heat to half its volume. Then add the beef stock and cook for a few minutes, stirring and scraping the bottom of the pan.

6. Place the fillets on a warm platter in layers—first the pork, then the veal, then the beef. Cover them with the hot sauce, then top them with the pepper strips and chanterelles.

<u>Yield: 4 servings</u>

NOTE: To clarify butter, cut it into pieces and melt it slowly in a saucepan so that the milk solids sink to the bottom of the pan in the form of a milky residue, leaving a clear yellow liquid on top. Strain the liquid through cheesecloth into a container, leaving the milky residue behind, and you have clarified butter.

VANCOUVER

TERRACE GRILL, BAYSHORE INN. Because of its spectacular bay and mountain setting, Vancouver is thought of as Canada's San Francisco. But its restaurants are not all that bewitching. In fact, the careless visitor will find himself in a run-of-the-mill steakhouse if he doesn't watch out.

The alternatives worth exploring are the many Chinese places along East Hastings Street in Vancouver's Chinatown or the restaurants where good fresh British Columbia fish, ocean or fresh water, is on the bill of fare. I think it outrageous for anyone, while in Vancouver, not to sample the superlative British Columbia salmon, and a good place to do the sampling is the Bayshore Inn's Terrace Grill, which serves the fish up in memorable fashion, stuffed and baked. Chef Everett Miller says he prefers a nice small salmon if he can get it; otherwise he produces his specialty with a center cut or a fillet. In any event the result is not to be confused with those cross-cut salmon steaks that so often arrive overdone, tough, and dry. Here the fish is cooked long enough to be firm and no more. And it comes with a complete dinner for under $10.

In the same price range there is a bouillabaise that can also be recommended to the fish-minded. This tasty seafood stew, Bayshore Inn style, is served à la carte but makes a plentiful dinner. And for anyone looking for an alternative to fish, there is almost any cut of steak, British Columbia being a prime Canadian source of top-grade beef. Or there is Chef Miller's delicious butter schnitzel, which is made of seasoned ground veal and served with a sour cream sauce.

All meals are accompanied by one of Vancouver's superb picture-window views, for the Terrace Grill is on the frontage of Burrard Inlet, a busy harbor frequented by ships of many flags. Rising abruptly across the inlet are the dramatic Capilano Mountains, green in summer and snow covered in winter. Stanley Park, complete with zoo and monumental Northwest Coast Indian totem poles, lies to the left, and downtown Vancouver is minutes away to the right.

The Bayshore Inn is on Georgia Street at Cardero Street. The phone number is 682-3377. Howard Hughes chose the two top floors of the inn as a hideaway in 1972, but there is no record that the wealthy recluse's presence ever graced the Terrace Grill. The Grill is open from 6:30 A.M. to 1 A.M. and complete dinners start at not much more than $5 for chicken dishes and go up to more than $10 for such things as a steak and Alaska crab combination.

—*Jay Walz*

BOUILLABAISE
Based on the recipe of the Terrace Grill, Bayshore Inn, Vancouver

SAUCE

> ½ cup olive oil
> ½ cup julienne carrots, 2 inches long
> ½ cup julienne celery, 2 inches long
> 1 cup onions cut lengthwise into fine slices
> 8 cloves garlic, finely minced
> 4 medium tomatoes, peeled, and cut into ½-inch cubes
> pinch crumbled saffron
> ½ cup dry sauterne
> 1½ quarts fish stock (recipe below)
> bouquet garni (parsley sprig, pinch of dried thyme, and ½ bay leaf tied in cheesecloth)
> 1 tablespoon black pepper
> salt

16 clams in shell, thoroughly washed
8 mussels in shell, scrubbed and debearded
1 pound lobster tails in the shell, cut into 1½-inch pieces
½ pound jumbo shrimp, shelled and deveined
½ pound scallops
½ pound salmon, cut into 1-inch cubes or 2-inch-long pieces
½ pound striped bass, cut into 1-inch cubes or 2-inch-long pieces
½ pound halibut, cut into 1-inch cubes or 2-inch-long pieces

1. In a large saucepan heat the olive oil over medium heat. Add the carrots, celery, and onions and sauté them until they soften. Add the garlic and cook for 3 minutes. Add the tomatoes, saffron, and sauterne and cook until all the alcohol in the wine has vaporized, leaving only the wine essence.
2. Add the fish stock, bouquet garni, and pepper. Salt sparingly to taste. Allow to simmer slowly for at least an hour.

(CONTINUED)

3. Put the clams, mussels, lobster tails, shrimp, and scallops in the bottom of a large, heavy pot that has a cover. Fill the pot with the simmering sauce and add the cut-up fish.
4. Bring to a boil, reduce heat, and simmer, covered, for just 10 minutes.
5. Transfer the seafood to a large warm platter or individual soup bowls. Pour the bouillabaise into a serving bowl or tureen. Discard any clams or mussels that have not opened. Accompany with plenty of hot garlic bread.

Yield: 4 servings

FISH STOCK

3 cups canned clam juice
2 cups water
1 cup dry sauterne
1½ pounds rinsed fish bones and heads and shrimp shells
1 chopped onion
1 carrot, sliced
1 rib celery, cut in 2 or 3 pieces
bouquet garni (2 sprigs parsley, pinch of dried thyme, and 1 bay leaf tied in cheesecloth)
4 black peppercorns
½ teaspoon salt

Put all the ingredients in a large saucepan. Bring to a boil and simmer for 30 minutes. Strain and use.

Yield: 1½ quarts

NOTE: 1½ quarts of stock are needed to make the bouillabaise, but as the stock can be frozen and reserved for later use, this recipe may be increased if desired. Also, should the recipe as given yield less than 1½ quarts, simply add enough water or clam juice to bring it up to the correct amount.

BAKED STUFFED SALMON
Based on the recipe of the Terrace Grill, Bayshore Inn, Vancouver

2½ pounds fillet of salmon (a tail end of salmon cleaned, boned, and cut into 2 fillets) or, if available, a whole small salmon, cleaned and gutted
salt

black pepper
3 cups prepared herb-seasoned bread stuffing
1 teaspoon minced dill
lemon wedges

1. Preheat the oven to 350 degrees.
2. Season the nonskin side of the fillets or the inside of the whole salmon with salt and pepper.
3. Combine the dill with the stuffing.
4. If using fillets, place the stuffing in an ovenproof casserole or baking dish and place the fillets over the stuffing, skin side up. If using a whole salmon, place the stuffing in the fish and close the cavity with skewers, toothpicks, or needle and thread.
5. Bake until the salmon is just firm, about 40 minutes for the fillets, about 12 minutes per pound for a whole salmon. Serve hot garnished with lemon wedges.

Yield: 6 servings

BUTTER SCHNITZEL
Based on the recipe of the Terrace Grill, Bayshore Inn, Vancouver

2 tablespoons butter
1 cup chopped onion
1¼ pounds coarsely ground veal
1 egg, lightly beaten
1 teaspoon salt
¼ teaspoon black pepper
2 teaspoons Maggi seasoning
6 slices white bread, trimmed and cubed
4 tablespoons heavy cream
butter
1 cup sauce smitane (recipe below)

1. Melt the butter in a skillet and sauté the onion until soft and translucent.
2. Combine the onion with the veal, egg, salt, pepper, Maggi seasoning, and cubed bread; mix well. If you have a fine grinder, put the entire mixture through it. If not, pound the mixture with a meat mallet or other suitable implement so that the bread cubes are thoroughly mashed and well blended with the meat.
3. Mix in the cream by hand and form into 4 equal oval-shaped portions.

(CONTINUED)

4. Fry the portions in butter, for about 15 minutes or until they are golden brown, turning them once or twice. Place them on a warm platter, spoon the sauce smitane over them, and serve.

Yield: 4 servings

SAUCE SMITANE

1 tablespoon butter
1½ tablespoons grated onion
½ cup dry white wine
1¼ cups sour cream, at room temperature
salt
white pepper

In a small saucepan, melt the butter, add the grated onion, and sauté, stirring, until the onion is soft and golden. Pour in the wine and simmer until all the alcohol has vaporized and the wine is reduced to its essence. Stir in the sour cream and, while stirring, just heat through. Strain through a sieve and season with salt and white pepper. Return to the saucepan and heat again when ready to serve.

Yield: 1 cup

WINNIPEG

THE FACTOR'S TABLE. Winnipeg, capital of Manitoba, one of Canada's "Prairie Provinces," has a number of attractions. There is the Royal Ballet of international renown. There is the headquarters of one of the world's most fabled institutions, the three-century-old Hudson's Bay Company. And best of all, as far as I am concerned, there is the Factor's Table in the Fort Garry Hotel, where the magical Winnipeg goldeye is at its best.

The hotel, one of those old Canadian National Railway chateaux, is on the site of long-gone Upper Fort Garry, the Hudson's Bay Company stronghold and trading post at the confluence of the Red and Assiniboine rivers. The decor of its oak-beamed main dining room recalls the hall of the chief factor, as Hudson's Bay trading post managers were called. And it was at the factor's table that the boss wined and dined travelers, who for the most part were explorers, fur traders, and an occasional missionary.

The "chief factor" today is none of these. He is Nicholas Marchak, the *chef de cuisine*, whose Ukrainian-Canadian parents taught him as a child how to prepare such specialties of the house as sweetgrass buffalo pie. (Sweetgrass, the buffalo's favorite forage, has become the government's trademark for the finest meat produced from overpopulated herds in national parks, notably Wood Buffalo National Park in northern Alberta.) Chef Marchak also prepares pheasant under glass and other dishes reflecting a wide-ranging cosmopolitan cuisine. But it is his way with the prairie specialty of specialties, the Winnipeg goldeye, that really makes my mouth water.

This troutlike fish used to abound in several of the shallow prairie lakes, but overfishing has made it a growing rarity. One hears, disturbingly, that the only "Winnipeg goldeye" sold in most fish stores and delicatessens in these parts now comes from the United States—from cultivated lakes in Minnesota. At the Factor's Table, however, one is served *genuine* Winnipeg goldeye, usually from Lake Winnipeg north of the city, when it is available.

The delicacy that is placed upon one's plate—one whole peeled goldeye —has an orange-gold color and an aroma of oak wood smoke. One hears it has also been soaked in brine, but the special treatment is a trade secret of a Winnipeg fish company. "It requires little preparation," Chef Marchak told me. And, indeed, should you be fortunate enough to obtain a Winnipeg goldeye, the recipe is short:

"Remove the skin. Usually the head and tail are left on. Spread a little butter over the top of the goldeye, place in a pan and heat for six minutes in an oven at 400 degrees. Serve with lemon."

Some restaurants are said to substitute smoked tullibee for the hard-to-get goldeye. Tullibee has similar characteristics, including firm, flaky flesh, and some chefs swear their customers can't tell the difference between it and goldeye. But connoisseurs disagree, saying tullibee is inferior. In any event, to spare his guests any doubt, Chef Marchak serves his goldeye complete with head, for goldeye is toothless, tullibee has teeth. For this reason a fastidious Winnipeg gourmet refuses to touch any fish called goldeye if its head is removed.

Dinners at the Factor's Table, including soup, entree, side dishes, and beverage, run from about $5 to more than $10 for such specialties as whole live lobster, which has to be imported for ever so many hundreds of miles. The pheasant, the wonderful buffalo pie, a choice pepper steak, and the magnificant goldeye are all priced somewhere in between. The wine cellar offers an extensive selection of imported wines that are moderately priced by Canada's rather high standards.

The Factor's Table, in the Fort Garry Hotel, is at 222 Broadway. The phone number is 942-8251. Lunch is served from 11:45 A.M. to 2:30 P.M. and dinner from 5:45 P.M. to 10 P.M.

—*Jay Walz*

SWEETGRASS BUFFALO PIE
Based on the recipe of the Factor's Table, Winnipeg

The buffalo meat used at the Factor's Table comes from overpopulated herds in Canadian national parks. "Sweetgrass," in fact, is the Canadian Government's brand name for it. In the United States, buffalo—or to be more precise, bison—is available at butcher shops that carry game and specialty meats. If buffalo meat is unavailable, try this recipe with beef chuck instead.

2 pounds buffalo chuck, cubed
salt
black pepper
flour
4–5 tablespoons butter
4 tablespoons corn oil
2 onions, minced
2 cloves garlic, minced

2 ribs celery, finely chopped
1 teaspoon finely chopped parsley
1½ cups claret
1¼ cups (10 ounces) veal stock (recipe below)
1 tablespoon tomato paste
1 bay leaf
½ teaspoon dried thyme
½ teaspoon prepared English mustard
4–5 cups cooked vegetables (small white onions, carrots, and peas)
sugar
½ pastry recipe (see pp. 25–26, steps 1 through 4)

1. Preheat the oven to 350 degrees.
2. Season the cubes of meat with salt and pepper and roll them in the flour until they are generously coated.
3. In a skillet heat 2 tablespoons butter and the corn oil and brown the meat over high heat on all sides. Transfer the meat to a casserole with a cover.
4. Clean the skillet in which the meat was browned, or use another skillet, and heat 2 tablespoons butter. Sauté the minced onions, garlic, celery, and parsley until lightly browned and spoon over the meat in the casserole.
5. Combine the claret, veal stock, tomato paste, bay leaf, thyme, and mustard and add to the casserole. Cook, covered, in the oven for about 2 hours, or until the meat is tender.
6. Sauté the cooked carrots in a skillet with a little butter, sprinkling them with sugar so that they become glazed and slightly browned. Combine them with the cooked white onions and the cooked peas.
7. Take the casserole out of the oven and add the cooked vegetables.
8. Roll the dough ⅛-inch thick, large enough to cover the casserole. Press along the edges to seal and make several slits in the center of the dough for steam to escape.
9. Brush the dough with the beaten egg white so the crust will glaze, let dry, put the casserole back in the oven, and bake until the crust is golden brown, about 15 to 20 minutes.

Yield: 4 servings

VEAL STOCK

2 pounds veal bones
water to cover plus 3 quarts water
1 medium onion, peeled

(CONTINUED)

1 carrot
1 rib celery
1 teaspoon salt
2 black peppercorns
bouquet garni (1 sprig parsley, pinch dried thyme, ½ bay leaf tied in cheesecloth)

1. Put the veal bones in a large, heavy pot with water to cover, bring to a
   boil, and cook for about 5 to 10 minutes. Pour off the water, wash off
   the bones, wipe off any scum that remains on the pot, and fill with 3
   quarts of water.
2. Return the veal bones to the pot and add all the other ingredients. Bring
   to a boil, reduce heat, partially cover, and barely simmer for about 4
   hours.
3. Strain the stock, let cool, then place it in the refrigerator. When it is
   chilled, remove any fat that has congealed on the surface. The stock is
   now ready. Use amount recipe requires. The remaining stock can be
   frozen for future use.

Yield: 1 quart

PHEASANT UNDER GLASS À LA CRÈME

Based on the recipe of the Factor's Table, Winnipeg

*At the Factor's Table this dish, as its name implies, is served
under a glass bell, but at home the bell can be dispensed with.*

1 pheasant, disjointed
¼ teaspoon salt
white pepper
flour
2 tablespoons butter
4 tablespoons dry white wine
1½ cups heavy cream
cayenne
1 tablespoon lemon juice

1. Ask your butcher to disjoint the pheasant or do it yourself as follows:
   Cut off the legs and thighs. Insert a knife between neck and wing, cut
   about 1 inch, then hold carcass with knife and pull breast off carcass

by grasping the collar bone and wing. Turn the carcass around and repeat as above. Trim the breast by removing the collar bone. Trim the legs by chopping off excess bone from the drumsticks.

2. Wipe the pheasant pieces, cut off any fat, and season the pieces with the salt and white pepper. Dredge them liberally with flour.

3. Preheat the oven to 325 degrees.

4. Melt the butter in an ovenproof pan or casserole that can be covered. Dip one side of the pheasant pieces in the melted butter, then turn and place dry side (skin side) down in the pan. Place the pan in the oven and cook the pheasant, covered, for about 40 minutes, turning once.

5. Remove the pan from the oven. Uncover, pour in the wine, then the cream, and finally dust the pheasant lightly with the cayenne. On top of the stove bring the wine and cream to a boil, then place the pan in the oven, uncovered, and cook for 15 minutes more.

6. Remove from oven, add the lemon juice, and serve.

Yield: 2 servings

China, People's Republic of

PEKING

SHOU TU K'AO YA TIEN, also known as PIEN YI FANG. There are 20 or more fine restaurants available to foreigners in Peking (and many, many more if the foreigner speaks Chinese and enjoys small street cafes catering exclusively to Chinese patrons). But of the top half dozen eating places the one I enjoy most is Shou Tu K'ao Ya Tien, or the Capital City Roast Duck Shop, an establishment usually referred to simply as Pien Yi Fang, which means "reasonably priced restaurant." Its atmosphere is completely Chinese and its rendering of its most famous dish is superb. That dish, in which it has specialized since its founding in 1855, is Peking duck, a special breed of duck that is artificially fed for 30 days prior to being killed, then pumped full of air like a balloon to separate the skin from the carcass, then roasted in a special oven, sliced, and finally eaten, both crackling skin and delicious meat, rolled up in pancakes with crunchy bits of vegetables and various sauces. The great Peking duck restaurant Chüan Chü Te', established in 1864, is much more Westernized than Pien Yi Fang.

Pien Yi Fang is only a gunshot from the great Tien-an Men Square in a small *hut'ung*, or alley, near the *Ch'ien Men*, or Central Gate, of the Forbidden City, once the residence of the emperor. Like most Peking restaurants, Pien Yi Fang is open to the street and crowded with Chinese diners at small tables close together. Foreigners make their way through the packed first-floor dining room and go upstairs to a private dining room plainly furnished but redolent of generations of Chinese cooking. Service is supervised by Pien Yi Fang's director, a cheerful and knowledgeable restaurateur who watches every detail of the presentation of the Peking duck—itself a formidable art. Foreigners usually bring wine with them, from their own cellars if they are diplomats or else from the stocks of the larger hotels. *Mao t'ai*, the 140-proof Chinese liquid fire, is available, also beer and soft drinks. The Chinese dine early and a 7 P.M. reservation is usual. By the time dinner is over (about 9:30 or 10) the restaurant is empty. Reservations should be made 24 hours in advance if at all possible. Peking duck should be ordered as it is the house specialty, and the entire dinner can be duck, starting with hors d'oeuvres of crispy webbed feet and duck liver pâté. Other dishes can be arranged by those able to discuss their choices with the director in Chinese, but the foreigner is advised to leave the entire menu up to the restaurant, which will not disappoint him.

Pien Yi Fang is on Hsien Yu Keu, the first *hut'ung* to the left in Ch'ien Men Wai. The phone number is 75-05-05. The place is open for lunch and dinner, and a meal will run about $5 to $6 a person exclusive of liquor. There is no service charge and tipping is not customary.

—Harrison E. Salisbury

China, Republic of
TAIPEI

For unimaginably good food, you need only come to Taipei on the island of Taiwan. In this capital city of Nationalist China every style of Chinese cuisine is represented, and the dishes are prepared, moreover, by chefs who dare not let their standards down, as they often do when they are lured abroad, because their customers are simply too knowledgeable and demanding. Most westerners who have been able to visit both mainland China and Taiwan say that the food here is equal to the best there. And with access to the mainland still severely limited, Taiwan is *the* place for the tourist to experience authentic, excellent Chinese cooking—and at very reasonable prices.

The problem is which restaurants to recommend. There are so many fine ones that to choose is far from easy. Here are three of my favorites, each specializing in the cuisine of a different region of the mainland.

MANDARIN RESTAURANT (HWA SHIN). For one of my first meals in Taipei, friends took me to the Mandarin to introduce me to the glories of Hunan cuisine and I have been hooked ever since. The Mandarin's owner, Peng Chang-kuei, is one of the greatest modern Chinese chefs, a man whose former students are now master chefs in restaurants all over the world. Furthermore, Mr. Peng is something of a living legend among Chinese gourmets because he personally developed a number of dishes now regarded as classics, creating some in their entirety and adapting others from traditional recipes which he felt were deficient in that they called for too stark a seasoning. Mr. Peng's creations are still hot enough to win applause from the pepper-loving natives of Hunan (famous even in Taiwan as the province of Mao Tse-tung), but the seasoning is a subtle blend of tastes rather than just being fiery.

Don't fail to order the spice- and honey-preserved ham, which is baked in clay and is sweet rather than hot; the sliced fish in chicken soup, which is more interesting than it sounds; the chicken à la viceroy; and the silver thread rolls (*yin szu chuan*), which are nice for soaking up the sauce in the dish listed on the English side of the menu as "Bean Curd With Peng's Cooking." (A more graceful translation would be "Peng's Bean Curd.") Beer or rice wine (ask for aged wine, served warm) go well with Hunan food.

In Taipei any restaurant with carpeting and tablecloths is luxurious, and the Mandarin has both, plus wood-paneled walls, so it is comparatively high class. It is also fairly large, with a spacious main dining area and private rooms off to the side for groups of ten or more. The atmosphere is pleasant, the service is polite and efficient, and some of the waiters even speak passable English.

The Mandarin's address is 16 Nanking East Road, Section 1, second floor (above the lobby of the Asia Hotel). The phone number is 51-33-55. The restaurant is open every day of the year from 11:30 A.M. to 2:30 P.M. and 5:30 to 9 P.M. except for a few days of vacation around the Chinese New Year. A meal for four people, including tax and service charge, should come to about $15. No tipping is necessary, but it is polite to leave whatever small change is left over from paying the bill.

While the Mandarin is conveniently near most of the major hotels, it is in an area of no particular sightseeing interest. There is a downtown branch of the Mandarin, however, that is in the heart of the West Gate District, Taipei's busiest shopping and entertainment area. An after-dinner stroll in the neighborhood is a good way to get a vivid impression of Taipei's active street life—hawkers selling goods from open storefronts, peddlers of food and lottery tickets, crowds walking and window-shopping. The branch is on the second floor of the Peace Hotel at 150 Chunghua Road (tel: 33-97-89) and the food, prices and hours are the same as at the main restaurant.

PHOENIX RESTAURANT. When the Phoenix opened in 1972, word quickly spread that its food was among the best in town. A major reason for its success, and one known only to a few customers, was that the Phoenix had lured away the skilled chef from Taipei's best known and longest established Szechuan restaurant. Some of the outstanding Szechuan-style dishes offered by the Phoenix are dry-fried string beans, shredded beef with chile sauce, diced chicken with peppers, prawns with chile sauce, and Szechuan duck or camphor tea-smoked duck. Tell the waiter (most understand some English) if you do not like your food too hot, as many (though not all) Szechuan dishes are highly spiced. Be sure to order a plate of pancakes (*yo bing*), which are not listed on the menu. Several of the dishes, such as the string beans and shredded beef, are at their best wrapped inside a pancake to make a sort of sandwich. Drink beer or rice wine.

The Phoenix occupies the whole of a nine-story building, with public dining rooms on the two lowest floors, the kitchen at the very top and private rooms and banquet halls in between. The decor is fairly elegant by Taipei standards. A small foyer, dominated by a large chandelier and a red-carpeted staircase, leads to the first-floor dining room, which is really more of a mezzanine. Reflecting the mythological association of the restaurant's name, the walls are decorated with scenes from antiquity—Greek, Roman, and pre-Columbian as well as Chinese. The menu is in Chinese and English.

The Phoenix is in the same area as the main Mandarin restaurant and so it is also convenient to the major hotels. Its address is 1–2 Nanking West Road and the phone number is 52-53-05. Except for a brief vacation around the Chinese New Year, it is open every day from 11:30 A.M. to 2 P.M. and 5:30 to 9:30 P.M. The price of a meal will vary considerably according to how many and which dishes your party orders, but you can enjoy a feast at the Phoenix for not much more than $3 a person, including tax and service charge. As for tip, just leave the small change from your bill.

CHIH MEI LOU. A colleague of mine, James P. Sterba, a *New York Times* correspondent with considerable experience in Asia, once wrote that in Taipei he prefers to eat in restaurants that "look like hardware stores." That way, he said, he could be sure that the management had not gone after the tourist trade, with the inevitable decline in standards that this involves. Mr. Sterba presumably had in mind a restaurant like the Chih Mei Lou (which translates, ironically, as the Bringing About Beauty restaurant).

While no one would actually mistake it for a hardware store, the Chih Mei Lou is not much to look at. The paint has faded, and the interior has obviously not been refurnished since the grand opening two decades ago. But if the restaurant is not a visual delight, there is that much less distraction from the food. The Peking-style dishes are superb.

The specialty of the house is Peking duck, prepared with ducks from the restaurant's own farm. The dish should be eaten by placing a slice of duck meat or duck skin and a piece of leek dipped in bean-paste sauce onto a pancake and folding the sides of the pancake in toward the center to make the equivalent of a sandwich. When you order Peking duck you also get a large bowl of duck soup and a dish made from eggs, duck fat, and scallions.

The duck alone can easily be enough for three or four people, but the fried shredded pork and vermicelli salad makes a good appetizer, and larger groups may want to order such additional tasty dishes as fish slices in wine sauce or braised chicken fillet with chestnuts. The Chinese are not known for their desserts as a rule, but restaurants serving food from Peking (still called by the old name of Peiping by the Chinese Nationalists) offer an especially good way to end a meal. It is cubed bananas in hot sugar syrup. The pieces are dipped in the water bowl that is provided to keep them from getting too sticky.

The Chih Mei Lou is in the bustling, lively West Gate area, not far from the Mandarin branch. The address is 162 Chunghua Road and the phone numbers are 33-42-14 or 36-58-62. It is open from 11:30 A.M. to 2 P.M. and 5:30 to 9:30 P.M. every day of the year except for the usual few days' vacation at Chinese New Year's time. The restaurant is medium sized, with 20 or 30 tables, and the menus are in English as well as Chinese. The waiters do not speak English here, but you can easily get what you want by pointing to it on the English menu. In the unlikely event that you run into some difficulty, there may well be a Mandarin-speaking American graduate student at the next table who can help. The Peking duck is less than $6 with all the trimmings, so a party of four could still order several other dishes and wind up with a bill in the neighborhood of $10. Rice wine or beer goes fine with the food, and as the check includes a service charge, no tipping beyond small change is customary.

One last word about dining out in Taipei that applies equally to all restaurants: The Chinese eat dinner early (they may take a late night snack of noodles or dumplings), so that after 7:30 P.M. you may find the best dishes already sold out and by 9 the waiters often start piling chairs on empty tables. So do as the Chinese do and sit down to your evening meal early.

—*Donald H. Shapiro*

CHICKEN À LA VICEROY
Based on the recipe of the Mandarin Restaurant, Taipei

This dish is also known as Duke Tso's Chicken.

1 3-pound chicken, cut into bite-size pieces
1 egg white
3 tablespoons dark soy sauce

(CONTINUED)

oil for deep frying
4–5 dried hot red peppers, seeded and halved
3 cloves garlic, minced
1 tablespoon crushed and chopped fresh ginger
1 teaspoon cornstarch
1 tablespoon white vinegar
sugar
salt

1. In a bowl mix well the chicken pieces, egg white, and 1 tablespoon soy sauce.
2. Heat the oil in a large frying pan. Fry the chicken until light brown, turning frequently. This takes about 15 to 20 minutes. Drain and remove chicken to a plate
3. Remove all but 1 tablespoon oil from the pan. Add red pepper and sauté until pepper turns black. Add garlic and ginger and sauté a few seconds.
4. In a bowl dissolve the cornstarch in vinegar and remaining soy sauce. Add this to the pan together with the chicken. Cook, stirring, at a sizzle over high heat for 30 seconds. Add sugar and salt to taste and serve hot.

Yield: 4 to 6 servings

PENG'S BEAN CURD
Based on the recipe of the Mandarin Restaurant, Taipei

4 ounces lean pork, cut into finest possible strips
2 cloves garlic, minced
1 dried hot red pepper, seeded and shredded
1 tablespoon fermented black beans
2 tablespoons vegetable oil
4 squares fresh bean curd
1 tablespoon dark soy sauce
1 teaspoon cornstarch
¼ cup water
salt

1. In a bowl mix together pork, garlic, pepper, and black beans.
2. In a skillet heat the oil over medium heat and add the pork mixture. Cook, stirring, at a sizzle for 3 minutes.
3. Add bean curd and soy sauce and cook at a simmer, stirring, for 2 minutes. The bean curd will break up into large chunks so stir gently.

4. Dissolve cornstarch in water and add to the simmering bean curd mixture. Cook, stirring, till sauce simmers and thickens. Season with salt if necessary and serve hot.

<u>Yield: 2 to 4 servings</u>

DRY-FRIED STRING BEANS
Based on the recipe of the Phoenix Restaurant, Taipei

2 pounds fresh string beans, tips cut off
1 cup vegetable oil
1 teaspoon chopped fresh ginger
4 ounces ground pork
1 tablespoon dry sherry or chinese rice wine
1 teaspoon sugar
1 tablespoon dark soy sauce
2 tablespoons chopped scallions
1 teaspoon white vinegar
salt

1. Heat oil in a skillet over high heat. Add beans and cook, stirring, at a loud sizzle for about 10 minutes. The skin should turn lightly golden. Drain and set beans aside.
2. Remove all but 1 tablespoon oil from the skillet. Add ginger and ground pork and stir-fry 3 minutes for pork to cook.
3. Return string beans to skillet and add wine, sugar, soy sauce, scallions, vinegar, and salt. Stir to mix, and serve hot.

<u>Yield: 4 servings</u>

FISH SLICES IN WINE SAUCE
Based on the recipe of Chih Mei Lou, Taipei

SAUCE

2 cloves garlic, minced
2 tablespoons dry sherry or chinese rice wine
1 teaspoon sugar

(CONTINUED)

1 teaspoon cornstarch
1 tablespoon light soy sauce (see note)
2 tablespoons water
salt

F I S H

3 tablespoons dried tree ears (see note)
2 cups water
¾-pound fillet of sea bass, cut into 1-inch-by-2-inch chunks
1 egg white
3 tablespoons vegetable oil

1. Make the sauce by combining all the sauce ingredients in a cup.
2. Boil the tree ears in the water for 2 minutes to soften and cook them. Drain the tree ears, and line a serving platter with them.
3. In a bowl combine the fish chunks and egg white and mix well.
4. Heat the oil in a skillet and add the fish. Fry gently until cooked through (the fish should stay white and not turn brown). It is not necessary to turn the fish pieces.
5. Add the sauce and bring to a simmer to thicken. Arrange fish and sauce on the bed of tree ears and serve at once.

Yield: 2 servings

NOTE: Light soy sauce and tree ears, the latter a mushroomlike fungus that grows on the bark of trees and is sold dried in plastic bags, may be purchased in Chinese groceries or stores carrying oriental food specialties. See "A Note About Food Sources," page 290. If unavailable, you may omit them.

Colombia

BOGOTÁ

RESTAURANT EDUARDO. Choosing a restaurant in Bogotá can be a frustrating experience. There are many first-rate ones and outward appearances are of no help. And interestingly, almost all of the finer places have opened only in the last few years. Before then Bogotaños with money prudently dined at home because of the intense poverty and concomitant violence that surrounded them. Today, however, the rapid growth of the northern suburbs has put more distance between them and the squalid southside slums, and there is also more money about because of growth in the economy.

Restaurant Eduardo, about four miles from the downtown section of Bogotá, is one of the more popular of the new chic gastronomic oases. The cuisine is international because members of the new monied class are fully familiar with local dishes and prefer steak and lobster to rice and beans. Specialties of the house are flaming lobster and shrimp dishes and charcoal-broiled meats. The restaurant's decor is rustic Dutch. (Curaçao and Aruba, both Dutch islands in the Caribbean, are favorite vacation spots of the new Colombian middle class.) Despite the Dutch decor, however, a trio of strolling musicians plays foot-tapping Colombian folk music.

Restaurant Eduardo is at 11th Avenue and 89th Street. Reservations are in order and the phone number is 364-387. Don Eduardo, the owner, opens at noon and starts closing at 1 A.M. Food is still relatively inexpensive in Bogotá, and dinner for two, including aperitif and a bottle of fine Chilean wine, is around $12. Strangers should ask their hotel taxi driver (taxis, too, are relatively inexpensive in Bogotá) to pick them up after dining because most residents of the district in which Restaurant Eduardo is located have their own cars and taxis are often rare late at night. Another tip: Foreign liquor is heavily taxed and so is quite expensive in relation to food (scotch, for instance, is $1.50 a drink). And remember, Bogotá's altitude (about 8,500 feet) serves to double the impact of alcohol in one's oxygen-short bloodstream.

—H. J. Maidenberg

Czechoslovakia

PRAGUE

SANTA CLARA. Under the Prague Zoo is the Santa Clara, a cavelike, intimate place that was once a wine cellar. Its small size and location away from the center of town impart a particularly cozy atmosphere that the other wine-cellar restaurants in the Czech capital cannot match. Unusual, too, are the Santa Clara's resident crickets, which roam free. They were removed once, but the customers missed the background noise of their chirping and so they are back, in limited numbers.

The Santa Clara holds only about 25 diners and they sit on sheepskin-covered wooden benches. The service is fairly typical for a Czech restaurant, which is to say, accommodating. The specialty of the house is fondue, both cheese and beef, the latter accompanied by a variety of excellent sauces.

The Santa Clara is at U Trojskeho Zamku 9. The phone number is 84-12-13. It is open for dinner only, seven days a week, from 7 P.M. to midnight, and a meal runs about $8 a person. Aside from a visit to the zoo, there's nothing much to do in the area unless the idea of a pre-dinner stroll through nearby vineyards attracts you.

OPERA GRILL. For a restaurant more centrally located than the Santa Clara, try the Opera Grill. It, too, is a small one-room affair, but the 20 or so diners it holds sit in huge upholstered chairs amid a Meissen decor while a piano tinkles in the background. There is probably a menu but you may never get to see it. Before each course the owner will discuss what he can offer for that course. One dish he probably will recommend is the house specialty, crêpes stuffed with mushrooms, ham, and veal and topped with asparagus tips and grated parmesan cheese. The clientele is quite select—Czechs with money, diplomats, and tourists who have been told about the place. The wines are both local and imported.

The Opera Grill is at Divadelni 24, in a small square near the opera house. The phone number is 26-55-08. Dinner only is served, starting at 7 P.M., and it will cost around $10 to $12 a person. Book a table in advance. The restaurant closes for a month's vacation in the summer, usually in July.

Since both the Santa Clara and Opera Grill serve dinner only, for lunch try one of Prague's many taverns, especially if you like beer. The taverns serve wine, too, but Czech draft beer is unsurpassed and should be sampled. The taverns are known to many Czechs by their distinctive beers—dark, light, regional, or whatever—with the food of strictly secondary interest. Ask your hotel receptionist to recommend a nearby tavern or to give you the name and address of his own favorite. The waiters may not speak English, and you may share your table with others, but you will enjoy the experience.

—*James Feron*

OPERA GRILL SPECIAL
Based on the recipe of the Opera Grill, Prague

*This recipe for crêpes stuffed with ham, veal and mushrooms
can be made with omelets if preferred. Simply substitute the
omelets for the crêpes and proceed with the filling and garnish
as given below.*

CRÊPES

1 egg
1 egg yolk
8 tablespoons flour
salt
sugar
1 teaspoon melted butter
1 cup milk
vegetable oil or butter

1. Put the egg, yolk, flour, and a pinch of salt and sugar into a blender container. Blend at low speed to combine. Add the melted butter. Blend again at low speed, gradually adding the milk. Cover and blend at top speed for 1 minute or until the batter is the consistency of light cream.
2. Cover and refrigerate, letting the batter rest at least an hour before using.
3. Heat a 6 to 7 inch crêpe pan which has a light coating of vegetable oil or butter over moderately high heat. When the oil is just beginning to smoke, remove the pan from the heat and pour 3 to 4 tablespoons (a scant ¼ cup) of batter into the middle of the hot pan. Tilt the pan in every direction so the batter runs over the entire surface of the pan. Return the pan to the heat for 60 seconds. Loosen crêpe and when brown lift it out (do not cook the other side). Grease the pan again and repeat the procedure until you have used up all the batter.
4. Keep the crêpes warm by covering them with a dish or setting them in a low oven.

Yield: About 8 to 10 crêpes, 1/16 inch thick.

NOTE: The crêpes may be made several hours ahead of serving time or even be kept for several days in the refrigerator. Reheat in low oven before using.

FILLING

¼ pound mushrooms, sliced
3 tablespoons butter
1 tablespoon lemon juice
1 cup veal stock (see page 94) or ½ cup canned beef bouillon and ½ cup canned chicken broth
1 egg yolk, lightly beaten
½ cup heavy cream
½ cup finely chopped cooked ham
½ cup finely chopped cooked veal

1. Place the mushrooms, 1 tablespoon butter, and the lemon juice in a saucepan with a tablespoon or two of water. Bring to a boil and simmer over low heat for 10 minutes. Add the liquid from this mixture to the veal stock.
2. Heat the veal stock to a simmer. Off heat, add the egg yolk, cream, and 2 tablespoons butter. Cook, stirring, over very low heat until mixture thickens. Do not allow liquid to boil.
3. Add the mushrooms, ham, and veal.

(CONTINUED)

ASSEMBLING AND GARNISH

4 mushrooms, chopped and sautéed
8 asparagus tips
freshly grated parmesan cheese
1 tablespoon butter

1. Preheat the broiler.
2. Fill the crêpes, one at a time, placing the filling on the cooked side of each and rolling up.
3. Place the rolled crêpes on a shallow ovenproof dish. Sprinkle with the mushrooms, place an asparagus tip on each crêpe, sprinkle with parmesan cheese, and dot with butter. Brown under the broiler.

Yield: 4 servings

Denmark

COPENHAGEN

PLAZA HOTEL RESTAURANT. Right in the middle of Copenhagen, just across from the Central Station, near the world-famous Tivoli Gardens and the shop-lined pedestrian street called Stroget, is the Plaza Hotel, an elegant establishment whose motto is yesterday's charm with today's comfort. If you want to stay in the old five-story building with its 120 rooms and ten suites, you should try to make reservations at least a month ahead because you will be competing for accommodations with the likes of Victor Borge, the comedian, and Birgit Nilsson, the opera singer. But even if you can't get a room at the Plaza, you shouldn't deny yourself the pleasure of a meal in its restaurant, which is indubitably the best in Copenhagen and has the finest French kitchen in northern Europe.

Before you enter the restaurant, have an aperitif in the Library Bar, a beautiful room filled with antique furniture and books from floor to ceiling through which guests may browse. Once in the restaurant, with its tasteful decor and effortlessly efficient service, you can watch the kitchen staff finish the preparation of your dinner out in the dining area.

I can heartily recommend the fillet of veal with morels in a glazed cream sauce, a specialty of the Plaza's kitchen. Another magnificent dish is the fillet of turbot poached in white wine and served with chopped hazelnuts and a mousseline sauce. The Plaza's house wine is really good, or you can enjoy a bottle from its cellar.

The hotel is at 4 Bernstorffgade. The phone number is 14-92-62. The restaurant is open every day from noon to midnight except Christmas Eve. A lunch or dinner, including service charge and the house wine or wonderful Danish beer, should run between $8 and $15, but it can go higher if several specialties are ordered. Book a table in advance.

—Steffen Gram

FILLET OF VEAL WITH MORELS
Based on the recipe of the Plaza Hotel Restaurant, Copenhagen

4 6-ounce fillets of veal, cut ½ inch thick
white pepper
3–4 tablespoons butter
20 morels (see note)
¾ cup dry white port
⅓ cup dry white wine
1 tablespoon meat glaze (recipe below)
⅓ cup heavy cream
salt

1. Season the fillets with white pepper and sauté them in 2 tablespoons butter for 10 minutes. Remove the fillets and keep them warm.
2. Drain the morels, wash them well, and dry them with paper towels. Cut each morel in half and sauté for 10 minutes in the same skillet in which the veal was sautéed.
3. Pour the port and white wine over the morels. Add the meat glaze and simmer until about ⅔ of the liquid is absorbed.
4. Add the heavy cream and simmer until the sauce is thick.
5. Stir in about a tablespoon of butter and taste for seasoning. Add salt and freshly ground white pepper if necessary.
6. Lightly brush the fillets with butter. Place them in a serving dish and pour the sauce over them. Serve immediately.

Yield: 4 servings

MEAT GLAZE (*glace de viande*)

Meat glaze is any stock boiled down until it has been reduced to the consistency of a syrup that will become a firm jelly when cooled. A veal-based glaze is the most useful and adaptable. About 3 cups of veal stock will yield about a ½ cup of glaze.

To make the glaze, skim any fat off the stock (see page 94) and strain the stock if necessary. Then bring it to a boil in an uncovered saucepan and boil it slowly until it has reduced by half. Strain it through a very fine sieve into a smaller saucepan and continue to reduce it until it becomes a syrup that lightly coats a wooden spoon. Watch it very carefully during this latter stage as it is very easy to burn. Strain the syrup into a jar and when it has cooled and turned into a jelly, cover it with a screw top and store it in the refrigerator. It will keep for several weeks under refrigeration. A small amount of glaze stirred into a sauce or soup will enhance its flavor. In addition, glaze dissolved in water may always be used instead of stock.

NOTE: Morels, edible wild mushrooms, are available canned or dried in gourmet food shops. If the morels are dried, soak them in warm water for an hour before using them.

Ecuador

QUITO

EL CONQUISTADOR. Quito was probably the best kept secret in South America before the 1972 oil boom. If not the continent's most beautiful capital, it is its cleanest, most colonial, and at the same time most Indian city.

But Quiteños of means, whatever their racial makeup, have, like too many people in South America, a negative attitude toward Indians. Consequently their culture and food reflect their tenacious hold on Ecuador's Spanish heritage. So much so, in fact, that European Spaniards are often embarrassed by it.

Among Quito's many new restaurants that cling to traditional menus as well as cater to the hordes of foreign businessmen lured to Ecuador by the oil boom is El Conquistador. Featured are Spanish seafood dishes, paellas, and pastries. As for meats, a favorite is *ternera* Oscar, a dish of white veal, artichoke hearts, and other vegetables. El Conquistador, named for the Spanish conquerors, also serves excellent steaks and chops and fresh, crisp salads that invariably include the luscious avocados grown in valleys below this 9,300-foot-high capital.

El Conquistador is in the new Hotel Colon Internacional at Amazonas and Patria Avenues in the heart of the northside business district, a short taxi ride from the colorful colonial streets of downtown Quito. Don Gerardo Muñoz, the maître d'hôtel, would be the first to advise newcomers to Quito to eat and drink lightly the first day or so because of the altitude. The lack of oxygen slows the digestion of food. The altitude also makes nights chilly despite the fact that Quito is only about 20 miles south of the equator.

El Conquistador is open for lunch every day from 11:30 A.M. to 3 P.M. and for dinner from 6:30 to 11:30 P.M. The phone number is 521-300. Lunch runs $5 or more and dinner about $9 a person, including a cocktail.

—*H. J. Maidenberg*

TERNERA OSCAR
Based on the recipe of El Conquistador, Quito

*At El Conquistador this dish is served with small peas,
saffron rice, and artichoke hearts stuffed with béarnaise sauce.*

4 slices veal, about 3½ ounces each
4 tablespoons butter (approximately)
4 tablespoons finely chopped onions
2 tablespoons flour
1⅓ cups beef stock (see page 95) or canned beef bouillon
1 teaspoon tomato paste
salt
black pepper
4 tablespoons heavy cream
4 tablespoons cognac, warmed

1. In a skillet, sauté the veal in butter until golden brown. Remove and keep warm.
2. Add the onions to the skillet and sauté until limp. Add the flour and stir to a smooth paste over very low heat. Let the flour color slightly. Add the beef stock and tomato paste and bring to a boil. Simmer gently for 4 to 5 minutes. Season with salt and pepper. Add the cream and stir to mix.
3. Add the cognac to the sauce and ignite.
4. Pour the sauce over the veal slices. Serve at once.

Yield: 2 servings

LANGOSTINOS EPICUR
Based on the recipe of El Conquistador, Quito

When this dish is served at El Conquistador, the maître d'hôtel forms a large ring of rice on the guest's plate and places the shrimp, mushrooms, and lots of sauce in the middle.

6 tablespoons butter
2½ tablespoons flour
1 cup chicken stock (see page 101) or canned chicken broth
salt
black pepper
1 cup dry white wine
¼ cup Pernod
1 teaspoon curry powder
½ teaspoon dried tarragon
pinch dried thyme
1 bay leaf
30 large fresh shrimp, shelled and deveined, with heads removed
2 cloves garlic, minced
2 tablespoons finely chopped onions
2 cups small fresh mushroom caps
½ cup heavy cream
¼ cup cognac

1. To make the sauce, melt 2 tablespoons butter in a saucepan. Off heat, stir in the flour until a smooth paste is achieved. Return the pan to the heat, add the chicken stock, and cook, stirring, until the sauce is thick and smooth. Season with salt and pepper.
2. Add the wine, Pernod, curry powder, tarragon, thyme, and bay leaf. Stir to blend. Correct seasoning. Remove from heat.
3. In a large, heavy skillet, melt 4 tablespoons butter and sauté the shrimp, garlic, onions, and mushrooms over high heat for 3 minutes.
4. Add the sauce to skillet, cover, and simmer slowly for 6 to 8 minutes. Add the cream, stir to blend, add the cognac, ignite, stir, and serve immediately.

Yield: 4 servings

Egypt

CAIRO

ALADIN'S. Cairo is not exactly a city for gourmets, but I like Aladin's. It is a cozy if cavernous place with a good bar behind an ornamental Egyptian wood screen and a huge window with Aladin and the giant painted on it.

The Egyptian hors d'oeuvres at Aladin's are splendid. Among them are boiled eggplant with garlic, vinegar, paprika, and green pepper; *baba ghanouj*, a spread made of grilled eggplant and sesame paste; and *tahina*, which is made with sesame oil, lemon juice, garlic, and vinegar. Other hors d'oeuvres include yogurt with cucumbers and sautéed chicken livers. Ask the waiter to bring you all the hors d'oeuvres, together with a bottle of Ptolémés, a dry Egyptian white wine. Incidentally, outside of the luxury hotels where you can eat American food at American prices, Aladin's is one of the few places in Cairo where white wine comes properly chilled and in an ice bucket.

After you have feasted on the hors d'oeuvres, you might try an Egyptian main dish such as *tulli*, a veal stew with tomatoes, peas, carrots, green peppers, and artichokes; or *kofta*, patties of meat, raisins, almonds, and hazelnuts. There are also Italian dishes on the menu and fish from the Mediterranean. The grilled shrimp, when available, are excellent, and so is the *dorade* and the *loup de mer*. I've never made it through to dessert, but the waiters talk about it with affection. The clientele is composed mainly of Egyptians and travelers from neighboring Arab countries, and the diners have an air of more or less mysterious business about them rather than leisure.

Aladin's is at 26 Sherif Street. The restaurant is usually uncrowded but you might want to phone ahead; the number is 54107. A full meal runs about $5 to $7.50 a person with wine but without cocktails, and as in all good Cairo restaurants a foreigner is expected to leave about 10 percent in tips democratically distributed (by the customer himself) to everyone from the headwaiter, to the waiter, to the boy at the door. Lunch is served starting at 1:30 P.M. and dinner from about 8:30 until past midnight. Aladin's is open seven days a week, all year. It is air conditioned and located in the business district, with good leather stores—particularly handbags—nearby.

—*Henry Tanner*

TULLI
Based on the recipe of Aladin's, Cairo

1 pound stewing veal, cut into 1-inch cubes
3 tablespoons butter
1 pound tomatoes, cut into thick slices
1 pound carrots, cut into 1-inch rounds
1 pound fresh or frozen green peas
2 artichoke hearts (see note)
4 green peppers, seeded and cut into 8 wedges
½ cup water
salt
black pepper

1. In a heavy casserole sauté the veal in butter until light brown.
2. Add the tomatoes, carrots, peas, artichoke hearts, green peppers, water, salt, and pepper. Bring to a boil, cover, and simmer for about 1 hour.
3. Preheat the oven to 350 degrees.
4. Place the casserole in the oven for about 30 minutes to finish cooking. Serve hot over white rice.

Yield: 4 servings

NOTE: To prepare the artichokes, pull off all the tough leaves by bending back and snapping off. Cut across the artichoke right above the heart, slicing off the rest of the leaves. Scrape away the hairy choke with a sharp knife. Cut off the stem and trim the bottom of the heart. Halve the hearts, rub with lemon, and use in recipe as directed. Canned or thawed frozen artichoke hearts can be substituted.

KOFTA
Based on the recipe of Aladin's, Cairo

Although veal is preferred, this dish can also be made with ground beef.

1 pound ground veal
2 small onions, finely chopped
½ cup raisins
½ cup coarsely chopped almonds
½ cup coarsely chopped hazelnuts
salt
black pepper

1. Preheat the oven to 350 degrees.
2. Combine all the ingredients in a mixing bowl. Mix thoroughly. With moistened hands, form mixture into 8 to 10 small patties, about 2 inches in diameter.
3. Place the patties on a greased baking sheet and bake for about 1 hour, or until golden brown. Serve with white rice.

Yield: 4 servings

Eire–see Ireland

England

CASTLE ASHBY

THE FALCON. Northamptonshire is not generally regarded as tourist territory. In fact, this agricultural county's main claim to fame, apart from the lovely flat greenness of its farmland, is that its central position gives it more neighboring counties—nine, to be exact—than any other county in England. Northamptonshire's pastoral charm, uncelebrated though it may be, is always within easy reach of travelers meandering through the Midlands. And for such travelers the Falcon makes a suitable stop.

A hotel that was formerly a farmhouse, the Falcon dates back to the sixteenth century. It is situated in the village of Castle Ashby, a cluster of fieldstone houses on the estate of the Marquess of Northampton not far from his ancestral home. While the Falcon's restaurant may not be a temple of haute cuisine, what it does offer is good food, well served, in the cozy surroundings of an English inn and the tranquillity of a rural setting.

A visit to the Falcon should begin with some draft beer or a gin and tonic in the cellar bar with its stone walls, beamed ceiling, and polished barrels for tables. It used to be the farmhouse dairy and is reached by descending a steep flight of winding stairs. Afterwards, proceed to the dining room, which seats 70 persons and overlooks a well-kept lawn and garden where roses bloom as late as December in mild winters.

This is hunting country, and the Falcon's specialties are pheasant, quail, hare, and venison, according to season. Also roast duck with orange sauce. The duck is always listed on the menu; the game dishes are not, and patrons should telephone ahead to inquire which are being served on any particular day. For a country restaurant the menu is extensive and far from insular. The first courses usually available, for example, include *escargots bourguignon*, on the one hand, and corn on the cob (which is pretty exotic to an Englishman) on the other.

Farther down the card, however, it's well to choose typically English dishes like the grilled Dover sole, the roast chicken and bacon or the roast joint of the day. The roast beef and voluminous Yorkshire pudding are hearty and tasty, and so is the steak and kidney pie, the meat immersed in a wonderful gravy beneath a crisp, flaky pastry crust. The vegetables, broccoli and spinach among them, are grown locally and delight city dwellers who have forgotten how good fresh vegetables can taste. There is also a cold buffet of various salads—ox tongue salad, ham salad, chicken salad, and duck salad—as well as cold lobster or salmon with mayonnaise.

The desserts often include a delicious blackberry and apple tart and, from the rolling cart, pastries, peach flan, and trifle. Assorted cheeses are available, too, and for those of large appetite the Falcon maintains an old English custom, that of a savory dish served *after* dessert. Sardines on toast and Welsh rarebit are examples. Coffee, which can be taken while one is sunk into a deep chair in the lounge, comes with petits fours.

The wine list is quite comprehensive, with London-bottled burgundies and bordeaux as well as German, Italian, and Portuguese wines.

The Falcon serves lunch from 12:30 to 2 P.M. and dinner from 7:30 to 9 P.M., six days a week. Lunch only is served on Sunday. The average cost of a meal with wine is about $7.50 a person. The resident manager of the hotel is Mr. M. Ward and the phone number is Yardley Hastings 200.

Castle Ashby is about eight miles southeast of Northampton and 63 miles north of London. It lies about 12 miles east of the Newport Pagnell exit of Motorway 1, England's main north-south highway.

—*Stanley Carr*

STEAK AND KIDNEY PIE
Based on the recipe of the Falcon, Castle Ashby

2 pounds stewing steak
¼ pound lamb kidneys, washed and trimmed
salt
black pepper
2 tablespoons butter
1 small onion, finely chopped
1 clove garlic, finely minced

¾ teaspoon worcestershire sauce or to taste
pinch of dried rosemary
1 tablespoon flour
½ teaspoon gravy browning sauce (such as Gravy Master or Kitchen Bouquet)
1 short pastry crust (recipe below)
1 egg
1 tablespoon milk

1. Cut the steak into pieces about 3 inches long, 1½ inches wide, and ⅓ to ½ inch thick. Cut the kidneys into small cubes. Season the meat with salt and pepper.
2. Melt the butter in a heavy saucepan, add the meat, onion, garlic, worcestershire sauce, and rosemary. Cover the pan and let the meat stew in its own juices over a low flame for about an hour, stirring occasionally.
3. Preheat the oven to 350 degrees.
4. Blend the tablespoon of flour with a little cold water and add it to the meat and juices in the pan to make a gravy. Add the browning sauce and let simmer for a few minutes until the gravy thickens.
5. Place the meat and gravy in a not-too-deep baking dish. There should be enough gravy to come at least halfway up the side of the dish. If there is not, add enough beef bouillon to bring it up to that level.
6. Cover the dish with the pastry crust, seal and trim the edges. Beat the egg and milk together and lightly brush the dough with the mixture. Cut several gashes in the top.
7. Bake for approximately 30 to 40 minutes, until the crust is lightly browned. Serve hot.

Yield: 4 servings

SHORT PASTRY CRUST

2 cups sifted all-purpose flour
pinch of salt
5 tablespoons very cold margarine
4 tablespoons shortening
2–4 tablespoons ice water

1. Sift the flour and salt into a chilled bowl. Cut in the margarine and shortening quickly with a pastry blender or 2 knives until the mixture resembles fine crumbs.
2. Add the water gradually, adding just enough to hold the dough together.
3. Shape the mixture into a ball, pressing lightly. Place the ball on a lightly floured board and roll it out until it is large enough to cover the baking dish.

LONDON

L'ETOILE. London has its share, likely more than its share, of French restaurants. Most of the expensive ones are styled to match their prices, with a certain grandeur or up-to-date stainless chic. But if you prefer marble and tile, the flavor of pre-war Paris untouched by interior decorators, try the Etoile. Outside there is a sign with a faded blue star (or is it green?): "Hôtel et Restaurant de L'Etoile." It could be the Left Bank. Inside is one long, narrow room with the same half-dozen waiters always bustling about. Very comforting. Very English, too: The waiters pretend to be nothing else. That is why I do not call it L'Etoile but *the* Etoile.

For me, the high point of a meal here is the rolling cart of hors d'oeuvres. I do not mean little dishes of pickles and tidbits from which one makes up a plate. I mean separate platters of superb creations, any one of which makes a memorable opening. Cold turbot with prawns and olive oil is almost always among them, and a delicious sea bass, and *salade niçoise*, and dressed crab, and asparagus in season, and a dozen other dishes that make decision a torment.

After that my own inclination is toward a self-denying main course, such as *paillard de veau*, a thin, tender veal steak broiled and served with lemon. But for those who wish, there are traditional French bourgeois dishes such as tripe and brains, or rack of lamb, or *steak au poivre*.

The vegetables are worth mentioning, too, because they are fresh and enterprising: very often edible-podded peas, for example, and *ratatouille*, the eggplant-zucchini-tomato-onion-pepper casserole of Provence. Fruit is a strong entry in what we call dessert and the upper-class English call pudding. As soon as strawberries or raspberries appear, the Etoile will have them, and also fresh peaches or figs served with a dash of lemon when in season.

Wines: an extensive list, really impressive. Among the whites I would not look farther than a delicate, flinty sancerre—Clos de Paradis '70 at $5.50. I am a claret man, so I shall stick to those among the reds and say that they range from Cos d'Estournel '63 at $7.75 to Cheval Blanc '64 at $32.50.

The opening cold turbot costs about $3, *steak au poivre* is about $4.50, and $1.50 or so will get you strawberries and cream. That means cream. The menu, carrying out the Etoile's old-Paris flavor, is appropriately hard to read, being handwritten in green, red, and blue on a blue card.

The Etoile is at 30 Charlotte Street, near Tottenham Court Road and not far from the Post Office Tower with its revolving view of London at the top. Charlotte Street is great for wandering, full of Greek restaurants and German delicatessens and the greatest hardware (brass and bronze and the like) store ever. The Etoile's phone number is 636-7189 and you must book ahead. Lunch is served from 12:30 to 2:30 P.M., dinner from 6:30 to 10 P.M., and the restaurant is closed Saturday and Sunday.

—*Anthony Lewis*

TURBOT À LA MONEGASQUE
Based on the recipe of L'Etoile, London

Although this cold fish salad is always made with turbot at L'Etoile, flounder or other similar firm, white-fleshed fish could be substituted if turbot is unavailable.

3½–4 pounds turbot
2 whole onions
1 sprig parsley
6 black peppercorns
1 teaspoon salt
½ pound peeled cooked prawns or medium shrimp
1 onion, chopped
3 sprigs parsley, chopped
juice of 3 lemons
4 tablespoons olive oil
white pepper
1 cup mayonnaise
black olives for garnish

1. Simmer the turbot, whole onions, parsley, peppercorns, and salt in enough water to cover the fish for 10 to 12 minutes, or until fish is cooked. Leave to cool.
2. Clean and remove the bones. Place the cooked turbot in a large bowl and mash.
3. Add the prawns, onion, parsley, lemon juice, olive oil, and pepper. Mix gently. Let the mixture marinate for 1 hour.
4. Serve on a bed of lettuce with mayonnaise and black olives.

Yield: 4 servings

INIGO JONES. The first great English architect, and the one who helped introduce the Palladian style of columns and classic proportions to Britain, was Inigo Jones (1573–1652). One of his buildings that still stands is St. Paul's Church, Covent Garden, backdrop for Eliza Doolittle's flower-selling. In the nineteenth century the church built a handsome mission house down the street, and that mission house is now a restaurant: the Inigo Jones.

It may well be London's aesthetically most pleasing. There are spacious rooms on two floors, with lots of distance between tables. Set here and there are stained glass windows from original designs by William Morris. (The building was a stained glass factory before its latest conversion.) There is a harpsichord in the foyer, and in the evenings someone plays Bach and Clementi.

The food is notable also, and more adventurous than almost anywhere else in London. Among soups, for example, there is *topinambour*, a mixture of Jerusalem artichoke and cucumber, or a fish soup garnished with slices of rolled spinach pancakes, or an iced avocado soup. Other first courses include hot fresh salmon in puff pastry, salmon soufflé, and a *pâté parfait* served on a cold artichoke heart with a sauce of sour cream and cranberry.

Simple dishes are available for those who prefer them: a first-class grilled calf's liver, for one. But the main courses also include some in which the chef's ingenuity and taste are evident, an example being a diced beef fillet in a sauce of brandy, cream, and fresh green peppercorns. The desserts appear in the usual way of a good English restaurant, on a rolling cart: fresh fruit salad, trifle, rich *gâteaux*, the lot.

The Inigo Jones is at the corner of Garrick and Floral Streets in the Covent Garden area. Walk down Garrick Street a few steps and you are in the West End theater district. Floral Street leads to the Royal Opera House. Reservations are essential at the Inigo Jones, and the restaurant's phone number is 836-6456. Prices, which include a 15 percent service charge, range from $2.50 for the artichoke-cucumber soup and around $4 for the salmon in puff pastry to $6 for calf's liver and $6.50 for the diced fillet of beef. The wine list is interesting if not grand: $5 for a fresh muscadet or the house beaujolais villages at the modest end, and on up through such a superb claret as Chateau Gruaud Larose '64 at $22. The Inigo Jones is open for lunch Monday through Friday from 12:30 to 2:30 P.M., for dinner Monday through Saturday from 6 P.M. to midnight.

—Anthony Lewis

PAYSANNE DE BOEUF NIGELLE
Based on the recipe of Inigo Jones, London

6 tablespoons butter
3 tablespoons flour
1 teaspoon tomato paste
½ cup dry sherry
2 cups beef stock (see page 95) or canned beef bouillon
20 green peppercorns (see note)
2 pounds fillet of beef, cut into small cubes
½ cup heavy cream

1. Melt 3 tablespoons butter, stir in the flour, tomato paste, half the sherry, and the beef stock. Cook gently for 15 minutes or longer until sauce is quite thick.
2. Crush the peppercorns and poach them in the remaining sherry over low heat for 10 minutes. Add to the beef stock mixture when that begins to thicken.
3. Melt the remaining 3 tablespoons butter in a large pan and fry the meat in it. Add the juice from the pan to the sauce. Set the meat aside.
4. Simmer the sauce for 5 minutes. Then, while still simmering, add the heavy cream
5. Add the meat, bring to a boil, and serve.

Yield: 4 servings

NOTE: Green peppercorns are available in cans, packed either in water or vinegar. If you use the vinegar-packed variety, wash and drain them before using.

RULES. London is a town where the best restaurants are not authentically English. Rules, however, is worth a visit because of its atmosphere and long history. It was founded in 1798 by Thomas Rule in the heart of Covent Garden and a number of stories about it have grown up. The small door that leads onto a landing of narrow steps, for instance, was supposedly built for Edward VII so that he could arrive and leave unnoticed with Lillie Langtry. The waiters also tell stories of visits by Dickens, Thackeray, Galsworthy, H. G. Wells, George Bernard Shaw, and Sean O'Casey.

The food is good and the service pleasant and attentive, even though it is hardly the finest restaurant in London. The continental restaurants—Greek, French, and Italian—are really my favorites, but for visitors who want an English atmosphere, Rules is the place. It is cozy at the ground floor and upstairs tables, and there are wood paneling, red frilly lampshades, a swirling ceiling fan, and English prints of scenes and people long gone. I suggest the smoked salmon as an appetizer, to be followed by one of several English dishes on the large menu—perhaps jugged hare and red currant jelly, or roast beef and Yorkshire pudding, or pheasant in season. There is also an excellent chicken pancake mornay. For dessert, if you want to go all-English, have the black currant and apple pie with thick fresh cream poured over it. Or if you feel like relaxing the stiff upper lip by then, try the crêpes suzette.

Rules is at 35 Maiden Lane, near the Royal Opera House. The phone number is 836-5314. Appetizers range in price from about $2 for avocado with shrimp to more than $3 for lobster cocktail. The smoked salmon appetizer is $2.50. Entrées range from around $3 for the jugged hare and $3.50 for the roast beef and Yorkshire pudding to $7.50 for a whole pheasant. Meals are served from noon to 3 P.M. and 6 to a little after 11 P.M. Monday through Friday. Closed Saturday, Sunday, and for three weeks in August.

—Alvin Shuster

CHICKEN PANCAKES MORNAY
Based on the recipe of Rules, London

8 crêpes (see page 58)
½ large boiling chicken (2–2½ pounds of chicken)
salt
black pepper
1 onion, sliced
1 carrot, quartered
bouquet garni (2 sprigs parsley, ½ teaspoon dried thyme, 1 bay leaf tied in cheesecloth)

SAUCE

4 tablespoons butter
2 tablespoons flour
2 cups chicken stock (see steps 2, 3 and 4)
salt
black pepper
1 teaspoon heavy cream (optional)

grated gruyère or parmesan cheese

1. Make the crêpes and reserve.
2. Place the chicken in a heavy pot and barely cover it with cold salted water. Add the pepper, onion, carrot, and bouquet garni. Bring to a boil, lower the heat, and simmer, partially covered, for an hour or so, or until the meat falls easily from the bones. Skim the scum from time to time during the simmering.
3. Remove the chicken from the broth and let it cool. Pick the meat from the bones and cut it into fine shreds.
4. Strain the stock and set aside 2 cups for the sauce. Store the rest in the refrigerator for another use.
5. To make the sauce: Melt the butter in a pan, but be careful not to brown it. Add the flour and cook over very low heat for 5 minutes, stirring constantly. Put in the chicken stock and mix well. Bring the mixture to a boil and let it boil for about 5 minutes. This will reduce the mixture to about ⅓ of its quantity. Season it with salt and pepper. If a richer sauce is desired, and if the stock is not too rich, add a teaspoon of heavy cream.
6. Reserve a small amount of the sauce to moisten the top of the crêpes. Fold the shredded chicken into the rest of the sauce. Add salt and pepper if necessary.
7. Place the chicken mixture inside the crêpes, roll them up, place them in an ovenproof serving dish, and moisten them with the reserved sauce.
8. Sprinkle grated cheese liberally on top and heat in a preheated broiler for 4 or 5 minutes or until nicely browned. Serve hot.

Yield: 4 servings

ON A TRAIN

BRITISH RAIL BREAKFAST. As James Reston remarked years ago, the Europeans have invented a marvelous new mode of travel. It allows the traveler to read his newspaper, doze or look at the scenery while he moves, without worrying about traffic. This wonderful creation is called a railroad. Or, as they say in Britain, railway.

It is possible not only to travel on trains but also to eat on them—and in style. The French would claim the food honors, and doubtless they would be correct. But the English are better than the French at breakfasts, on trains as in hotels and homes. Enter the restaurant car at, say, 8 o'clock in the morning on your way to Manchester or York. The tables are covered with white linen. There are mounds of butter on each, and a jar of Chivers thick-cut marmalade. If things are working well, a waiter in a white jacket will approach soon after you sit down and offer you tea or coffee at once.

Then the menu. Choices are simple. Continental breakfast costs a dollar and change. That offers an opening of fruit juice or corn flakes or porridge, then toast or rolls in limitless quantities, with coffee or tea. But who would have the self-restraint to stop at a continental breakfast?

For two dollars and change there is the full breakfast. After the same openers comes what the menu calls the Grill Tray. That means two eggs any style, plus bacon, plus sausage, plus tomato, plus grilled mushrooms, plus sautéed potatoes, plus fried bread. Yes, fried bread. That is a very English dish that is exactly what it says it is. They probably fed it to Oliver Twist, but my children swear by it.

Or instead of the eggs and meat you may have fish: grilled kippers or poached haddock. I go for sausages myself and consider British Rail's to be of a superior tangy type. In fact, the only weakness in the breakfast is the toast, which is uninteresting. They should add health bread.

On a busy morning the service of breakfast on a British train is theater. Instead of taking individual orders, the waiters come through with huge trays, letting everyone take what he will: first trays of half grapefruits and juice, then cereal, then platters of lovely greasy fried eggs, then fish, baskets of toast . . . . David Storey, who made a locker room into drama, could write another play.

Most intercity trains in Britain have restaurant cars, but it is advisable to check ahead of time. And they do serve meals other than breakfast. Once a woman opposite me at lunch ordered steak and kidney pudding, while I had fresh grilled salmon. She admired my salmon and said she hated steak and kidney pudding. Why, then, had she ordered it? "White wine," she said, "does not agree with me."

—Anthony Lewis

Ethiopia

ADDIS ABABA

THE KOKEB. Addis Ababa, the headquarters of the Organization of African Unity and the United Nations Economic Commission for Africa, is a cosmopolitan city of more than three-quarters of a million people. In it you can find restaurants serving French, Italian, Chinese, and other foreign dishes. The Kokeb serves nonindigenous dishes, too, but its real forte is excellent Ethiopian cuisine.

The word "kokeb" means "star" in Amharic, the language of the predominant people of Ethiopia, and it is appropriate because the restaurant is on the top floor of a tall building with a star on its roof that lights up at night. This star is the beacon by which those seeking the true delights of Ethiopian cooking set their course.

The way up to the Kokeb is in a glass-sided elevator from which you gain a widening vista of the city as you ascend. Addis Ababa itself is at an elevation of 8,000 feet and is ringed by the peaks of a mountainous plateau. The Kokeb's comfortable, well-stocked bar looks right out over the city and is an ideal spot from which to view a rose-pink sunset above the ring of mountains.

The decor of the Kokeb is built around the centuries-old Coptic wall paintings and traditional furnishings that may still be found in the homes of the ruling Amharic aristocracy. There are the hide-covered round shields and spears of the fierce highland warriors, silver Coptic crosses, and portraits of dark-eyed Ethiopian women with fixed, distant stares. Floppy wicker baskets and hour-glass-shaped tables—*mesabs*—in reds, blues, and greens hold fruits, breads, and other sideboard stores.

The Kokeb's traditional dishes include thick, spicy stews, chopped beef, and chicken along with newly harvested vegetables like bright carrots and red onions, and such fruits as figs, oranges, and bananas. In addition to the traditional honey wine, *tej*, there is a wide variety of excellent low-cost Ethiopian wines that resemble those of Mediterranean countries. Ethiopian beers are also excellent. Coffee, which Ethiopians say originated in their country, is usually served black. If taken in traditional style, it may be flavored with honey, a lump of butter, and a pinch of salt.

What makes dining at the Kokeb or other Ethiopian establishments an extra pleasure is the wonderful natural courtesy of Ethiopians, which is combined with an impressive natural dignity. At the Kokeb you will be greeted by a handsome Amharic gentleman in Western dress or an even more attractive Amharic woman wearing either the latest Western fashion or the traditional *shama*. The latter is a loose-fitting but graceful long dress with a shawl or stole that is deftly draped over the shoulder to display the Coptic pattern. It is also worn by the waitresses.

The Kokeb is on Menelik II Avenue adjacent to Africa Hall, which houses the Organization of African Unity and the United Nations Economic Commission. The phone number is 40-89-03. The restaurant is open every evening, and dinner is usually served until about 10:30 P.M. A three- or four-course Ethiopian meal with Ethiopian wine should cost around $6. A 10 percent tip is standard, but the service may move you to make it 15.

—Brendan Jones

SEGANA DORO WAT
Based on the recipe of the Kokeb, Addis Ababa

Ethiopians usually eat stews, such as this one of lamb and chicken, with a thin bread called indjara, *which is made of* teff, *a grain virtually unobtainable outside Ethiopia. A portion of the stew is placed on an* indjara, *a strip is torn off, wrapped up, and popped into the mouth. A pleasant custom at dinner parties is the selection and wrapping of a choice morsel by one diner, who then feeds it to a fellow diner as a token of affection or esteem. In Western homes, in the absence of* indjaras, *the stew could be served with rice.*

4 cups sliced onions
8 tablespoons (1 stick) butter
2 pounds stewing lamb, cut into 2-inch chunks

(CONTINUED)

½ cup lemon juice
1 3-pound chicken, cut into serving pieces
4 tablespoons flour dissolved in 4 tablespoons water
½ teaspoon ground red pepper
½ teaspoon paprika
½ teaspoon ground ginger
salt
black pepper
8 large carrots, cut into 2-inch rounds
2 large tomatoes, cut into thick slices
8 hard-boiled eggs, peeled

1. In a large heavy casserole, brown the onions in the butter. Add the lamb, lemon juice, and enough water to cover. Cover and braise for 30 minutes.
2. Add the chicken pieces and braise for another 30 minutes, or until meat is nearly tender.
3. Stir the flour solution into the stew, then add the red pepper, paprika, ginger, salt, black pepper, carrots, and tomatoes. Cover and simmer until the vegetables are done, about 25 to 30 minutes.
4. Gash the eggs lightly in several places and add to the stew a few minutes before serving.

Yield: 6 to 8 servings

France

LES BAUX-DE-PROVENCE

LA BAUMANIÈRE. The medieval mountaintop castle of the Princes of Provence and the surrounding village of Les Baux, once fallen into rocky, brooding ruins, are today alive again, thanks to a vast restoration undertaken by the French government. Rebuilding was prompted by the grandeur of the site and its romantic history. Les Baux was a power in the Middle Ages, dominating scores of cities and towns, and now it is something of an artistic community with specialists in ceramics and hand-woven or hand-printed textiles. There are pleasant little artisan shops and a superb panorama of Provence from the crags above the castle.

Below, in the valley, about halfway between Arles and Avignon, is one of France's best and most agreeable restaurants, La Baumanière. It is thoroughly Provençal, from its light sauces soaked with fresh herbs to its sturdy rustic furniture and broad tiled terraces with flowers that sparkle against the dull silver olive groves beyond. Winter is the best, brightest time to go. Early spring can be gray and bone-chilling from the mistral, which blows off the Alps, and summer is likely to be hot.

La Baumanière is also a hotel, with charming rooms furnished in authentic Provençal style, antiques and all. But it is small and reservations should be made as far ahead as possible. There is horseback riding, and several chateaux and old farms in the neighborhood are worth a visit.

The cuisine is a special delight for those who like full flavor without the heaviness of cream and butter so favored in northern France. The menu is extensive, drawing on both the most delicate Mediterranean seafood and the tender young lamb of the hills. Raymond Thuilier, the owner, manager, and master chef, relies much more on the savory bouquet of local herbs than on the garlic and red pepper staples of nearby Marseilles. His *rouget à la nage au basilic* (red snapper in basil sauce) will set even jaded palates afloat. And his scrambled eggs (with hollandaise sauce and shrimp, ham, or tomato mixed in) show what heights even a normally commonplace dish can attain.

The address of the restaurant is Oustaù de Baumanière, Les Baux-de-Provence. The phone number is 97-33-07. It is open for lunch and dinner all year and Thuilier says that closing time is whenever the last guest leaves. He is, incidentally, a restaurateur of the old school who believes that guests deserve a gracious welcome, counts in old francs, and is delighted to show off his rambling, polished kitchens. The price of a meal will run from about $25 to $35 a person, excluding wine and a 15 percent service charge. Hotel rooms with bath range from about $40 to $60 a night.

—*Flora Lewis*

ROUGET À LA NAGE AU BASILIC
Based on the recipe of La Baumanière, Les Baux-de-Provence

At La Baumanière this dish of red snapper with basil sauce is made with fresh local herbs and olive oil from the first cold pressing of fresh olives. Raymond Thuilier, La Baumanière's owner and master chef, describes the finished product thus: "You will find all of the Mediterranean and Provence in your dish, and the snappers will have retained their original flavor."

SAUCE

½ cup olive oil
1 clove garlic, crushed
a sprig of fresh fennel (or a pinch of dried)
a sprig of fresh rosemary (or a pinch of dried)
10–12 fresh basil leaves (or 1½ teaspoons dried)
a sprig of fresh coriander
1 medium tomato, peeled and chopped
salt
white pepper
a pinch of paprika

Make the sauce by combining all the sauce ingredients and let the mixture stand for several days for the herbs to soak well in the oil.

COURT BOUILLON

2 cups white wine (preferably the same wine you will serve with the dish)
1 quart water
1 teaspoon white vinegar
salt
white pepper
1 bay leaf and a pinch each of dried thyme, fennel, rosemary, and basil tied in
   cheesecloth
2 orange slices
2 lemon slices

FISH

1 dozen mussels, cleaned and debearded
2 1-pound red snappers, head and tail intact, cleaned and ready for cooking
fresh basil leaves

1. Make the court bouillon in a large pot by combining all of its ingredients
   and 4 of the mussels. Bring to a boil, then simmer for about 30 minutes.
2. Take a little of the court bouillon (a cup or less), put it in a small pot
   over low heat, add the remaining mussels, cover, and let steam about 10
   minutes, or just until the mussels open. Discard any that do not open.
3. While the mussels are steaming, bring the large pot of court bouillon to
   a boil again, remove it from the heat, and gently place the snappers in
   it. Leave the snappers in the court bouillon for about 5 to 6 minutes, or
   until done. If necessary, put the pot back over low to medium heat to
   fully cook the fish. Do not let the snappers boil as they should be firm
   and impeccably formed in the serving platter.
4. Carefully remove the snappers from the court bouillon and place them on
   a warm platter, cover with the sauce, add a few fresh basil leaves and the
   steamed mussels, and serve.

Yield: 2 servings

SCRAMBLED EGGS WITH HOLLANDAISE
Based on the recipe of La Baumanière, Les Baux-de-Provence

6 eggs, farm fresh if possible
4 tablespoons butter
2 tablespoons water

(CONTINUED)

4 tablespoons hollandaise sauce (recipe below)
salt
black pepper
6 tablespoons either chopped cooked shrimp, ham, or fresh tomato

1. Beat the eggs, preferably with a wire whisk, as for an omelet.
2. Put the butter and water in a saucepan. Heat until the butter is melted.
3. Add the eggs. With one hand, hold the saucepan by the handle and agitate the pan vigorously at the edge of the heat. With the other hand, constantly stir the eggs. The agitating and stirring are to keep the eggs from coagulating as what is wanted is not an omelet but very soft scrambled eggs, practically a cream. This requires constant watching and some practice as the heat must be neither too high nor too low.
4. As soon as the eggs reach a thick, creamy consistency, stir the hollandaise sauce into them rapidly and vigorously with a wire whisk. Remove from the heat, season with salt and pepper, and quickly add the shrimp, ham, or tomato.
5. Serve immediately, very hot, in cups, small bowls or preferably in hollowed-out brioches.

Yield: 2 servings

BLENDER HOLLANDAISE SAUCE

3 egg yolks
2 teaspoons lemon juice
½ teaspoon salt
white pepper
8 tablespoons (1 stick) butter

1. Place the egg yolks in a blender container with the lemon juice, salt, and pepper. Cover and blend at top speed for 3 seconds.
2. Melt the butter in a small saucepan and heat it until it foams.
3. Turn the blender on at top speed and pour in the butter in small dribbles. The sauce should become a thick cream by the time ⅔ of the butter has been added. Continue pouring until the butter is all blended and the sauce thickened, but do not pour in the milky residue at the bottom of the butter pan.
4. The sauce is now ready for use. If not used at once, it should be refrigerated in a tightly sealed jar and the desired amount carefully reheated over very low heat before use.

Yield: 1 cup or more

LA NAPOULE-PLAGE

L'OASIS. This restaurant in a village five miles west of Cannes is just what its name implies—a happy relief from the scores of fair-to-middling eating places, many of them quite expensive, that dot the French Riviera. L'Oasis is expensive, too, but I have found that the money is well spent, for the dishes are lovingly prepared by Louis Outhier, the chef and proprietor.

The restaurant, set in a delightful flower garden, is decorated with the art of the region—coastal scenes, white villas with gaily tiled roofs. Fresh flowers are on every table, and the tables are large enough for dining at ease. Moreover, the waiters are accustomed to leisurely eaters, men and women who savor their food, and the service is admirable.

Because L'Oasis is on the Mediterranean, its principal dishes are fish. I recommend the turbot, that most delicate of products of the sea, poached in champagne, a taste delight you will not soon forget. Another specialty is *langouste Belle Aurore,* a sauced lobsterlike preparation that my palate finds utterly splendid. Other possibilities are *loup en croûte,* the *loup* being a local fish that is cooked in a flaky pastry crust, and *sole au Noilly,* which is prepared with white wine, mushrooms, cream, and vermouth. One can also order various chicken and veal dishes, but my feeling is against it here, for L'Oasis is a temple of haute cuisine whose goddess is fish. Pay your respects to her and you won't be disappointed.

Monsieur Outhier's wines are Bellet and Bandol, both products of the south of France and both excellent. He has others, of course, of great repute, but I think you will be happy with his first choices.

The address of L'Oasis is simply La Napoule-Plage and it is a short drive from Cannes along the seacoast. The village itself is gay with color and well worth a stroll that you may want to undertake as a *digestif.* The restaurant's phone number is 38-95-52. It is open for lunch and dinner every day except Tuesday and it closes for vacation for a month or more in winter. À la carte main courses run from about $7 up. There are also several fixed-price meals ranging from something over $12 to almost $25, not counting wine and a 15 percent service charge.

—Alden Whitman

SOLE AU NOILLY
Based on the recipe of L'Oasis, La Napoule-Plage

2 2-pound sole, filleted, with heads and bones saved for stock

FISH STOCK

heads and bones of sole
¾ cup dry white wine
salt
1 tablespoon white pepper
bouquet garni (2 sprigs parsley, ½ teaspoon dried thyme, 1 bay leaf
tied in cheesecloth)
1 small onion, sliced
3 cups water

10 mushrooms, finely chopped
4 tablespoons butter
¾ cup dry vermouth
1¼ cups plus 3 tablespoons heavy cream
4 egg yolks
1 tablespoon lemon juice

GARNISH

3 small truffles, very finely sliced
2 tomatoes, peeled and quartered

1. To prepare the fish stock, place the fish heads and bones in a large saucepan. Add the wine, a pinch of salt, the pepper, bouquet garni, onion, and water. Simmer for about 20 minutes and strain.
2. Meanwhile, sauté the mushrooms in 2 tablespoons butter. Set aside on the lowest possible heat.
3. Fold the fillets lengthwise and put them in a skillet with the remaining 2 tablespoons butter. Pour the vermouth over and add about 1½ cups of the fish stock. Cook over medium heat until the liquid is about to boil. Turn the heat down so that the fillets cook, without boiling, for about 5 minutes, or until the fillets turn white.
4. Remove the fillets carefully, so as not to break them. Put the fillets aside and strain the broth, which will be the base for the sauce.
5. Add a pinch of salt, not more, to the broth, which should not be insipid. Stir and taste. Adjust seasoning if necessary.
6. Heat the broth slowly to reduce it. It should lose ⅘ of its volume and become a flavorful concentrate.
7. Off heat, add 1¼ cups heavy cream and beat vigorously with a wire

whisk. Then heat the sauce, bringing it slowly to the boiling point. Remove the sauce from the heat.

8. In a small bowl, combine the egg yolks, 3 tablespoons heavy cream, and a dash of lemon juice, stirring carefully. Add to this 2 tablespoons of the hot sauce, stir, then add to the main sauce. The sauce is now ready.

9. Top the fillets with the sautéed mushrooms. Then lay the fillets on a dish, sprinkle with the remaining lemon juice, and pour the sauce over.

10. Garnish with the sliced truffles and tomato wedges and serve. In the restaurant it is additionally garnished with tiny pastry crescents and presented in a basket wrapped in a white cloth.

Yield: 4 servings

PARIS

Paris is, of course, a movable feast. If I had only 36 hours to spend there, I'd cable for reservations at least two weeks ahead (a must) to dine in two little spots that are, in the view of many connoisseurs, each the best of its kind.

ALLARD. For the old bistro par excellence, with solid Burgundian food and the finest beaujolais and burgundies available, I'd revisit Allard, just off Place St. Michel in the Latin Quarter. I'd let the patron, André Allard, pick the wine according to my purse and recommend the plat du jour, but I'd lean toward Fernande Allard's fish with *beurre blanc*, followed by duck with turnips (if turnips are in season) or guinea hen with lentils or a marvelous lamb stew or, or, or. . . .

Allard is at 41 rue St.-André-des-Arts. The phone number is 326-48-23. One can eat for about $15 to $20 a person, including service charge and a modest wine. Or one can spend more. Allard is open for lunch and dinner every day except Sunday. It is closed Christmas and Easter, for a week or so in spring, and for a month or more in summer.

LE VIVAROIS. For the finest haute cuisine in Paris I'd head for the staid 16th arrondisement and Le Vivarois. Here I'd let Madame Peyrot, one of the most knowledgeable maîtres d'hôtel in Paris, choose the wine, and I'd ask her husband, a shy and brilliant chef, to choose the food. It changes with the marketing and his own genius, but among the dishes he is famous for are his duck pâté, veal kidneys, and oxtails braised in champagne. The decor is modern.

Le Vivarois is at 192 Avenue Victor-Hugo. The phone number is 504-04-31. One can eat, service charge and wine excluded, starting at about $15 to $25 a person. The restaurant is open for lunch and dinner Tuesday through Saturday, for lunch only on Sunday and is closed all day Monday. It also closes on some holidays and for a good part of the summer.

—*John L. Hess*

LE NAVARIN
Based on the recipe of Allard, Paris

This lamb stew, a great country dish, is the plat du jour
at Allard on Thursdays and Fridays, where it is served with a
casserole of potatoes. We are indebted to Karen Hess for
obtaining the recipe from Fernande Allard.

3½–4 pounds lean lamb, cut into 1½-inch cubes
3–4 tablespoons butter or chicken fat
2 medium onions, chopped
1 clove garlic, crushed
1 tablespoon tomato concentrate or paste
1 tablespoon flour
1 cup dry white wine
veal stock (recipe below)
bouquet garni (2 sprigs parsley, ½ teaspoon dried thyme, 1 bay leaf tied in
     cheesecloth)
2 teaspoons salt
black pepper

1. In a large heavy pan quickly sauté the lamb in 2 tablespoons of butter or fat until it is brown on all sides. Lift out the meat and, using more fat if necessary, sauté the chopped onions until golden. Set aside the onions with the meat.
2. In a bit more fat, add the garlic, tomato concentrate, and flour. Stirring constantly, cook gently for a few minutes.
3. Return the meat to the pan and continue cooking, turning over and over, for 5 more minutes.
4. Add the wine and enough stock to cover the lamb mixture, reserving about 1 cup of the stock if you intend to make the casserole of potatoes. If there is not enough stock left to cover the lamb mixture, add a little water.
5. Add the bouquet garni, salt, and pepper. Cover and cook over very low heat for about 40 minutes, or until the lamb is tender.
6. Remove the lamb to a warm serving dish. Reduce the sauce by about half. Salt and pepper if necessary. Strain the sauce over the meat. Serve with the following casserole of potatoes if desired.

Yield: 4 to 6 servings

CASSEROLE OF POTATOES

6 firm potatoes, cut into chunks
2 tablespoons chicken fat or butter
salt
black pepper
1 cup veal stock (recipe below)

1. Preheat the oven to 375 degrees.
2. Use 1 tablespoon of the chicken fat or butter to coat a casserole. (Almost any ovenproof dish of suitable size will do.) Lay the potatoes down, salting and peppering as you go, taking into account the saltiness of the stock.
3. Cover the potatoes with the stock, adding a little water if necessary, and dribble the remaining fat or butter about. Cover the casserole with foil and bake until the liquid is pretty well absorbed, about 1 hour.

Yield: 4 to 6 servings

VEAL STOCK

3–4 pounds veal knuckles and veal shin
3–4 quarts water
2–3 carrots
2 onions, quartered
1 rib celery, halved
2 teaspoons salt
1 teaspoon black peppercorns
bouquet garni (2 sprigs parsley, ½ teaspoon dried thyme, 1 bay leaf tied in cheesecloth)

1. Cover the knuckles and shin with cold water and very slowly bring to the barest simmer. Add the vegetables, salt, and peppercorns. Skim off the worst of the scum as it rises. Partially cover the pot and simmer for 5 hours, making sure there is never more than the slightest suspicion of a boil.
2. Strain and cool, uncovered. Store in the refrigerator. Lift off the fat and you have lovely homemade veal stock. Make it the day before you need it.

Yield: 4 to 6 cups

QUEUX DE BOEUF BRAISÉES AU CHAMPAGNE
Based on the recipe of Le Vivarois, Paris

*Here are oxtails braised in champagne as prepared by Claude
Peyrot of Le Vivarois. This is truly haute cuisine, and the
procedure is broken down into four steps—making the
beef stock, the oxtails, the oxtail garnish, and the sauce.
Karen Hess, who got the recipe from M. Peyrot, says "it is
adapted only in the sense that chefs tend to speak in short-
hand . . . and to be damnably imprecise about amounts." She
goes on to say, "I supplied the mirepoix, stock, etc. And most
suggested amounts. Even so, a great deal of leeway is
necessary in amounts—salt, for instance. It depends on how
much was in the stock and is the butter salted; butters vary in
saltiness, even salt varies in saltiness, to say nothing of
people's tastes. . . . It is my suggestion on Meaux mustard.
M. Peyrot said 'Champenoise' and Meaux is on the edge and
available in import shops. Also, he said fresh tarragon; I
personally would omit rather than use dried."*

*And now, the queux de boeuf braisées au champagne. The
stock is made the day before you need it. In addition, the
oxtails may be braised the day before, leaving only the final
two steps for the day the dish is to be served.*

BEEF STOCK

**3–4 pounds beef bones, cracked
small piece of soup beef
2–3 carrots, diced
2 onions, quartered
1 rib celery, halved
2 teaspoons salt
1 teaspoon black peppercorns
bouquet garni (2 parsley sprigs, pinch of dried thyme, 1 bay leaf tied in cheesecloth)**

1. Cover the bones and meat with cold water and, very slowly, bring to the barest simmer. Add all the rest of the ingredients. Skim off the worst of the scum as it rises. Put a cover on the pot but leave it a bit to one side. Be sure that there is always only the slightest suspicion of a boil and continue cooking for about 5 hours.
2. Strain and cool, uncovered. Store in the refrigerator. Lift off the fat and you have lovely homemade broth. Make it the day before you need it.

Yield: 3 cups

NOTE: Any unused stock may be frozen for 2 to 3 months or refrigerated. If refrigerated, bring to a boil every 2 or 3 days.

(CONTINUED)

OXTAILS

Mirepoix

3 onions
3 carrots
2 ribs celery
1 thin slice raw ham
1–2 tablespoons butter
2 fine whole oxtails
2–3 tablespoons olive oil
salt
black pepper
1 cup champagne
beef stock
3 cloves garlic
2 fresh tomatoes, quartered
bouquet garni (2 parsley sprigs, ½ teaspoon dried thyme, 1 bay leaf tied in cheesecloth)

1. Finely chop the *mirepoix* vegetables and the ham. Place them in a large heavy pot (dutch oven type), and cook gently in the butter for about 12 minutes, until tender but not brown.
2. Cut the oxtails at the joints. Sauté in the olive oil until golden brown, turning frequently. Salt and pepper the pieces.
3. Arrange the pieces on top of the *mirepoix*. Pour the champagne over and add enough beef stock to cover. The exact quantity varies with the size of the pot. Add the garlic, tomatoes, and bouquet garni.
4. Bring very slowly to a bare simmer, cover, and allow to continue thus for 3 to 4 hours until the meat is very tender. Uncover and cool the meat in the broth.

GARNISH

8 tablespoons (1 stick) butter, melted over hot water (as in a double boiler)
2–3 tablespoons French mustard from Champagne (Moutarde de Meaux) mixed with a little French champagne
2 cups freshly made bread crumbs (Take good quality stale bread, crumb it and sift through a coarse sieve. A nuisance, but very different from dried crumbs.)

1. Allow the pieces of meat to drain very well (not losing any of the juice) and wipe with a paper towel. Reserve the braising liquid for the sauce. Paint each piece of meat with the butter, then the mustard mixture, then roll in the bread crumbs.

2. At serving time, place the pieces of meat under a preheated broiler and grill until a beautiful golden brown, turning frequently. Serve with champagne sauce.

NOTE: May be prepared through step 1 two hours before serving time; cover with foil and keep cool.

CHAMPAGNE SAUCE (start 45 minutes before serving time)

1 shallot (or large scallion), chopped
8 tablespoons (1 stick) unsalted butter
1½ cups excellent French champagne
braising liquid from the oxtails, strained
1 tablespoon chopped fresh tarragon
1 teaspoon Meaux mustard

Choose a good heavy pot (not aluminum). Allow the shallot or scallion to soften in 1 tablespoon butter over very low heat. Add the champagne and, over higher heat, allow it to reduce to ½ cup, or less. Add the braising liquid and continue to reduce, skimming now and then, until the sauce assumes a definite consistency of heavy cream. Add the tarragon. Remove from heat and with a wooden spoon beat in the remaining butter, a bit at a time. Add the mustard and check for salt and pepper. This sauce is a very fragile emulsion of extraordinary intensity of flavor. You may vary the amount of butter to suit your preference in taste and texture.

Yield: 4 to 6 servings

NOTE: When you add the braising liquid and start the reduction, begin grilling the meat so that it will be done by the time you start whipping in the butter. You must time it in this way as the sauce will not stand. Should the sauce separate, add 2 ice cubes and gently whisk to recovery.

L'ORANGERIE. There are times in Paris when the very thought of another vast menu, of still more rich cuisine, can kill the appetite. The beauty of L'Orangerie is that it doesn't have any menu, and very little cuisine. Diners are first served a fine smoked ham, then a huge basket of fresh raw vegetables—radishes, celery, green peppers, cucumber, fennel, cauliflower, tomatoes, scallions, etc. The only choice is whether to have steak or lamb chops for the main course, both grilled over an open fire and served with baked potato, and then sherbet, fruit, or tart for dessert.

Since the cooking is either utterly simple or absent altogether, as with the raw vegetables, there is no way to hide the slightest flaw in the ingredients, invariably as handsome as they are tasty. Another reason why L'Orangerie is special, particularly for reporters working six hours ahead of New York time, is that it stays open until 3 A.M. On the other hand, it isn't open for lunch, which is officially why it doesn't appear in the Guide Michelin, though I suspect the lack of cuisine has something to do with it too.

Because of its late hours, its handsome medieval-Paris atmosphere on the Ile St. Louis, its impeccable service and refreshing food, when it opened L'Orangerie was a great success with "le Tout Paris," the even more snobbish French equivalent of the Four Hundred or the Beautiful People. It has passed from high fashion now, but cabinet ministers and actors and such are still frequently to be seen and there is always a crowd. Reservations are essential and can be made after 4 P.M.

There is room for about 50 people under L'Orangerie's vaulted ceiling, typical of Paris of the twelth to fifteenth centuries. Flowers, sturdy old furniture, and the table settings add to the atmosphere of pre-Renaissance luxury. The Ile St. Louis, and the Ile de la Cité just across a narrow footbridge at its tip, are the oldest parts of Paris and contain some of its most splendid monuments as well as fascinating streets lined with antique shops and old book and print stores.

Notre Dame is on the Ile de la Cité. The cathedral has attractive public gardens and behind them, honoring those sent to Nazi death camps, is the little-known Memorial to Deportees with its small but impressive museum. The Conciergerie, where the court waited to be hauled to the guillotine during the French Revolution, the Sainte Chapelle, and the Palais de Justice are nearby. There is a bright flower market on the Quai aux Fleurs on the right bank of the Ile de la Cité, but it is closed by the time L'Orangerie opens.

L'Orangerie is at 28 Rue St. Louis en l'Ile. The phone number is 633-9398. It is open every day from 8 P.M. to 3 A.M. except for August, when it closes for the month. There is a single price of roughly $17.50 for the set meal, which includes wine, coffee, and service charge.

—*Flora Lewis*

LE POT AU FEU. This is a restaurant at which you must absolutely make reservations well in advance. Even a letter before your arrival in France wouldn't hurt. The reason why tables are so much in demand has nothing to do with the restaurant's location, for it is on a gloomy street in Asnières, a suburb to the west of Paris. There is nothing remarkable about the decor either, and the service, though performed by skilled young waiters, is relaxed. What counts at Le Pot au Feu—and accounts for its tremendous success—is the food. Under Chef Michel Guérard it has already become a legendary center of the revolution taking place in French cooking.

Chef Guérard is typical of the new chefs in that he traces his revolutionary roots to Fernand Point of Vienne and is pushing still further in the direction of the sophisticated simplicity at table that the late Monsieur Point began. Take Guérard's *fricassee de volaille*, duck fricassee with vinegar, which descends from the Point recipe of the same name. It is not a dish that requires the time and talents of a quartermaster general. Stock must be made ahead of time, but, apart from that, the process, like the end result, is a paradigm of purity. There is nothing fussy here, nothing heavy—no garnishings of artichoke bottoms, carved truffles, and piped potatoes. A chef of an earlier generation might scoff and say: "You've got nothing but duck pieces and a vinegar reduction." The modern answer is that no one wants all those edible curlicues on the side any more. What the best young French chefs are about is exactly this kind of *plat*, one that emphasizes the major ingredient—in this case, duck—cooks it magnificently and distills a subtle sauce without an army and a fortune. And few do it better than Michel Guérard.

Getting to Le Pot au Feu involves a short taxi ride out of Paris, but it is well worth the effort to dine on Guérard's duck, his *mousseline de St. Jacques*, a delicate preparation of scallops with a lobster sauce, or his other specialties. The restaurant, with its wood-paneled dining room, is at 50 Rue des Bas, Asnières, and the phone number is 733-00-71, but please check before setting out in case success has forced Le Pot au Feu, as now seems likely, to move to larger quarters. The restaurant serves lunch and dinner Tuesday through Saturday, dinner only on Monday. It is closed Sunday, on some holidays, and during the month of August. One can eat for around $20, including service charge, or one can spend considerably more, depending on choice of dishes and wine.

—*Raymond A. Sokolov*

FRICASSEEE DE VOLAILLE
Based on the recipe of Le Pot au Feu, Asnières

1 4-pound duck, cut into serving pieces
2 heads garlic, unpeeled
6 tablespoons unsalted butter
1½ cups wine vinegar
¾ cup tomato sauce

(CONTINUED)

1 teaspoon tomato paste
3 cups veal stock (recipe below)
2 cups chicken stock (recipe below)
fresh tarragon (optional)

1. Brown the duck pieces, turning occasionally, with the garlic heads, in 4 tablespoons butter, until the skin is crisp and the meat is almost tender. Pour off all the fat.
2. Deglaze the pan with ¾ cup vinegar. To deglaze, simply stir the vinegar around in the pan without removing the duck pieces; the vinegar will dissolve the duck juice and brown particles in the pan and become the base of the sauce. Do not allow liquid to reduce more than slightly.
3. Degrease the liquid off the heat by allowing it to stand for a few minutes to let the fat to rise to the top, then skim it with a spoon to take off as much fat as possible. If there is any remaining fat, strips of paper toweling can be drawn across the surface to soak it up.
4. Deglaze again with the remaining ¾ cup vinegar, reducing slightly.
5. Add the tomato sauce, tomato paste, veal stock, and chicken stock. Reduce the liquid by about ¼ over moderately high heat.
6. Remove the pan from heat. Drain the duck pieces, put them into an ovenproof dish, and reserve in a low (250 degree) oven.
7. Working quickly so that the duck pieces do not dry out, put the cooking liquid through a fine strainer, mashing the garlic heads thoroughly. If the sauce is too thin, reduce it further in a clean pan.
8. Add the remaining 2 tablespoons of butter to the sauce. Pour it over the duck pieces on a serving platter, sprinkle with a little fresh tarragon, and serve.

Yield: 4 servings

VEAL STOCK

2 pounds veal shank (meat and bones) cut into 1–2-inch sections
1 tablespoon butter
1 carrot, diced
1 medium onion, chopped
4 scallions, chopped
1½ cups dry white wine
warm water
1 teaspoon salt
½ teaspoon dried thyme
4 sprigs parsley
1 bay leaf

1. Preheat the oven to 450 degrees.
2. Put sections of veal shank in a pan and brown them in the oven, about 1 hour, turning so that all sides brown but do not burn.
3. Meanwhile, heat the butter in a skillet and sauté the carrot, onion, and scallions until the carrots are softened and shiny and the onions are translucent.
4. Put the meat and vegetables in a large, heavy pot. Cover and place over very low heat for 20 minutes. Uncover, add ½ cup wine, raise the heat as high as it will go, and let the liquid evaporate until the meat juices in bottom of the pot turn brown. Repeat this process twice, with ½ cup of wine each time.
5. Cover the contents of pot with warm water, bring to a boil, add the salt, thyme, parsley, and bay leaf. Simmer, uncovered, for 5 to 6 hours. Add more water if needed.
6. Strain the stock, cool at room temperature, refrigerate, and skim the resulting layer of fat off the top of the stock prior to using. Measure the stock and if less than 3 cups, add enough water to bring it up to 3 cups.

Yield: 3 cups

CHICKEN STOCK

3 pounds chicken necks, wings, and backs
1 onion, peeled and stuck with 1 clove
1 carrot, sliced
4 ribs celery, each cut into 4 pieces
1 thin slice of lemon
10 peppercorns
bouquet garni (2 sprigs parsley, ½ teaspoon dried thyme, and 1 bay leaf tied
     in cheesecloth)
10 cups water
salt

1. Place all the ingredients in a large saucepan and bring to a boil. Simmer, uncovered, for 1½ hours, skimming the surface of scum as necessary.
2. Strain through cheesecloth. Boil the strained liquid rapidly, uncovered, to reduce the stock to about 7 cups. Skim off all the fat. Refrigerate and use as required.

Yield: 7 cups

ROANNE

TROISGROS. This is an establishment that already has all the accolades that a nation of gourmets can give it. It is a "great" restaurant that really is superb.

First of all, it is quite without the fuss and formality—and the theatricality—of a number of other "greats" of France. You don't go to Troisgros to be seduced by the decor, or to see and be seen. (Though I have to admit that once when I was there in walked John Lennon and Yoko.) The interior is pleasant enough, and outside the view is of a nondescript railway station in a nondescript provincial town 250 miles south of Paris.

You go to Troisgros to eat—exquisite things like *escargots de Bourgogne, pâté de grives au genièvre, soupe de moules, sole à la ciboulette, escalope de saumon à l'oseille, steak au fleurie à la moelle, oeufs brouillés aux truffes* . . . . Portions are copious, but not heavy. The dessert cart would tempt a saint twice. You are urged to try a slice of this cake, a bit of that *sorbet*, a handful of wild strawberries with a glob of that wonderful thick fresh cream—all on a plate together.

Troisgros, which was started in 1930 by the Troisgros family, is now in the hands of two brothers, Jean and Pierre Troisgros. Both underwent the classic French culinary training of working in other restaurants. Like many of the best younger chefs of France, they served under Fernand Point at the Pyramide in Vienne.

Their menu is not one of those vast tomes listing 90 variations on a sole. It is, in fact, quite short, but with no one dish even remotely resembling another, and each of them of the utmost refinement. The emphasis is always on the food, and what you eat is not tarted up with unnecessary crescents of puff paste or sprigs of parsley. Food is put in front of you, on the largest and most practical dinner plates I have ever seen, and allowed to speak for itself.

At least one of the jovial brothers frequently comes out of the large kitchen to talk with guests. But if you don't want to talk you don't have to. The waiters are knowledgeable, helpful and, best of all, friendly. They do not, for example, make a monumental and unnecessary fuss about decanting in front of a candle flame a bottle of burgundy that is still too young to have thrown any sediment.

The wine list is short, but excellent. The family comes from Burgundy, and the brothers have stayed, happily, with the wines they know. There is a house brand of blanc de blanc champagne, a fine Meursault, a simpler red burgundy that you order by the carafe. After coffee the waiter automatically pours 12-year-old *marc de Bourgogne* into your still warm cup.

Troisgros is at the Place de la Gare. The phone number is 71-26-68. It is open for lunch and dinner, and closes for vacation for several weeks in January. A meal is, of course, not cheap, but unless you go overboard on truffles and champagne you shouldn't have to spend more than $25 a head.

—*Clyde H. Farnsworth*

LA SOUPE DE MOULES
Based on the recipe of Troisgros, Roanne

This mussel soup can be prepared well ahead of dinner and reheated when necessary. Since it contains no butter, it can also be eaten chilled.

FISH STOCK

bones of 3 sole
2 good-size pieces conger eel (see note)
1 pound any small white-fleshed, non-oily sea fish (halibut, cod, striped bass)
2 quarts water

½ cup dry white wine
2 large shallots, finely chopped
4 pounds mussels, preferably small ones, cleaned and debearded
1 cup finely diced carrots
2 large onions, finely diced
3 leeks (white part only), finely diced
1 tablespoon olive oil
2 cloves garlic, finely chopped
5 ripe tomatoes, peeled, seeded, and finely chopped
½ teaspoon powdered saffron
½ cup heavy cream
pinch of dried thyme
salt
white pepper

1. Make a fish stock by putting the bones and fish in a large saucepan. Add the water, bring to a boil, then simmer, uncovered, for 30 minutes. Strain through a fine sieve and set aside.

(CONTINUED)

2. Put the wine, shallots, and mussels in a large pot. Cover, and cook over high heat for a few minutes, shaking the pot often, until the mussels open. Then remove the mussels from their shells (discard any that are firmly closed) and put the shelled mussels back in their cooking liquid. Set aside.
3. Sauté the carrots, onions, and leeks in the olive oil without browning. Add garlic, tomatoes, saffron, and fish stock. Simmer for 40 minutes.
4. Just before the dish is ready to be served, add the cream, thyme, mussels and their cooking liquid. Heat, without boiling, correct the seasoning, and serve very hot in large bowls.

Yield: 8 servings

NOTE: If conger eel is unavailable, you will not be able to duplicate Troisgros' stock exactly, but for the eel substitute an additional ½ pound of fish or fish bones.

ESCALOPE DE SAUMON À L'OSEILLE
Based on the recipe of Troisgros, Roanne

8 4-ounce salmon scallops, prepared as in step 1

FISH STOCK

2 cups water
½ pound fish bones or fish (see step 2)
1 carrot, finely chopped
1 onion, finely chopped
¼ cup dry white wine

½ cup dry white wine
¼ cup Noilly Prat dry vermouth
1–2 shallots, or 2–4 scallions (white part only), finely chopped
2 tablespoons heavy cream
4 tablespoons sorrel, without stalks or center spines, cut into large strips
8–10 tablespoons butter, softened
salt
white pepper

1. The scallops are cut in exactly the opposite fashion from a salmon steak —that is, from front to back, in fillets. Cut out any gray or discolored spots, pick out all small bones with a tweezer, and flatten the scallops

between 2 sheets of wax paper with a meat pounder or rolling pin until they are about ¼ inch thick.

2. Now make the fish stock. The fish can be whiting or preferably the bones of what the French call *poisson noble*—sole. Put all the ingredients for the fish stock in a saucepan and cook for 10 to 15 minutes, then strain.

3. In a saucepan of enameled cast iron or tinned copper, heat 1 cup of the stock, the dry white wine, and vermouth. Add the shallots and simmer until the shallots have softened.

4. Add the cream and cook, beating with a whisk, until the sauce has thickened.

5. Add the sorrel and let it cook for no more than half a minute.

6. Remove from the heat and add 6 to 8 tablespoons of butter, little by little, beating constantly. Check for seasoning. Keep the sauce hot on a very low flame, preferably on an asbestos pad, while you cook the salmon.

7. Season the salmon with salt and pepper.

8. Melt 2 tablespoons of butter in a skillet until it almost smokes. Sauté the salmon on both sides over high heat for about 5 to 7 minutes.

9. To serve, pour the sauce onto a hot platter and arrange the salmon on top of the sauce.

Yield: 4 servings

ROUEN

AUBERGE DE L'ÉCU DE FRANCE. Rouen, which was severely damaged in World War II during the Allied invasion of Normandy, has done a remarkable job of modernizing its urban and river dock facilities and also of restoring its flavorful Norman character. On the Place du Vieux Marché, where Joan of Arc was burned at the stake in 1431, is L'Auberge de l'Écu de France, a bare-beamed, gabled house built in 1606. It has flowering window boxes and an interior decor of fine old faience, burnished copper pots, and crisp white linen. The rooms have wisely been kept small, so that the place looks rather like an inn on the square might have appeared in the angry days when Joan was tried and martyred. There is a little Joan of Arc museum with a junky souvenir shop nearby, but the Auberge has a good deal more of an authentic feel about it.

The menu is large and contains many Norman specialties with rich cream sauces, including a *St. Pierre au Noilly,* in which the fillets of St. Pierre, a white-fleshed fish, are poached in vermouth and chopped shallots before butter and cream are added. The service is careful and therefore not too fast. René Guggenbuhl, nephew of the proprietor, worked on the luxury liners *France* and *Liberté,* and he performs the elaborate ritual of preparing *caneton à la rouennaise* at your table. This is a duck dish, an intricate and unusual demonstration of haute cuisine that attracts the stares of other diners, so prepare to be in the spotlight if you order it. But it is worth the attention and the wait, succulent but not heavy, and so satisfying that you may find it impossible to go on to the luscious *profiteroles* on the dessert menu. Portions are large, but as a whole duck is needed for the duck press part of the ceremony, the *caneton* must be ordered for two. Take heart, however: There are compelling incentives to walk off even the most substantial lunch, for many of the glories of Rouen—the cathedral, the Church of St. Maclou, the big clock, the best museums—are all within easy strolling distance.

The address of L'Écu de France is simply Place du Vieux Marché. The phone number is 71-46-30. Lunch is served from noon to 2:30 P.M., dinner from 7 to 9:30 P.M., and the place is open every day except for several weeks in summer, when it is closed for vacation. The cheapest meal is about $4. There is an enormous "gastronomic" menu of five courses for about $7.

Drinks and a 12 percent service charge are extra. A meal of prawn bisque, duck, salad, wine, and coffee for two should come to something more than $30.

—*Flora Lewis*

ST. PIERRE AU NOILLY
Based on the recipe of L'Écu de France, Rouen

St. Pierre, a white-fleshed fish not found in American waters, is called John Dory in English. In L'Ecu de France's preparation of this dish, the fillets are decorated with fleurons—miniature puff-paste crescent pastries akin to croissants. The home cook can substitute sole or other white-fleshed fillets for the St. Pierre and omit the fleurons.

2 fillets of St. Pierre, sole, or other flat, white-fleshed fish
½ cup dry vermouth
2 shallots, chopped
½ cup heavy cream
2 tablespoons butter
salt
white pepper

1. Poach the fillets in the vermouth in a skillet over medium heat for about 12 minutes. Add the shallots. Simmer for another 2 to 3 minutes. As soon as the fillets are cooked, transfer them to a warm serving dish.
2. Add the cream, butter, salt, and pepper to the liquid in the skillet. Stir well. Simmer for 3 minutes.
3. Pour the sauce over the fillets and serve.

Yield: 2 servings

CANETON À LA ROUENNAISE
Based on the recipe of L'Écu de France, Rouen

*At L'Écu de France the final stages of this duck dish are
prepared at the table with a spirit flame and a silver chafing
dish, not to mention a duck press. This allows such highlights
as the grilling of the legs and wings over the flame and the
flambéing of the slices of duck. Finally the carcass is put into
the press and all the juices are extracted and added to the
sauce. However, the home cook can prepare the dish in the
kitchen, using broiler and stovetop, and since a duck press is
not exactly a common household utensil, we have suggested
an alternate method of preparing the sauce. It's not as great
as the real thing, but it's a good deal better than no* caneton
à la rouennaise *at all.*

**1 4–5 pound duckling
5 tablespoons butter
2 shallots, finely chopped
¾ cup dry red wine
5 tablespoons Dijon-type mustard
salt
black pepper
½ cup cognac
¼ cup red bordeaux wine**

1. Place the duckling with its neck, heart, gizzard, and liver in a large saucepan in which there is about 3 inches of simmering water. Cover and allow to steam for about an hour.
2. Remove the duckling from the saucepan; reserve the liquid and duck liver.
3. Broil the duckling in a preheated broiler, 4 inches from the heat, for 15 minutes on each side. Watch carefully to see that it doesn't brown too much. Place the duckling on a carving dish.
4. Heat 1 tablespoon butter until it foams, add the shallots and sauté them for about 7 minutes. Add the red wine and reduce it to ⅓ its original volume.
5. Cut the wings and legs off the duck and cover them thickly with the mustard; season with salt and pepper. Grill them over a blazing spirit flame or broil them in a preheated broiler.
6. Carve the remaining meat into thick slices, 4 to 6 slices from each breast. Lay the sliced meat in a buttered chafing dish. Add salt and freshly ground black pepper. Pour cognac over slices, ignite, and flame the meat.

7. Chop the cooked liver finely, mash it, and knead in 4 tablespoons of butter. (A quick method is to put the liver and butter into a blender container and puree.) Add this paste to the reduced red wine and shallots. Then add the bordeaux.
8. Put the duck carcass in a duck press and extract the juices. If you do not have a press, reduce by half 1 cup of the liquid in which the duck was steamed. Add the juices from the press (or the reduced liquid) to the sauce prepared in Step 7. Simmer and gently pour over the slices of duck.
9. Place the grilled legs and wings around the sliced duck meat and serve.

Yield: 2 servings

Germany

BERLIN

KOTTLER'S ZUM SCHWABENWIRT. At a time when more and more West Berliners seem to be patronizing drugstores, pizzerias, and places serving Greek, Turkish, or Chinese food, an old-fashioned German restaurant is becoming almost a rarity. But such an establishment is Kottler's, founded in 1924. It is one of the oldest restaurants in West Berlin and one of the few remaining where genuine German dishes are a specialty.

The food at Kottler's is cooked and served with pride, and the menu almost always includes game of some sort—venison, wild boar or even, for those who like it, ibex, flown in from the Austrian Alps. My own favorite is not game but *sauerbraten*, the wonderful marinated pot roast that Kottler's serves with potato dumplings and apple sauce. Another favorite of mine is *spätzle*, handmade noodles, served as a dish by themselves with a salad or as an accompaniment to such main courses as succulent broiled leg of veal in cream sauce.

The restaurant is still in its original premises on the ground floor of an apartment house built before World War I in a turn-of-the-century part of town, in a borough known as Schöneberg, about eight city blocks from the downtown heart of West Berlin. It is the area where Christopher Isherwood lived in the 1930s when he wrote his *Goodbye to Berlin*, a book that later became the basis for the play *I Am a Camera* and the musical and movie *Cabaret*. Isherwood described the houses on Motzstrasse, where Kottler's stands, as "monumental shabby safes" containing the "tarnished valuables

110

of a bankrupt middle class." Some of the buildings have gone, but the neighborhood still gives that impression. There are lots of antique shops in the vicinity as well as a number of (rather seedy) night spots. The decor of the restaurant itself is quaint and Old Worldly, the atmosphere one of quiet competence.

The address of Kottler's Zum Schwabenwirt is Motzstrasse 30, Berlin 30, and meals are served from noon to midnight seven days a week. The phone number is 24-38-93. À la carte prices range from $3 or more for a snack to around $5.50 for the *sauerbraten* and $6 or so for the leg of veal in cream sauce with *spätzle*. The wine list offers 110 French and German reds, whites, and rosés. My favorite is a Kaiserstühler Weissherbst, a German rosé from the Baden area. A one-liter bottle is just over $8, and a quarter of a liter is served for a little over $2.

—Ellen Lentz

SAUERBRATEN
Based on the recipe of Kottler's Zum Schwabenwirt, Berlin

Here is one of the classics of German cuisine as prepared by Chef Hermann Hartmann of Kottler's.

½ pound bacon or larding pork
3–4 pounds top-quality beef round, in one piece

MARINADE   (1 quart)

1⅓ cups red wine vinegar
2⅔ cups water
1 onion, sliced
2 sprigs parsley
2 medium carrots, sliced
1 rib celery, sliced
1 leek (white part only), sliced
2 bay leaves, crumbled
12 black peppercorns, crushed
6 whole cloves

4 tablespoons cooking oil
1 tablespoon salt (approximately)
3 tablespoons butter
3–4 cups dry red wine

(CONTINUED)

1 tablespoon flour
3 tablespoons raisins soaked in brandy to cover
salt
black pepper
sugar

1. Ask your butcher to trim the meat of all outside fat and lard it with 8 to 10 strips of larding pork or bacon, or use a larding needle yourself and draw the strips through the meat.
2. Make the marinade by combining the vinegar and water in a large pot and adding all the other marinade ingredients securely tied in cheescloth. Bring to a boil and let cool.
3. Place the meat in a nonmetallic container and add the marinade. The marinade should completely cover the meat. Marinate at room temperature for 3 to 4 days.
4. Remove the meat from the marinade and pat it very dry. Remove the cheesecloth package of vegetables, open it, and let the vegetables dry.
5. Preheat the oven to 350 degrees.
6. Heat the oil in a large skillet. When the oil is just below the smoking point, put in the meat and brown it all over until it is dark brown. Then salt it generously.
7. Heat 2 tablespoons butter in a pan and sauté the dry marinade vegetables for a few minutes.
8. Transfer the meat and vegetables to a heavy casserole, place in the oven, and cook for about 1¾ hours, basting frequently with the marinade.
9. Put the red wine in a saucepan and reduce to about 2 cups by boiling over high heat.
10. When the meat and vegetables have cooked in the oven for 1¾ hours, add the reduced red wine. Continue cooking for 15 minutes more.
11. When the meat is done, discard the vegetables and strain the sauce through a sieve. Thoroughly blend the remaining tablespoon of butter and the tablespoon of flour in a saucepan and slowly add the strained sauce, stirring over low heat to thicken.
12. Add the raisins soaked in brandy and adjust the seasoning to taste with salt, pepper, and sugar.
13. Slice the sauerbraten, put the slices on a serving platter, and pour the hot sauce over the meat.

Yield: 6 to 8 servings

FRANKFURT AM MAIN

SOLBER-ERNST. In Frankfurt am Main, the city of Goethe, Schopenhauer, and big business, a traveler with a taste for simple German cooking can find succor immediately at the Solber-Ernst Inn, just a hop, skip, and jump from the main railway station on Baseler Square. "Solber," in the dialect spoken here, means "salted" meat, specifically pork and veal, a specialty of the region and of the house.

The people of Frankfurt have been going to Solber-Ernst ever since 1912. It takes its name from its longtime owner, Ernst Riedle, who retired a few years ago. The present owner, Kurt Deylitz, and his wife, Annemarie, the chief cook, carry on the Riedle tradition, so the main dishes remain pig's knuckle, knuckle of veal, salted pork chops, and the like. Served with sauerkraut and accompanied by a foaming glass of Bindung beer, they make filling meals for a song.

Herr Deylitz, a friendly blue-eyed fellow with a sharp nose, boasts that he is a native of Frankfurt, but in his case his home town is Frankfurt an der Oder, in East Germany. He and his Saxon wife have completely adapted to Frankfurt am Main and are gracious hosts. If he takes a liking to you, Herr Deylitz might serve you his favorite aperitif, Karlsbader Becher Bitter.

Solber-Ernst has room for 60 guests. The benches and chairs are comfortable, and the linen and silverware stacked neatly in the center of the table for the diners to take themselves make one feel cozy. The prices are extraordinarily reasonable—less than $2 for a blueplate special of kraut roulades (thin slices of beef wrapped around sweetened sauerkraut), potatoes, and a dessert of peaches and ice cream. *Frankfurter Rippchen*, one of the house's salt-pork specialties, is less than $3.

Solber-Ernst is at 2 Baseler Square. The phone number is 23-26-06. The place is open every day except Saturday from 11:30 A.M. to 3 P.M. and 5 to 10 P.M. It lies within a stone's throw of the Main River and there is a pretty embankment for strolling.

—David Binder

ANNEMARIE DEYLITZ'S SAUERKRAUT
Based on the recipe of the Solber-Ernst, Frankfurt am Main

2 pounds sauerkraut
1 tablespoon cooking oil
½ pound sliced bacon
1 medium onion, chopped
30 dried juniper berries and 1 bay leaf tied in cheesecloth
1 teaspoon sugar
2–3 cups water, or to cover
1 cup moselle wine

1. Put the sauerkraut into a colander and rinse it thoroughly under running water.
2. Cover the bottom of an enamel pot with the oil and bacon. Add the chopped onion and heat until very hot.
3. Add the sauerkraut, the sugar, and the cheesecloth-wrapped juniper berries and bay leaf. Add water to cover, put a lid on the pot, and simmer for 1 hour.
4. Add the wine. Salt to taste if necessary. Remove the cheesecloth bag and serve.

Yield: 4 servings

FRANKFURTER RIPPCHEN
Based on the recipe of the Solber-Ernst, Frankfurt am Main

At Solber-Ernst they do not slice this dish into individual
pork chops until it is served. The home cook can do the same
or else start with individual chops, which will more
conveniently fit into a skillet. In any event, the dish goes
wonderfully well with mustard, Annemarie Deylitz's
Sauerkraut, and a large glass of beer.

3 pounds pork rib chops
1 cup butcher's brine (see note)

1. Trim excess fat from the chops.
2. Liberally cover the bottom of a large skillet or pot with the brine. Add

the pork and enough water to cover the chops. The proportion should be approximately 3 cups of water to 1 cup of brine.

3. Bring to a boil, reduce heat, and simmer, covered, for about an hour. The chops are now ready to serve.

Yield: 3 to 4 servings

NOTE: Many butchers will provide butcher's brine. If the brine is unavailable do not attempt this recipe.

MUNICH

ST. GEORG WEINHAUS. In Munich, where it is easy to overeat or take in too much beer, the place to go in the evening for a pleasant change of fare is the St. Georg Weinhaus, an inn specializing in simple, delicious dishes and outstanding German wines.

The St. Georg Weinhaus is a family place, started more than 20 years ago by Franz Hummert, a native of the Bogenhausen section of Munich, who took his restaurant's name from the parish church of St. George. His mother, Martina, who is in her eighties, is one of the three regular cooks and her recipes for hearty soups and chops dominate the menu. She is the oldest working cook in Munich and still has the brown hair of her youth. A terrine of her lentil soup garnished with cubes of roasted sowbelly is a meal in itself.

The vaulted cellar rooms, five in all, are furnished in the solid-stolid dark-stained Upper Bavarian style and boast the massive beams of a 500-year-old farmhouse. The place seats 220. To the left is a bar and dance music, to the right candlelit tables and soft traditional music. The service, by waitresses either slender or sumptuous in flattering dirndls, is sweet and swift. Herr Hummert, formerly a wine salesman, keeps a stock of over 60 wines he selects himself in the Rhine, Moselle, Baden, and Franconia regions.

The St. Georg Weinhaus is a little off the beaten track at Prince Regent Square, but it is quickly reached from downtown by a Number 55 bus. There is also ample parking space nearby. Prince Regent Square is in a pleasant residential district about halfway between the major Munich museums and the Riem International Airport. Old-timers recall that it was the place where Adolf Hitler had a mistress a decade before he seized power in 1933. That was in the building across the square.

The St. Georg Weinhaus is open every evening except Sunday from 7 P.M. to 3 A.M. The clientele ranges from smartly dressed young couples to elderly regulars from the neighborhood. Prices are modest—$2 or less for the simple dishes and about $1 for a big glass of wine. Reservations should be made by phoning 47-83-18.

—*David Binder*

MARTINA HUMMERT'S LENTIL SOUP
Based on the recipe of the St. Georg Weinhaus, Munich

2 pounds ham marrow bones (if unavailable, substitute 2 pounds beef
  marrow bones plus a small slice of ham or smoked pork)
2 quarts water
1 pound lentils
1 pound fat salt pork, or 1 pound bacon in 1 piece
1 cup minced onion
3–4 tablespoons oil or butter
1 tablespoon flour
salt
black pepper
8 tablespoons white vinegar

1. Boil the marrow bones thoroughly in the water for about 30 minutes. Strain the resulting broth. Remove the marrow from the bones and set aside.
2. Place the lentils and salt pork or bacon in a large pot, add the broth, and bring to a simmer.
3. Sauté the onion in the oil or butter until golden.
4. Combine the marrow with the flour in a small skillet or saucepan and cook, stirring, over low heat until the mixture becomes a thickened paste.
5. Press the marrow paste through a sieve and stir it into the simmering lentil soup. Add the sautéed onion and stir. Continue to simmer the soup for about 30 minutes.
6. Remove the salt pork or bacon. Cut it into small cubes and roast the cubes in the oven for a few minutes until they are brown and crisp.
7. Salt and pepper the soup to taste. Pour it into large bowls. Add vinegar to each serving in the proportion of 1 tablespoon of vinegar to each cup of soup. Garnish with the crisp salt pork or bacon cubes.

Yield: 4 servings as a main dish, 6 to 8 as a soup course

MEXICO À LA MUNICH
Based on the recipe of the St. Georg Weinhaus, Munich

*This creation of Martina Hummert's of the St. Georg
Weinhaus is obviously neither really German nor Mexican.
But it makes a hearty, informal dish served over thick-sliced
white bread or buns.*

1 cup minced onions
2–3 tablespoons vegetable oil
½ pound ground beef
½ pound ground pork
1 pint sour cream
½ cup beef stock (see page 95) or canned beef bouillon
1 16-ounce can green peas
1 heaping tablespoon chili powder
black pepper
salt

1. Sauté the onions in the oil until golden brown. Add the ground meats and sauté until dark brown.
2. In another pot, combine the sour cream and the beef stock, stir in the peas, and cook until hot. Add to the meat.
3. Add the chili powder and pepper to the mixture. Salt to taste and cook, stirring occasionally, for 10 minutes, then serve.

Yield: 4 servings

Great Britain—see England

Greece

ATHENS

GEROFINIKAS. Wrapped around the trunk of the ancient palm tree that gives it its name, this is the restaurant I like best in all of Athens. It's the kind of place where each hors d'oeuvre is a masterpiece. It's also a good setting for a Balkan spy novel as it happens to be a favorite dining spot of domestic and foreign intelligence men. Those in the know can see them dining here regularly and eyeing one another with ill-disguised suspicion.

The Greeks from Turkey who run Gerofinikas really believe in expert preparation of flawless ingredients, and the kitchen, presided over by Chef George, is open for inspection by patrons. A warning, however: The sight of the steaming pots, the tidbits called *mezes*, and the overwheming array of syrupy oriental desserts can wreck the most resolute diet. Among the *mezes*, one of the choicest items is the *avgotaraho*—smoked mullet caviar shaped into a tiny loaf and covered with yellow wax. It is cut into thin slices and tastes great on buttered bread, provided you peel off the wax. A portion of 10 slices costs about $3.50.

In addition to the *mezes*, Gerofinikas serves everything from a $50-a-person champagne-and-smoked-salmon supper to a $7 lunch of eggplant salad, pilaf Ali Pasha, and lamb (in any form you choose) washed down with native white wine. It has the best selection of fish in town and its skewered swordfish is renowned.

Gerofinikas is not a place the Greeks have kept secret from tourists, but it is quite popular with permanent foreign residents of Athens, even those who are not spies. With good reason: Its refinement is in sharp contrast to the stylized vulgarity of other tourist places.

The approach to Gerofinikas from the street is through an old tunnel 30 yards long which recently was refurbished to eliminate the powerful smell of age. Inside Gerofinikas the atmosphere is warm and hospitable, and the lighting, in contrast to most Greek restaurants, is discreet. The air-conditioned dining room, with its dark wood-paneled walls, is vast, and on a narrow elevated platform along the far wall is a single row of tables for those who want to command a full view of the place. In the center of the room, not far from the fireplace and well-stocked bar, is a round table on which are displayed some of the restaurant's more elaborate dishes along with bottles of fine French wine and boxes of Havana cigars.

The service at Gerofinikas is among the best in the country, but Greece, unfortunately, is a country where industrialization and massive tourism have taken their toll of good service. Should you have any problem, however, Theodoros, the maître d'hôtel, will solve it with a smile and an enormous exudation of dignified goodwill.

Gerofinikas is at 10 Pindarou Street, a few yards from Constitution Square, the center of Athens. It is open every day and reservations are highly recommended as the place is packed for lunch, which is served from 1 to 4:30 P.M., and dinner, 7:30 to midnight. The phone number is 622-719. The average meal with wine and tips costs upward of $8 a person.

—*Mario S. Modiano*

EGGPLANT SALAD
Based on the recipe of Gerofinikas, Athens

At Gerofinikas this cold spread is made with eggplants that have been seared over a hot charcoal fire until their skins are charred. Purists insist the charcoal imparts a unique flavor, but cooks without a charcoal fire find that putting the eggplants under a hot broiler and turning them until all the skin is charred makes an acceptable substitute.

**5 pounds eggplant
1 tablespoon plus 1 teaspoon salt
juice of 3 lemons
1¼ cups olive oil
1 teaspoon sugar**

(CONTINUED)

1. Broil the eggplants whole over charcoal or in a broiler, turning them occasionally, until all the skin is charred and the eggplants are tender. The eggplants are done when a knife goes through them easily. Remove from heat and let cool enough to handle.
2. Put cold water in a bowl large enough to hold the eggplants and add 1 tablespoon salt and the juice of 2 lemons. Stir.
3. Peel the eggplants or cut them in half and spoon out the meat in large pieces. Put the eggplant flesh in the bowl of water. Let cool.
4. In a small bowl, combine the olive oil, juice of 1 lemon, 1 teaspoon salt, and the sugar.
5. Remove the eggplant from the water, place in another large bowl, and mash quickly. Blend in the olive oil mixture and beat, by hand or machine, until the eggplant spread is smooth and creamy. Chill before serving.

Yield: 8 to 10 appetizer servings, more as a cocktail spread

PILAF ALI PASHA
Based on the recipe of Gerofinikas, Athens

2 cups raw long-grain rice, soaked in lightly salted cold water for 20 minutes
14 tablespoons (1¾ sticks) butter
4 cups water
2 teaspoons salt
1 chicken bouillon cube
½ pound chicken livers, cut into small pieces
1 cup dark raisins
½ cup pine nuts
2 teaspoons ground cinnamon
dill

1. Drain the rice.
2. Melt 10 tablespoons butter in a large saucepan. Add the water, salt, and bouillon cube. Bring to a boil and add the rice.
3 Let the water come to a rolling boil, lower the heat, and barely simmer, covered, for about 30 minutes, or until all the liquid has been absorbed by the rice. Remove the saucepan from the heat and let it stand for 15 minutes.
4. While the rice is simmering, melt the remaining 4 tablespoons butter in a skillet and sauté the chicken livers until lightly browned. Then add the

raisins, pine nuts, and cinnamon. Sauté until the raisins are soft and the livers cooked.

5. Carefully, so as not to mash the grains, start transferring the rice to a serving platter with a slotted spoon, alternating the rice with portions of the chicken liver mixture. Reserve some of the mixture to spoon over the top of the rice. Garnish with a sprinkling of dill.

Yield: 6 servings

EPTA KARAVAKIA. For all of Greece's 10,000 miles of lace-like coastline, good fish is still a rarity in this country, and when Greeks discover a good fish restaurant they tend to keep it to themselves. So while swarms of foreign tourists are shepherded to the expensive fish restaurants along the enchanting Bay of Tourkolimano, the Greeks themselves flock to Epta Karavakia, which lies along the avenue linking Athens to the seaside and is deftly camouflaged by the trees lining the road.

That Epta Karavakia—the name means "seven little boats"—expects no foreign tourists is evident from its menu, which is handwritten in Greek. So the best bet is to head straight for the kitchen counter and Chef Michael Drivas, whose lack of English is largely made up by the expressive pride with which he unveils his basket of fish buried in shaved ice and demonstrates how lively his lobsters are.

The secret of Epta Karavakia's success is, first, the freshness of its fish and, second, Chef Michael's charcoal grill. My favorite is *lithrini*, a fish with a grayish pink skin and delicate white meat, the Greek equivalent of red snapper. Grilled and served with an olive oil and lemon sauce, it is delicious. Another wonderful main course is fillets of Greek sole, beautifully fried, their taste heightened by the chef's own strong sauce. On the side you can order a dish of *radikia*, a wild mountain herb that is boiled and served as a salad with oil and lemon. As an hors d'oeuvre don't overlook the fried baby squid, but their parents should be avoided as they tend to be rubbery.

In the summertime meals are served in Epta Karavakia's garden where, except for the trees and shrubs that protect its privacy, there is little to distract you from your fish and the sight of other diners devouring theirs. The service is quite good considering the low ratio of waiters to patrons, who may number up to 200 at any one time. In winter the main dining hall, which seats about 110, is used. Here Chef Michael's charcoal grill is in plain view, and so is the reason for the restaurant's name—seven brightly colored miniature sailboats hanging from the ceiling. The pastel-painted walls are decorated with life buoys, anchors, fishing nets, old boat lamps, and the like. Over the kitchen counter are crossed oars.

Epta Karavakia opened in 1960 and proved an immediate success. It is at 371 Syngrou Avenue, about four miles out toward the sea, and it is wise to reserve a table by phone: 933-3291. No one at the restaurant speaks English, but they get the message when it comes to a reservation. The place is open seven days a week, evenings only, from 7:30 P.M. to 3 A.M. A taxi ride from Constitution Square, the center of Athens, costs about $1.50, and there is a taxi stand just outside the restaurant for the return journey, which would cost slightly more after midnight. A fish dinner for four, with squid hors d'oeuvre, *radikia*, wine (a liter of chilled white *Demesticha* wine is about $4), cheese, and fresh fruit, comes to around $22 including service, although one usually leaves an additional 10 percent for the waiter.

—*Mario S. Modiano*

FRIED FILLETS OF SOLE WITH CHEF MICHAEL DRIVAS'S SAUCE
Based on the recipe of Epta Karavakia, Athens

The chef's sauce, his own vigorous version of a rémoulade, is equally good with the Epta Karavakia's fried jumbo shrimp, the recipe for which follows this fillets of sole recipe.

4 sole fillets, about 10–12 ounces each
salt
black pepper
flour
2 eggs, lightly beaten
olive oil
4 tablespoons butter
parsley sprigs
Chef Michael Drivas's sauce (recipe below)

1. Pound the fillets lightly so they will not curl in frying. Season them with salt and pepper and sprinkle them with flour on both sides.
2. Put the fillets, one at a time, between the palms of your hands and pat them. Dip each into the beaten egg and let the excess egg drip off.
3. In a large, shallow pan, heat about an inch of olive oil until a light haze

rises from the surface. In another large pan put the butter and start to melt it just before you begin to fry the fish.

4. Fry the fillets in the hot olive oil for about a minute on each side. Carefully remove them from the oil, dip them in the melted butter, and serve them garnished with parsley and accompanied by Chef Michael Drivas's sauce.

Yield: 4 servings

CHEF MICHAEL DRIVAS'S SAUCE

1 teaspoon worcestershire sauce
¾ teaspoon curry powder
¾ cup mayonnaise
1 teaspoon Dijon-type mustard
1⅓ tablespoons ketchup

Slowly stir the worcestershire sauce and curry powder into the mayonnaise. Then stir in the mustard and ketchup. If the sauce is made ahead, stir before serving as it tends to form a crust.

Yield: about 1 cup

FRIED JUMBO SHRIMP WITH CHEF MICHAEL DRIVAS'S SAUCE
Based on the recipe of Epta Karavakia, Athens

20 jumbo shrimp, 2–3 inches long
salt
black pepper
flour
2 eggs, lightly beaten
olive oil for deep frying
parsley sprigs
Chef Michael Drivas's sauce (recipe above)

1. Shell and devein the shrimp, leaving the tails on. Season with salt and pepper and place them in a bowl of flour.

(CONTINUED)

2. Shake off the excess flour and dip each shrimp into the beaten egg. Place each shrimp on a clean plate until all the shrimp are coated.
3. In a deep pot, heat the olive oil until very hot and steaming. Remove the pot from the fire and drop in the shrimp, one by one, letting them fry until golden—about 2 minutes. Speed is essential to prevent the shrimp from becoming too dry.
4. Serve garnished with parsley and accompanied by Chef Michael Drivas's sauce.

Yield: 4 servings

Holland—see Netherlands

Hong Kong

HONG KONG

JADE GARDEN. On the fourth floor of Star House, a two-minute walk from the busy ferry terminus in Kowloon, is the Jade Garden, which has become my favorite among this British colony's many Chinese restaurants even though it specializes in southern China's Cantonese cuisine and I have long been captivated by the food of northern, central, and western China, where I lived for many years. But the best Cantonese cooking, which the Jade Garden provides at prices moderate for Hong Kong, is superior here to the cuisine of other regions of China for the simple reason that the Cantonese, who constitute a clear majority of this colony's four million people, demand their accustomed fare and expert cooks can be found to produce it.

The authenticity and high quality of the Jade Garden's offerings are due in part to the fact that its patrons are overwhelmingly Chinese, not tourists, and its backers are responsible people in a colony filled with get-rich-quick-at-the-customer's-expense operators. Moreover, its cooks, including a specialist who prepares fine non-Cantonese dishes like Peking duck and Hangchow's beggar's chicken, and a head chef who has demonstrated his skills abroad before live and television audiences, have so far not joined the great trek of good, bad, and indifferent chefs to Africa, South America, and the United States, an exodus that has ruined many of my once-favorite Hong Kong eating places.

The Jade Garden is conveniently located—virtually next door to an

128

elaborate arts and crafts shop that Peking has opened, to the myriad boutiques of the Ocean Terminal, and the lobbies and shops of the Peninsula and Hong Kong Hotels. The restaurant's decor is a rather pleasant ersatz Chinese, and four people can lunch well for around $20, surcharge but not tips included. A party dinner for ten in a private room overlooking one of the most beautiful harbors in the world comes to something more than $100. The cost is less if delicacies and specialties like shark's fin soup, beggar's chicken, and whole steamed garupa are omitted in favor of house favorites like duck with taro, shrimp casserole, and assorted roasted meats.

The Jade Garden is open seven days a week from 11:30 A.M. to 11:30 P.M. Dishes can be selected on the spot from English menus and orders given to waiters speaking or learning English. Reservations can be made by calling Kowloon 66-13-26, but anyone planning a party will want to make a personal visit beforehand to discuss with the affable managers and courteous chefs the selection of dishes and order in which they are served. Real gourmets are welcome, after rush hours, to inspect the kitchen, talk with the chefs and watch them cooking.

—Peggy Durdin

STEAMED WHOLE FRESH FISH
Based on the recipe of the Jade Garden, Hong Kong

In Hong Kong no good Chinese chef will use a frozen fish or a dead fish, however recently extinct. In the United States live fish are not so easy to come by, but at least make sure the fish is very fresh.

1 1½-pound fresh garupa, sea bass, or flounder, with head and tail intact, cleaned and ready for cooking
2 scallions, cut into 2-inch lengths
3 thin slices fresh ginger, cut into finest strips
2 tablespoons melted chicken fat (see note) or vegetable oil
1 tablespoon light soy sauce
¼ teaspoon salt or to taste

1. Rinse fish well in cold water, pat dry, and place on a heatproof platter which will fit into the pot you will use for steaming the fish. Spread the scallions and ginger on top of the fish.
2. To steam the fish, use a covered pot large enough to hold the fish platter. Add 2 inches of water and bring to a boil. Place an inverted heatproof

(CONTINUED)

bowl or metal stand inside the pot so that it projects *above* the water. Lower the fish platter onto the stand. Keep water at a low boil to maintain steam, cover pot, and steam fish for 15 minutes.

3. Just before fish is ready, heat the chicken fat or vegetable oil in a small skillet, add soy sauce and salt. When the fish is ready, pour the hot oil mixture over the fish and serve at once.

Yield: 2 to 4 servings, depending on other courses

NOTE: To render chicken fat, pull it from the inside of a chicken. Place fat in top part of a double boiler or in a heatproof bowl over steaming water. Cook over very low heat until fat is rendered, about 30 to 60 minutes. Strain and use for cooking. Leftover fat can be stored in a covered jar in the refrigerator, where it will harden. Melt to use.

STEAMED CRAB
Based on the recipe of the Jade Garden, Hong Kong

1 12-ounce crab, or 2 smaller crabs
3 eggs, lightly beaten
4 ounces finely ground pork
⅓ cup water
½ teaspoon salt
1 teaspoon fermented black beans, chopped finely
1 teaspoon finely chopped scallions
1 teaspoon finely chopped garlic
yolk of 1 hard-boiled salted duck egg, mashed (optional)
¼ teaspoon MSG (optional)
¼ teaspoon chopped dried tangerine peel (optional)

1. Prepare the crab by holding body in one hand and shell in the other and prying apart. Rinse shell gently in cold water so as not to dislodge the tasty yellow matter. Drain and set aside. Scrape and discard the hairy gray matter from the crab body, keeping claws and legs intact. Chop body in half, then each half into 2 to 3 portions, making sure each portion has a leg or claw attached. Crack claws and larger legs as you go along. Place the crab parts on a large heatproof platter and steam until almost done, about 10 minutes. (See step 2, preceding page)
2. Meanwhile, in a large bowl, mix together eggs, pork, water, salt, black beans, scallions, garlic, egg yolk, and tangerine skin. The last two have no substitutes; omit if you don't have them.

3. In an earthenware or other heatproof casserole or bowl place the crab shell with the inside facing up. Into the shell pour the egg mixture, then place all the portions of crab on top to resemble an overturned crab. Place the casserole in a large pot and steam for 15 minutes.
4. Preheat the oven or broiler to high. Place the crab in the oven or broiler for a few minutes to brown. Serve at once.

Yield: 2 servings

Hungary

BUDAPEST

THE APOSTLES. It's hard to go wrong with Hungarian cuisine, assuming you can tolerate paprika sauces. The real problem is avoiding gypsy fiddlers, and at the Apostles you can. No music. The restaurant, Bavarian style, was founded around 70 years ago and the present manager still remembers when Hungarian aristocrats used to come to dine. The kitchen turns out a fine goose liver in—you guessed it—paprika sauce, with potatoes and onions. Good sausages, good stuffed cabbage, first-rate strudel, and five kinds of beer, some of it drawn with a nineteenth-century pump still operating without difficulty. Diners sit in boxlike booths around a large wooden table accommodating perhaps 50 or 60 people in all. The name of the place comes from paintings of the apostles on the windows.

The restaurant is at 4 Kigyo Street, by the Danube and near the Duna Intercontinental Hotel, the Ferncui Church, the Historical Museum, and the Csok Gallery. The phone number is 38-11-91. A meal costs around $7 a person and the Apostles is open from 11 A.M. to 11 P.M. every day.

HATARCSARDA. As an alternative to the Apostles, you might try Hatarcsarda, a fine country restaurant on the Danube about ten miles from the center of Budapest. The wooden furniture is in Hungarian folk style and there is a garden shaded by weeping willows. The manager will encourage you to suggest what you might like, offer his own ideas, and produce an agreeable meal. Try pork chops in slices: they are soaked in milk, then cooked in hot lard with salt, paprika, pepper, and onions. The stuffed cabbage is also excellent.

Hatarcsarda is on Highway 10 between Szentendre and Leanyfalu. You can reach it by taxi for about $3 or by train or bus for only a few forints. You can also reach it inexpensively by boat—the Danube cruisers dock near the restaurant and although the trip takes longer by river than by road or rail, in summer it is quite pleasant. Hatarcsarda's phone number is 14-36-60. A meal should run in the neighborhood of $7 a person and the restaurant is open from 8 A.M. to midnight.

—*James Feron*

STUFFED CABBAGE
Based on the recipe of the Apostles, Budapest

1 pound pork, finely diced
¼ pound bacon, diced
½ cup raw rice
1 egg
salt
black pepper
1 teaspoon paprika
8 large cabbage leaves
2 pounds sauerkraut
¼ cup smoked pigs' tails, sliced] if unavailable, substitute ½ pound head
¼ cup smoked pigs' ears, sliced] cheese
1 cup sour cream

1. Combine the pork, bacon, rice, egg, salt, pepper, and paprika and set aside.
2. Obtain the cabbage leaves by cutting the core out of the head of cabbage and carefully loosening and removing the leaves one by one. Place the leaves in a pot of boiling water and let boil just until they are flexible. Trim off the heavy center rib.
3. Divide the meat mixture into 8 portions. Place each portion at the rib end of the leaf. Roll toward the tip, jelly-roll fashion, tucking sides in. When all the leaves are filled, place them in a deep pot.
4. Wash and drain the sauerkraut and add it to the pot, together with the tails, ears, and enough water to prevent scorching. Cook slowly for 2 hours over medium heat, adding water if necessary. (If using head cheese, do not add until 20 minutes before the stuffed cabbage is done.)
5. Serve with the sour cream.

Yield: 4 servings

Iceland

REYKJAVIK

HOTEL SAGA RESTAURANT. Call the Saga your friendly hotel. Everybody working in it really seems to *care*. At the desk there are huge smiles, good mornings and good afternoons and good nights, sleep well. And this kind of interest extends to the dining room, where waiters look you in the eye, are happy to discuss the menu, and will even hasten to lower the Muzak if you so desire.

In Reykjavik there are four or five good restaurants. None is perceptibly superior to any other. The cuisine is basically Danish (it wasn't so long ago that Iceland was under the Danish crown), the dishes are similar and most of the chefs seem to have come out of the same school at the same time. What the Hotel Saga Restaurant has that the others don't is a view. It is on the top (eighth) floor of the building, and eight floors is about as high as buildings in Reykjavik go. On a sunny day you look across the bay on the north toward Akranes, Snaefellsnes, and the Esja Mountains, on the west to the open ocean, on the south toward Loftleidir Airport, where domestic jets and light planes are constantly in motion. It's all relaxing and breathtakingly lovely. The city is spread around you—Reykjavik, with its little white buildings, gaily colored roofs, and broad streets.

The restaurant has its Icelandic specialties, mostly built around fish. For a thousand years the Icelanders have been living on fish and they do wonderful things with it. Crustaceans, too; the lobster tails, sweet, not much bigger than huge shrimp, are as succulent and tender as any lobster in the world. You will want to try the herring tray; it is wheeled up and makes a fine lunch: herring in wine, pickled herring, herring in curry sauce—name it and it's there. Cold beer goes well with it, though Icelandic beer is virtually nonalcoholic and there is no other kind available. The classic accompaniment is chilled Brennevin. That is the Icelandic national drink; they fondly refer to it as Black Death. It is like an aquavit and packs a wallop. The fourth or fifth time you pick yourself up off the floor after downing a slug, you begin to like it.

The herring tray comes in handy at dinner, too; it makes a fine starter. After that, Icelanders go in for cream soups, one tasting like the other because a hearty beef stock permeates them all. The main course can be lamb or pork, both good. There is little native beef, but Iceland raises its own sheep and pigs. A rack of baby lamb for a party of four is as beautifully prepared at the Saga Hotel as in any two-star French restaurant.

And, of course, there is fish, including salmon that was alive a few hours ago. At the Saga fillets of plaice, halibut, cod, or such local wonders as goosefish always seem to come out perfectly, with a light crust and an indescribably sweet, moist taste.

Standard desserts are pancakes with whipped cream or the local delicacy, *skyr. Skyr* is a yogurtlike milk product. Most people put a little sugar on it; some add whipped cream. Local cheeses are so-so. Coffee is very good.

You might ask the chef for items that are not on the menu. The various smoked meats—smoked lamb, especially—are delicious. There are also different varieties of smoked fish that are worth trying.

Wines are offered but nothing is outstanding. The French reds—bordeaux and burgundy—are of recent vintage and not estate bottled. The German white wines are a better buy. Standard hard liquors and cocktails are available.

The Saga serves breakfast, lunch, and dinner seven days a week. No liquor on Wednesday. Reservations are mandatory Friday, Saturday, and Sunday nights. *Everybody* in Reykjavik eats out on the weekends. A meal for two, with cocktails and wine, will run about $30, including 15 percent service charge. There is no tipping in Iceland. Indeed, some waiters resent tips. The bartender at the Saga's eighth-floor lounge will give you a look icier than the glacier around Hekla if you leave a tip. The Saga is in a residential part of town on a square called Hagatorgi and its phone number is 20-600.

—*Harold C. Schonberg*

HOTEL SAGA GRATIN
Based on the recipe of the Hotel Saga Restaurant, Reykjavik

6 ½-pound plaice or flounder fillets
1 cup dry white wine
1 pound cooked lobster meat
1 pound cooked shrimp, shelled and deveined
½ pound cooked and shelled mussels (about 1½ pounds in shell)
1 tablespoon butter
1 tablespoon flour
1 cup sliced cooked mushrooms (1 pound raw)
1 cup heavy cream (approximately)
1 cup hollandaise sauce (see page 88)
½ cup grated parmesan or cheddar cheese

1. Poach the fillets in white wine for 5 to 7 minutes. Strain and save the liquid.
2. Place the fillets in a large buttered gratin or other ovenproof dish. Add the lobster meat, shrimp, and mussels.
3. In a saucepan, melt the butter and make a roux by blending in the flour. Add the liquid in which the fish poached and stir over low heat until it thickens.
4. Combine the mushrooms with enough heavy cream to make 2 cups of mushrooms in cream. Add the mushroom mixture and hollandaise sauce to the fish stock and pour over the seafood.
5. Sprinkle with the grated cheese and place in preheated medium oven or under a broiler until the dish is heated through and the top is golden brown. Serve with toast and butter or rice.

Yield: 6 servings

India

CALCUTTA

THE AMBER. Calcutta is a nightmare city of over eight million people. Cows and homeless families alike sleep in the squalid streets. In the midst of this urban catastrophe you somehow don't expect to find good eating in comfortable bourgeois surroundings, but the Amber provides just that. It is a cheerful place, a favorite haunt of the upper middle class, and the feeling it conveys is one of prosperity and a full stomach.

Journalists, writers, middle-level executives, and their families have been coming to the Amber for more than 15 years. But they come, surprisingly, not to eat the Bengali specialties of eastern India but the rich curries and barbecued meats of northern India. In fact, although Calcutta is the capital of the state of Bengal, it is hard to find a good Bengali restaurant here. The local people seem to prefer to eat their delicately spiced cuisine in their own homes.

The Amber's menu, therefore, is full of the *tandoori* chickens and mutton kebabs that have become popular all over India. But a happy marriage between the *tandoori* ovens of the north and the resources of the Bay of Bengal can be found in the artfully spiced fish *tikka* or *tandoori* prawns. Another excellent dish is chicken *reshmi kebab*, in which the chicken is cut into cubes, marinated in a mixture of butter, lemon juice, soy sauce, brown sugar, onion, garlic, and spices, threaded onto skewers and grilled. Among the curries, the chicken *sag*, a mild curry mixed with a paste of finely minced spinach, is particularly good. The breads, which are not indigenous to this predominantly rice eating area of India, are excellent. Try the *kabli nan*, a bubbly flat bread with chopped peanuts embedded in the crust.

Besides its food, the Amber offers speedy service and low prices. (A whole *tandoori* chicken costs a little more than a dollar—and chicken is always the most expensive meat in India.) Because of this, the place is so popular that more than a simple reservation is required to get a table. Do call ahead, announce your presence when you get there, and then keep a close eye on the regular patrons, who may be trying to get a table ahead of you. And be prepared to complain, because one of them invariably will. Another thing: Remember that no restaurant in Calcutta is allowed to serve meat on Thursday.

The Amber, with its liveried waiters, clean white tablecloths, and vine-covered walls, is at 11 Waterloo Street. The phone numbers are 23-3477 and 23-6746. The restaurant is open every day from 12:30 to 3 P.M. and 6:30 to midnight. A three-course dinner for four, including tip and fresh lime sodas as the beverage, costs around $8. Liquor is very expensive and not very good, so try Indian beer if you don't like lime sodas.

—*Judith Weinraub*

CHICKEN RESHMI KEBAB
Based on the recipe of the Amber, Calcutta

1 pound skinned and boned chicken breast, cut into ½-inch cubes
3 tablespoons melted butter
2 teaspoons ground coriander
1 medium onion, minced
1 clove garlic, minced
2 tablespoons soy sauce
1 tablespoon lemon juice
1 teaspoon brown sugar
salt
black pepper

1. Make a marinade in a bowl by combining all ingredients except the chicken. Add the chicken cubes and mix thoroughly. Cover and marinate in the refrigerator for 6 to 7 hours or overnight.
2. Thread the chicken cubes on skewers and place under the broiler or on a charcoal fire. Broil until the chicken cubes are cooked and a golden color, turning once. This takes about 5 to 6 minutes on each side. Serve hot.

Yield: 2 servings

DELHI

MOTI MAHAL. Delhi wallahs tell the story of the tourist who was taken to nearby Agra to see the Taj Mahal. "But this is all wrong," he complained. "I came to see the Moti Mahal."

Like the Taj, Moti Mahal is a must for tourists and Indians alike, and it is in striking contrast to most restaurants in Delhi, which are tucked away in air-conditioned corners of modern hotels. You make your way past street vendors selling garlands of jasmine, sweets, and movie magazines and enter a sprawling complex, part open air, part enclosed, part roof garden, the whole filled with the smoky odors of the *tandoori* ovens that have made Moti Mahal famous.

Eating at the restaurant is like eating in the largest family dining room in the world. All the cooks and waiters are, in fact, more or less related and came to India from Peshawar in Pakistan, where Moti Mahal got its start before the 1947 partition of the Indian subcontinent. The service is friendly, if a little rushed, and almost anyone will help you decipher the menu, which is half in English anyway. Most people eat with their hands, but forks are provided on request.

Practically everybody orders some kind of chicken, and the restaurant needs at least a thousand chickens a day to keep up with the demand. The most famous dish is chicken *tandoori*, in which the chicken is first marinated in a spiced yogurt and then roasted in a *tandoor*, a cylindrical sunken oven. In winter you can get fish *tandoori*, tasting better than you ever dreamed possible, and all year round you can ask for *burra kebab*, skewered chunks of lamb redolent of turmeric and coriander. Standard curries are also available. The somewhat primitive kitchen is open for inspection, but it is better to view it after you eat.

Background entertainment is provided by four or five musicians sitting cross-legged and chanting Qawalli, choruses of Persianized Urdu poetry full of love and loss. The patrons sometimes join in.

Moti Mahal is on Netaji Subhash Marg in Darya Ganj, just half a mile from the Jama Masjid, the largest mosque in India. It is open every day of the week from 10 A.M. to 2 A.M. and it's inexpensive. A dinner for four can cost less than $10. The phone numbers are 27-3661 and 27-3011. No liquor or wine is served.

—*Judith Weinraub*

CHICKEN TANDOORI
Based on the recipe of Moti Mahal, Delhi

At the Moti Mahal the tandoor in which this dish is cooked is fired with layers of wood and then with charcoal that is heated white. Western cooks may substitute an ordinary oven, an oven broiler, or an outdoor grill. If using an oven, preheat it to 450 degrees. If using an outdoor grill, have the charcoal at white heat before the chicken is put on.

2 2½-pound chickens, skinned and halved
1 teaspoon salt
juice of 2 limes or lemons
1½ cups plain yogurt
4 cloves garlic, minced
1–2 teaspoons cayenne
2 teaspoons ground cumin
1 teaspoon ground coriander
1 teaspoon ground ginger
½ teaspoon (or more) red food coloring
black pepper
melted butter for brushing chicken halves
2 limes or lemons, cut into wedges
1 tomato, sliced
1 onion, sliced

1. You can use the skinned chicken halves as they are, but it is better to cut off and discard the wings, the rib bones, and the backbones while skinning the halves.
2. With a sharp knife make shallow gashes all over the skinned halves and rub the chicken with the salt and then the lime or lemon juice.
3. In a large bowl combine the yogurt, garlic cloves, cayenne, cumin, coriander, ginger, red food coloring, and black pepper. Brush the chicken thoroughly with this mixture, getting deep into the gashes. Marinate the chicken in the mixture for 4 to 5 hours or overnight.
4. Preheat the oven to 450 degrees, or use a broiler, or start a charcoal fire and get the coals white hot.
5. Thread the chicken along its length on long metal skewers and cook for 5 minutes on one side, turn and cook for 5 minutes on the other side. Brush with melted butter and cook for 10 minutes more on each side, or until the chicken is done and the surface is golden brown.
6. Sprinkle with lime or lemon juice and black pepper, garnish with lime or lemon wedges and tomato and onion slices and serve hot.

Yield: 4 servings

BUTTER CHICKEN
Based on the recipe of Moti Mahal, Delhi

The basis of Butter Chicken is Chicken Tandoori. Unlike the latter, however, Butter Chicken is served in a sauce.

2 2½-pound chickens, skinned and halved
1 teaspoon salt
juice of 2 limes or lemons
1½ cups plain yogurt
4 cloves garlic, minced
1–2 teaspoons cayenne
2 teaspoons ground cumin
1 teaspoon ground coriander
1 teaspoon ground ginger
1½ teaspoons (or more) red food coloring
black pepper
melted butter for brushing chicken halves
1 tablespoon tomato paste
3 cups canned tomato sauce
8 tablespoons (1 stick) butter
½ cup light cream
4–5 fresh green chili peppers, seeded and sliced
salt

1. Prepare and cook the chicken as for Chicken Tandoori (preceding page) through step 5.
2. While the chicken is cooking, bring the tomato paste and tomato sauce to a simmer in a large saucepan. Add the stick of butter, stirring until it melts. Then add the light cream and stir until blended.
3. Add the chili peppers and cooked chicken. Season with salt and simmer for 3 to 4 minutes.
4. Remove the chicken to a deep platter, discard the chili peppers, and pour the sauce over the chicken.

Yield: 4 servings

Indonesia

JAKARTA

VIC'S VIKING. Improbably named and unpretentious, this is Indonesia's first and best buffet-style restaurant. It offers lunch and dinner guests, for around three American dollars, all they can eat of 25 or 30 dishes of Indonesian, Dutch, Chinese, or other origin. It puts its money into good home cooking instead of a fancy, faked Asian decor and is patronized by Indonesians, from teen-agers to cabinet ministers, as well as Western residents of Jakarta and tourists. Also, and importantly, unlike many eating places here, where food is usually cooked in the morning and left to be eaten cold the rest of the day, none of the items in Vic's repertoire of some 80 hot and cold dishes will give travelers queasy stomachs—unless, of course, they help themselves too liberally to Indonesia's delicious chili-and-spice-based sauces.

A family concern opened in 1970, Vic's Viking is managed by one of the family—a stocky, friendly Indonesian of Chinese descent named Victor Aguswinata who has made cooking his hobby since his camping-out days as a Boy Scout. He collects and pores over cookbooks, some of them gifts from faraway places sent by satisfied customers, and frequently joins his 18 cooks to prepare one or more dishes.

Two of my favorites at Vic's are squid in black ink and a salad called *rujak*, the latter offered by (but risky to try in) innumerable little stalls and somewhat unhygienic eating places all over this sprawling capital city with the air of a village. Made of chilled cucumber slices, small chunks of pineapple, and slices of a crunchy, slightly sour Indonesian fruit called *kedondong*, it is served with a sauce made of brown sugar, chilies, tamarind juice, and *trasi* (mashed shrimp cake), a favorite Indonesian ingredient.

One of Vic's specialties is seafood—fresh, not frozen. At a meal a guest is often offered three kinds of whole fish, steamed or baked over charcoal on banana leaves, and four or five different shrimp dishes, including *tempura* prepared by a cook who spent some time in Japan.

There is an enormous range of meat, fowl, and vegetables: four or five varieties of *saté* (cubed meat or poultry on a skewer) accompanied by a peanut sauce, which is bland, or a hot sauce of vinegar, sugar, salt, red chilies, and crushed garlic; chicken, marinated and taken out of sizzling deep fat three times for further application of sauce; rich Chinese pork dishes, labeled in red to warn strictly abstemious Moslems, and noodles of wheat or rice flour lightly fried with chicken, shrimp, and Chinese green vegetables. There is adequate food for more conventional tastes, too, but the Indonesian and other Asian dishes are superior to the Western.

The price of $3 or so, tips excluded, includes coffee and dessert. Try fresh fruits in season, among them a short banana more expensive and tasty than its longer cousin, pineapple, papaya, *mangosteen*, and *rambutan*. Less than hotel prices are charged for Australian, Indonesian, and Chinese wines and the usual Western drinks; scotch and soda, gin and tonic, or rum coke cost about $1.

Since guests all eat in a single, often crowded, sparsely decorated room, Vic's is not the place for formal dinners. Reservations can be made over Jakarta's erratic telephone system (the numbers are 52469 and 52452) or in person at Djalan Thamrin 31, within walking distance of the American Express office, the National City Bank, Jakarta's only real department store, and the major hotels, which tend to offer very dull food at high prices. Lunch is served frm 11 A.M. to 2:30 P.M., dinner from 6 to 10:30 P.M.

—*Peggy Durdin*

SQUID COOKED IN INK
Based on the recipe of Vic's Viking, Jakarta

At Vic's Viking this dish is prepared with langkuas *and* lemon grass. Langkuas *is a thick root of the ginger family; as a substitute the home cook can use fresh ginger. Lemon grass, as the name implies, is a lemon-flavored blade of grass and is available dried or in powdered form in some shops carrying Asian foods. It may be omitted if not available.*

(CONTINUED)

1 pound fresh squid
2 cloves garlic, minced
2 tablespoons vegetable oil
2–3 fresh red chili peppers, chopped and crushed (If a less hot dish is pre-
    ferred, seed the peppers.)
2 thin slices langkuas or fresh ginger
2-inch piece lemon grass (optional)
salt
white pepper
2 tablespoons Japanese sweet sake or dry sherry

1. Clean the squid but retain the ink sac and head tentacles. Cut each squid into 3 to 4 pieces.
2. In a skillet or wok over high heat, brown the garlic in the oil. Add the chili peppers, *langkuas* or fresh ginger, lemon grass, salt, and pepper. Stir-fry until fragrant.
3. Add the squid and stir-fry until they curl and become white, about 3 to 4 minutes.
4. Add the sake or sherry and cook, stirring, for about 2 minutes to allow the squid to finish cooking. Do not overcook or the squid will become tough.

Yield: 4 servings

ROAST FISH
Based on the recipe of Vic's Viking, Jakarta

*As Vic's Viking prepares this dish, the fish is roasted on a few
layers of banana leaves over an open charcoal fire. The home
cook can omit the banana leaves, however, and a regular
broiler can be used if cooking with charcoal is inconvenient.*

½ cup dark soy sauce
1 clove garlic, minced
1 small onion, finely chopped
1 tablespoon lime or lemon juice
3 fresh red chili peppers, seeded and finely chopped
½ teaspoon sugar
½ teaspoon salt
1-pound red snapper or other white-fleshed fish, with head and tail intact,
    cleaned and ready for cooking

1. To make the sauce, combine the soy sauce, garlic, onion, lime juice, chili peppers, sugar, and salt.
2. Prepare a charcoal fire and on it place a wire grid covered with a few layers of banana leaves, if available. Or preheat the broiler.
3. Brush the fish with the sauce, inside and out, and cook slowly until it is golden brown, about 20 to 30 minutes. Turn the fish frequently during cooking and baste it often with the sauce. Bring the fish to the table hot, with any remaining sauce.

Yield: 2 servings

FRIED FRYER
Based on the recipe of Vic's Viking, Jakarta

1 cup dark soy sauce
½ cup Japanese sweet sake or dry sherry
2–3 tablespoons sugar
½ teaspoon MSG (optional)
½ teaspoon black pepper
1 teaspoon salt
vegetable oil
1 2½–3-pound chicken

1. In a large bowl make a sauce by combining the soy sauce, sake, sugar, MSG, pepper, and salt. Soak the chicken in it for about 1 hour, spooning the sauce inside the body and turning the chicken frequently so that all parts of it are coated with the sauce.
2. Remove the chicken from the sauce and fry it in 3 to 4 inches of hot oil until golden brown, rotating it so all sides brown. In the course of frying, lift the chicken out of the hot oil 3 times, dip it in the sauce each time, and return it to the hot oil to continue frying.
3. When the chicken is done, chop it into serving pieces with a cleaver or cut it up with a knife or poultry shears and serve it hot.

Yield: 4 servings

Ireland

DUBLIN

THE KING SITRIC. This restaurant, at Howth, about eight miles from the center of Dublin, was opened a few years ago by Aidan MacManus, a young man with a flair for preparing food of distinction, and it soon established itself as one of this capital's premier-class eating places. After stints in the kitchens of some of the finest restaurants abroad, young Aidan returned home to Dublin to make his career because he became convinced, to use his own words, that "Ireland has the finest foods in the world." Chef MacManus regularly goes out to meet the fishing trawlers that arrive in the harbor at his doorstep and returns with the choicest of sole, brill, turbot, and plaice from the Irish Sea. As a result he has won the accolades of Dublin gourmets for his fish dishes.

I can heartily recommend the fillet of brill *deauvillaise*, a delicious dish perfectly complimented by a Valley of the Rhone white wine chosen by courtly headwaiter Denis Byrne, who is a wine connoisseur held in high esteem by discerning guests of the Sitric. You might start your meal with a superb *bisque de langoustine* and finish with a specialty of the house, meringue Sitric, covered with a chocolate sauce.

Besides the brill, another dish I am particularly fond of, either as an appetizer or as a main course, is scallops *à la bretonne*. I won't attempt to describe it except to say that as Aidan prepares it, it is fit for the gods. Live lobsters are available, too, from May to October.

In addition to its renowned seafood, the King Sitric also has excellent beef, lamb, poultry and, in season, game dishes on its menu. The choices include lamb kidneys *chasseur*, in a marsala sauce with mushrooms, and *entrecôte marchand de vins*, a jucy Irish steak in a red wine sauce. The cardinal rule of the Sitric is to serve "nothing frozen and nothing tinned." All the seafood is fresh, and what is available depends on the weather and fishing conditions. All the vegetables and fruits are fresh, too, whether they come from Irish farms or by air from abroad—fresh strawberries from Israel, fresh beans and eggplants from Kenya, fresh melons from South Africa.

Dinner is served in gracious candlelighted rooms adorned with antiques and old prints. The restaurant, once the residence of Howth's Harbor Master, overlooks the picturesque fishing harbor. The name King Sitric honors the Norse King Sitric III, who built the first Christian church in Howth in 1024.

If you are visiting Howth on a bright spring or summer day, here is something not to be missed: Take a cab ride from Dublin city, veer right at Sutton Cross (two miles from Howth), and drive slowly up to the summit of Howth Head. The panoramic view across Dublin Bay is superb. On the right can be seen the Sugar Loaf Mountains of Wicklow, and on the left (on a clear day) the Mourne Mountains in County Down. Or you could go deep-sea fishing with a guide on a boat from the harbor, or else visit Howth Castle and its grounds, where from May on the rhododendrons are in full bloom and make a beautiful display. In any event, work up a nice appetite for a glorious dinner.

The address of the King Sitric is East Pier, Howth, Dublin. The phone numbers are 32-52-35 and 32-47-90, and it is essential to reserve a table in advance. The restaurant is open for dinner only, Tuesday through Saturday, from 6:30 to 11:30 P.M. Closed Sunday and Monday. Dishes are à la carte, with most appetizers about $2. The fish dishes range from about $3 on up, with lobster and some other items priced according to size. The brill fillet is around $3.50. So are the lamb kidneys, while the *entrecôte marchand de vins* is about $5.50. Most vegetables and desserts, including the meringue Sitric, are around a dollar. Top-class French chateau wines can be had at prices considerably more reasonable than those charged in Dublin city establishments.

—*Hugh G. Smith*

FILLET OF SOLE DEAUVILLAISE
Based on the receipe of the King Sitric, Dublin

*At the King Sitric this dish is made with brill, which is
caught in European waters. However, gray sole or flounder,
though not quite so highly regarded by gastronomes, is very
similar to brill and can be substituted.*

1 medium onion, finely chopped
2 tablespoons butter
salt
black pepper
2 pounds gray sole or flounder fillets
1½ cups heavy cream

1. In an ovenproof skillet, sauté the onion in the butter until soft and translucent, but do not let it brown.
2. Preheat the oven to 350 degrees.
3. Salt and pepper the fillets, place them over the onion in the skillet, pour the cream over, and bring to a boil.
4. Cover the skillet and place in the oven for 12 to 15 minutes.
5. Carefully transfer the fillets from the skillet to a warm platter and return the skillet with the sauce to the top of the stove. Simmer the sauce to reduce its volume and thicken it (see note).
6. Season the sauce with salt and pepper and pour it over the fish. Serve with boiled potatoes.

Yield: 4 servings

NOTE: To help thicken the sauce, a *beurre manié* may be used. Make the *beurre manié* by blending 2 tablespoons flour with 1 tablespoon butter and form into tiny balls. With the skillet off the heat, gradually drop the balls, one by one, into the hot sauce, stirring gently. When all the balls have been dropped into the sauce, put the skillet on a low flame and simmer until the sauce thickens.

SCALLOPS À LA BRETONNE
Based on the receipe of the King Sitric, Dublin

*This dish is both a main course and an appetizer at the King
Sitric. As an appetizer the recipe will make 4 servings. The
dish may be prepared beforehand and reheated when
required, Chef Aidan MacManus says.*

1 pound bay scallops (if sea scallops are used, halve them)
salt
black pepper
1½ cups dry white wine
½ cup minced onion
6 cloves garlic, minced
8 tablespoons (1 stick) butter
4 tablespoons flour
2 tablespoons chopped parsley

1. Two pans are needed to prepare this dish. Wash the scallops and season them with salt and pepper. In one saucepan bring the scallops to a boil in the wine and cook for 1 to 2 minutes. The chef warns, "Do not boil the scallops too much as they will tend to toughen and lose flavor." Strain the liquid from the pan and reserve.
2. In the second pan, sauté the onion and garlic in the butter until the onions become translucent. Add the flour and blend thoroughly. Remove the pan from the heat and slowly add the reserved liquid, stirring carefully to blend well.
3. Return the pan to a very low heat and stir continuously until the sauce is of a creamy consistency. Simmer for an additional 10 minutes.
4. Add the scallops and parsley to the sauce. Season with salt and pepper to taste. Serve hot.

Yield: 2 servings

SHANAGARRY

YEATS ROOM RESTAURANT, BALLYMALOE HOUSE. Mr. and Mrs. Ivan Allen run this excellent establishment in County Cork as a family enterprise. From his 400 acres of rich farmland, including a separate mushroom farm, Ivan provides an abundance of fresh seasonal vegetables, dairy products, eggs, poultry, and lamb, while fish is brought in fresh daily from Ballycotton Harbor a few miles away. Mistress of the kitchen is Ivan's wife Myrtle, one of the finest cooks in Ireland.

When asked how she came to be such a surpassingly good cook, Mrs. Allen replied: "I am a farmer's wife and have not been trained as a cook. I was just interested, had a few good books, lots of good materials to hand, and a discriminating and appreciative husband. In addition, I had six children whose health, I firmly believed, rested on good food. I taught myself to cook sufficiently well to land myself a job as a cookery correspondent of the *Farmers' Journal*. Then when the family grew up I decided to specialize further, and we opened our own dining room for meals. As this house is big and roomy, we went into the hotel business in a limited way, too."

Commenting on the food she puts before her guests, Mrs. Allen said: "This part of Ireland is rich agricultural land—much the same soil, climate, and produce as Normandy. I have always believed we could produce and serve very good meals here. I was also convinced that the best food in Ireland, and elsewhere, is to be had in private houses—often country houses—like ours. Our menus, therefore, are based on what one would expect to get in such a house."

And what one gets when one sits down to dinner at Ballymaloe House's lovely Yeats Room, which is adorned with pictures by a distinguished artist, the late Jack B. Yeats (brother of poet W. B. Yeats), is superb. There is a choice of three of Myrtle Allen's delicious homemade soups, several varieties of fish taken from Ballycotton boats that day, main courses of meat, poultry, or game with a wealth of fresh vegetables, four mouth-watering desserts to pick from, and coffee and cheeses to round off the meal.

Among the dishes you might encounter on any given night are spinach soup or artichoke soup (both made with fresh vegetables from the farm), *pâté maison*, terrine of chicken, Myrtle Allen's famed cheese fondue made with cheddar, garlic, and chutney, cockles and mussels with mayonnaise, poached mullet, grilled salmon, bass baked in butter, roast farmhouse

150

chicken and bacon (the chickens range free and taste much better than those confined in coops), roast haunch of Ballinatroy venison, stuffed scallops of baby beef, and roast lamb with rosemary and garlic. If ham, pork, or duck are on the menu, you may be lucky enough to taste a delectable sauce made with Irish Mist liqueur and brandy that Mrs. Allen originated (it's also good on plum pudding and dessert soufflés and omelets). And speaking of desserts, those at Ballymaloe House regularly include such treats as sweet geranium soufflé, blackberry fool, praline ice cream, and almond meringue with peaches and cream. As for wines, a fine variety is to be had from Ivan Allen, who looks after the bar and cellar in the evening after his day on the farm. Modestly, Ivan does not claim to be an authority on wines. "We are not experts," he says. "We only know the good from the bad."

Ballymaloe House, which offers lodgings as well as food, is part of an old castle that has been rebuilt and modernized through the centuries, with the fourteenth-century keep remaining in its original form. There are 20 bedrooms, several with private bathrooms. In the old coachyard are several inexpensive rooms suitable for young people. A small gate lodge with one bedroom is ideal for honeymoon couples. All the rates are very reasonable by American standards. The amenities include a swimming pool, tennis courts, a nine-hole golf course, horses and ponies for riding, and a trout pool for the use of the guests. The beach at Ballycotton is about 20 minutes away by car. Two interesting places and good shopping centers in the vicinity of Ballymaloe House are the quaint coastal town of Youghal, with its carpet-making industry, and the city of Cork. It was to Cork long ago that a young man rode the 19 miles on horseback from Shanagarry to hear an impressive Quaker preacher named Thomas Low. As a result the young man emigrated to America, where he founded Pennsylvania. He was William Penn.

The address of the Yeats Room Restaurant is Ballymaloe House, Shanagarry, County Cork. The phone numbers are Midleton 62531 and 62506. The Yeats Room is open to visitors for breakfast, lunch, and dinner Tuesday through Saturday. On Sunday and Monday it is closed to the public and meals are served only to guests staying at Ballymaloe House. A magnificent full-course dinner, served from 7 to 9:30 P.M., costs around $9.50. Lunch (buffet only) is less than half that, and breakfast is about $2.50.

—Hugh G. Smith

BALLYMALOE CHEESE FONDUE
Based on the recipe of the Yeats Room Restaurant, Ballymaloe House, Shanagarry

2 cups grated cheddar cheese (about ½ pound)
1 tablespoon dry white wine
1 clove garlic, crushed
2 heaping teaspoons chopped parsley
2 heaping teaspoons sweet chutney

Melt all the ingredients together in a fondue pot and serve immediately, accompanied by bread cubes.

Yield: 2 servings

MYRTLE ALLEN'S IRISH MIST SAUCE
Based on the recipe of the Yeats Room Restaurant, Ballymaloe House, Shanagarry

Myrtle Allen serves this sauce with ham, bacon, pork, or duck. It's also good with plum pudding and dessert soufflés and omelets.

1 cup sugar
½ cup water
2 tablespoons Irish Mist liqueur
2 tablespoons brandy

1. Combine the sugar and water in a heavy saucepan, bring to a boil, and simmer gently until the mixture becomes a syrup the color of light amber.
2. Stir in the Irish Mist liqueur and brandy, simmer a few moments to blend. Serve immediately.

Yield: about 1 cup

Israel

TEL AVIV

ZION AND ZION EXCLUSIVE. The Zion Restaurant and its annex, the Zion Exclusive, are in the shabby Yemenite quarter of Tel Aviv. The Zion opens at 8 in the morning to serve laborers famished after a hard night's work in the busy fruit and vegetable market a stone's throw away. (The Zion Exclusive, being more exclusive, doesn't open until noon.) At midnight the Zion is packed with an after-movie crowd that overflows its three small rooms and spills out to tables set up on the sidewalk. During the day office workers, laborers, Israelis from other parts of the country, and foreign tourists replace one another at the restaurant to partake of its oriental bean soup, piquant dips, and grilled meats. There are no frills, but the atmosphere is genuine, the food is fresh, the portions are ample, the service is quick and friendly, and $4 buys a tasty and satisfying meal. It's strictly kosher, too.

At the back of the Zion, away from the bustle, is the Zion Exclusive, which caters to diners with more time and money. Here, too, the fare and milieu are authentic—but on another level. Uniformed waiters serve the popular *shashliks* and *kebabs* in grander style and the diners sit at wrought-copper tables. Choicer meats beyond the reach of the proletarians and clerks out front are offered. The specialties are incredible concoctions dreamed up by the manager, Gbaria Hani. About a hundred dishes are prepared daily. Most of them are mysterious, and for an intriguing experience the patron is advised to leave the ordering to Mr. Hani himself. The highly spiced entrée may turn out to be filled carrot or pear, and the compote may be sweetened garlic, radish, or artichoke. It can be quite an adventure and quite a meal.

The Zion and Zion Exclusive are at 28 Peduyim Street. The phone numbers are 58714 and 57323. The cost of a meal runs from about $4 to $8 at the Zion, including service but no drinks, and from about $12 to $16 at the Zion Exclusive, including service and wine. The Zion is open from 8 A.M. to past midnight. It closes Friday afternoon and doesn't reopen until Saturday night. The Zion Exclusive is open from noon to 3:30 P.M. and 6:30 P.M. to midnight. It is closed all day Friday and stays closed until Saturday night. Both the Zion and Zion Exclusive also close on Jewish religious holidays.

—Moshe Brilliant

ASPARAGUS SOUP
Based on the recipe of the Zion Exclusive, Tel Aviv

For this and the following recipe from the Zion Exclusive, we are indebted to Mrs. Moshe Brilliant, who spent a whole day in the kitchen with Chef Muhamad Grayeb Abu Shanab.

2 pounds canned asparagus
3 quarts water
1 tablespoon powdered instant chicken broth
1 pound uncooked white meat of turkey (if unavailable, substitute chicken),
      cut into small pieces
½ teaspoon salt
¼ teaspoon white pepper
1 quart soya milk (see note)

1. Drain the asparagus. Cut off the tips of the asparagus and reserve them for another use. (If used in the soup, the tips would not hold up in the cooking and would make the finished dish less attractive.)
2. In a large pot, combine all the ingredients except the soya milk and cook, partly covered, over low heat for 2 hours.
3. Add the soya milk and cook for an additional 30 minutes. Serve.

Yield: 16 servings

NOTE: Soya milk usually comes in powdered form and can be purchased where health foods are sold. Add water according to package directions to reconstitute to 1 quart liquid soya milk.

ARTICHOKE DESSERT

Based on the recipe of the Zion Exclusive, Tel Aviv

LEMON SYRUP

10 canned artichoke bottoms (see note)
2 slices lemon
1 cup sugar
1 cup water

FILLING

1 tablespoon pine nuts
1 tablespoon almonds
1 tablespoon walnuts
1 tablespoon raisins
2 tablespoons fine bread crumbs
1 tablespoon shredded coconut
1 teaspoon sugar
⅛ teaspoon rum extract
⅛ teaspoon vanilla extract
½ tablespoon rum
½ tablespoon cherry brandy

SAUCE

1 tablespoon sweet red wine
1 tablespoon dry rosé wine
1 tablespoon brandy or cognac
½ tablespoon rum
½ tablespoon cherry brandy
1 slice lemon
sugar

GARNISH

shredded coconut

1. Simmer the lemon slices, sugar, and water over low heat for 1 hour to make a lemon syrup.
2. Grind the nuts and raisins in an electric blender or a grinder. Or cut up the raisins and mash with the nuts by using a mortar and pestle or by wrapping in a piece of cloth and striking with a hammer.
3. Mix the ground nuts and raisins with all the other filling ingredients. Add about 4 tablespoons of the lemon syrup and mix well with the filling. Set aside.

(CONTINUED)

4. Put the artichoke bottoms into the remaining lemon syrup and simmer for 15 minutes.
5. Remove the artichoke bottoms from the syrup. Place equal amounts (about 1 tablespoon) of the filling on each bottom.
6. Combine all the sauce ingredients except the sugar and heat for 1 or 2 minutes. Add sugar to taste. Spoon the sauce over the filled artichoke bottoms. Garnish each bottom, with shredded coconut and serve. If desired, chill before serving.

Yield: 5 to 10 servings

NOTE: Artichoke hearts or bottoms are the edible base of the artichoke with the leaves and choke removed. The restaurant uses fresh artichokes, but canned artichoke bottoms are very satisfactory and sometimes more economical. If you cannot obtain canned bottoms or wish to make this dessert with fresh artichokes, proceed as follows: Pull off all the tough leaves by bending back and snapping off. Cut across the artichoke right above the heart, slicing off the rest of the leaves. Cut off the stem and trim the bottom of the heart. Put 1 quart of water and 2 tablespoons of lemon juice in an enamel saucepan. As you trim the bottom of each heart, drop it into the acidulated water. When the hearts are in the saucepan, bring the water to a boil and simmer for 30 to 45 minutes. Take the hearts out of the water, and with a spoon scrape away the hairy choke in the center of each heart. The filling will be placed in the resulting indentation.

Italy

BOLOGNA

RISTORANTE NERINA. There are scores of good restaurants in Florence, that glorious stronghold of tourism, but those listed in the guidebooks have lately been slipping in quality and service, and the plain ones are often better for wine than for food. So whenever I visit Florence and can manage it, I take the one-hour trip by car or train to Bologna, Italy's gastronomic capital, where people still care for good cuisine and are happy if visitors do, too.

Nerina's is named for Rina (Nerina) Della Libera, a native of Vicenza, who opened the place on a square near Bologna's Piazza Maggiore in the late 1950s. The restaurant has the mock-Alpine decor that Italians call rustic, and most patrons look like serious eaters. The service is quick and competent, and a meal at Nerina's can be combined with a visit to the immense fifteenth-century Basilica of St. Petronius, which is nearby, or with other sightseeing in Bologna's well-preserved historic center.

As is natural for Bologna, pasta dishes dominate Nerina's offerings. One glorious item is a large plate containing a selection of the restaurant's pasta specialties. Mrs. Della Libera says that all her pasta is homemade and that she never serves canned vegetables, and one is inclined to believe her. After the pasta I'm usually not much interested in the meat course, but Nerina's turkey, sausages, and cuts of various meats from the serving cart are always tempting.

The wines to be drunk in Bologna are the glorious foaming deep red

157

Lambrusco, a product of the nearby Modena-Sorbara area that travels badly, and Sangiovese and Albano from the Romagna. On two recent occasions I got superlative violet-scented Lambrusco at Nerina's.

The Ristorante Nerina is at 6 Piazza Galileo. The phone number is 23-21-56. Nerina's is open daily except Tuesday from noon to 3:30 P.M. and 7 to 11 P.M. There is a tourist menu at $5. An à la carte meal should run from $8 to $10, including wine and tip.

—Paul Hofmann

CHEF'S GOLDEN DROP

Based on the recipe of Ristorante Nerina, Bologna

½ pound lasagne

BÉCHAMEL SAUCE

4 tablespoons butter
4 tablespoons flour
2 cups milk
salt
black pepper

1 egg, beaten
1 cup thinly sliced mushrooms
1 cup thin strips of cooked ham

1. Cook the lasagne in plenty of boiling salted water until just done. Strain and keep warm.
2. Preheat the oven to 350 degrees.
3. While the lasagne is cooking, make the béchamel sauce: in a pan melt the butter over low heat. Remove the pan from the heat and add the flour all at once. Stir into a smooth paste. Return the pan to the heat, add the milk, and stir continuously until it thickens into a smooth sauce. Season with salt and pepper. Fold in the beaten egg and mix well with the sauce.
4. Place the lasagne in a deep ovenproof dish. Spread the mushrooms and ham on top and then pour the sauce over all. Bake for about 20 minutes or until the sauce bubbles and browns. Serve hot.

Yield: 2 servings

Florence—
see Bologna and Lucca

LUCCA

BUCA DI SANT'ANTONIO. Lucca is one of Italy's most delightful cities, and visitors to Florence should definitely take an hour's drive on the motorway to Pisa to see this architectural gem, enclosed on all sides by its seventeenth-century ring of walls and ramparts with their old tall trees. A quietly prosperous provincial capital, Lucca has three or four good restaurants. My favorite is Buca di Sant'Antonio. In winter a table near its fireplace with the flames crackling is one of the coziest corners in all of Tuscany.

Buca di Sant'Antonio is on a tiny square off the Church of San Michele, one of the best examples of the Pisa-Lucca Romanesque style. The restaurant is small, with two wainscoted ground-floor rooms and a second-floor section for the overflow of guests or local wedding parties. On weekends tables should be reserved in advance.

In the hunting season, which runs from September to December and a few weeks in spring, Buca di Sant'Antonio offers venison shot in the nearby hills. The house chianti is eminently drinkable. On one visit I was so taken with the wine that I bought a straw flask full of it and took it with me to Rome. Alas, the car ride didn't improve the wine; it didn't taste quite as good in Rome as it had in Lucca.

The service at Buca di Sant'Antonio isn't quick when the place is full, which it normally is, but it is always genial. Once when I praised the dark flat bread that is one of Lucca's specialties, the headwaiter slipped me a loaf free of charge after I had paid the bill and was about to go.

Buca di Sant'Antonio, owned by Franco Barbieri and Giuliano Pacini, is great for pasta dishes and risotto, Tuscan steak and, of course, venison. Most diners really don't mind that the choice of desserts is limited.

Buca di Sant'Antonio is at 1/5 Via della Cervia. The phone number is 43-681. It is open every day except Monday from noon to 3 P.M. and 7 to 10 P.M. A lunch or dinner with plenty of chianti and espresso costs $6 to $8. The restaurant closes for several weeks in summer, usually in July.

—Paul Hofmann

RISOTTO BUCA
Based on the recipe of the Buca di Sant'Antonio, Lucca

*At the Buca di Sant' Antonio this rice dish is prepared with
grated truffles, but at home it can be served without the
truffles if they are too difficult or too expensive to obtain.*

2 cups raw white rice
3 cups water
12 tablespoons (1½ sticks) butter
½ cup chopped onions
¼ cup dry white wine
1 cup chicken or beef stock (see pages 101 and 95) or canned chicken broth
    or beef bouillon
1 cup cooked green peas
salt
½–1 cup grated parmesan cheese
grated truffles (optional)

1. In a saucepan bring the rice and water to a boil. Boil about 5 minutes to allow the rice to absorb most of the water. Cover pot, lower heat, and simmer gently 20 minutes until the rice is done.
2. In a skillet sauté the onions in 8 tablespoons butter until limp, add the white wine, and bring to a boil to reduce slightly. Add the stock and green peas, and bring to a simmer. Then add the cooked rice and stir gently to mix. Season with salt. This rice dish is supposed to be more liquid than most.
3. Serve the rice very hot with a knob of butter (3 or 4 tablespoons), grated parmesan cheese, and truffles on top.

Yield: 6 servings

RABBIT WITH OLIVES AND POLENTA
Based on the recipe of the Buca di Sant'Antonio, Lucca

RABBIT

4 tablespoons olive oil
1 4–5-pound rabbit, cut into serving pieces
4 cloves garlic, minced
1 teaspoon dried rosemary
1 cup dry white wine

(CONTINUED)

salt
black pepper
2 cups chopped tomatoes
1 cup pitted black olives

P O L E N T A

6 cups water
2 teaspoons salt
2 cups finely ground cornmeal
butter (optional)
grated parmesan cheese (optional)

1. In a heavy pot heat the oil and lightly brown the rabbit pieces.
2. Add the garlic, rosemary, wine, salt, and pepper. Bring to a boil to reduce the wine slightly. Then add the tomatoes and enough water to barely cover the rabbit. Cover the pot and simmer for about 1½ hours, or until the rabbit is tender.
3. While the rabbit is simmering make the polenta (cornmeal mush): Bring the water and salt to a boil in a large pot. Slowly pour in the cornmeal stirring with a wooden spoon. Cook, stirring, over low heat, until the mixture is thick and smooth. Continue cooking and stirring over the lowest possible heat for about 20 minutes. Place the polenta on a large platter and add butter and grated parmesan cheese, if desired.
4. When the rabbit is tender, correct the seasoning, stir in the black olives and serve with the polenta.

Yield: 6 to 8 servings

MILAN

GIANNINO. Dynamic Milan, Italy's commercial, financial and publishing center, boasts many fine restaurants, some of them very expensive. Standards are high because there is more money and sophistication here than just about anywhere else in Italy. Yet despite all the fashionable new restaurants, whenever I am in Milan and can make it I have a meal at an outlying place that has been in business for more than 70 years, always in the hands of the same family.

The late Giannino Bindi, grandfather of the current managers, was an immigrant from Tuscany who at the end of the last century started a wine tavern in what was then the far southeastern outskirts of Milan, which is the chief city of Lombardy. The neighborhood has long since been enveloped by the growing metropolis, and now Giannino's is close to Linate Airport and just off the national highway and the Autostrada del Sole, the Milan-Rome motorway. Milan traffic being what it is, a trip by car from the center of town to Giannino's may take half an hour or more, but the restaurant is a convenient stop for anyone coming from or going to the autostrada.

The Guide Michelin gives Giannino two stars, the highest accolade bestowed on any Italian restaurant by the bible of French gastronomy. I don't subscribe to many Michelin appraisals in Italy, but Giannino's really deserves its two stars.

The former tavern, completely rebuilt after having been bombed out in World War II, is now a comfortable restaurant, and any patron who wants to can watch the work in the spotless kitchen where the founder's daughter, Ilda, and his grandchildren direct their experienced staff. The food at Giannino's is still basically Tuscan, but it also features Lombard dishes and other specialties of central and northern Italy. Definitely worth trying are fillet of sole Giannino, in which the fish is browned, flamed with brandy, and served with heavy cream, shrimp, boiled clams, and mushrooms; and the *bocconcini di vitello*, a dish of veal, wine, herbs, tomatoes, and other good things.

Giannino is at 8 Via Amatore Sciesa. The phone number is 54-29-48. It is open every day except Sunday from noon to 3 P.M. and 7 to 11 P.M. A lunch or dinner with wine and espresso costs $8 to $11. The restaurant closes for several weeks in summer, usually in August.

—*Paul Hofmann*

SOLE FILLETS GIANNINO
Based on the recipe of Giannino, Milan

2 ½-pound sole fillets
3 tablespoons flour
3 tablespoons butter
6–8 fresh shrimp, shelled and deveined
salt
black pepper
2 tablespoons brandy
1 dozen clams, boiled and shelled
1 cup sliced mushrooms
1 cup heavy cream

1. Flour the sole fillets lightly. In a skillet heat the butter and sauté the fillets until very lightly browned on both sides. Add the shrimp during the last 2 minutes of cooking. Season with salt and pepper.
2. Add the brandy and ignite. Arrange the shelled clams and sliced mushrooms on the fillets and pour the cream over to cover. Simmer very gently for 3 to 4 minutes for sauce to heat through and reduce slightly. Serve hot.

Yield: 2 servings

BOCCONCINI DI VITELLO
Based on the recipe of Giannino, Milan

½ cup flour
2½ pounds stewing veal, preferably from the shank, cut into small chunks
2 tablespoons vegetable oil
3 tablespoons butter
1 clove garlic, minced
2 tablespoons chopped onion
½ rib celery, chopped
½ cup dry white wine
2 cups chicken or beef stock (see pages 101 and 95), or canned chicken broth
    or beef bouillon
2 medium tomatoes, peeled, seeded, and chopped
½ teaspoon dried rosemary
½ teaspoon powdered sage or dried basil
2 tablespoons chopped parsley
salt
black pepper

1. Lightly flour the veal chunks and brown them in the oil and butter. Add the garlic, onion, and celery during the last 2 minutes of browning.
2. Add the wine and bring to a boil, then add stock, tomatoes, rosemary, sage or basil, and parsley. Bring again to a boil, cover the pot, lower the heat, and simmer for 1 hour or until the meat is tender. Season with salt and pepper and serve with rice.

Yield: 4 servings

NAPLES

LE ARCATE. Since Naples is sadly deteriorating and tourist business is falling off, restaurants that were once famous have tended to become scruffy. On several recent visits I found that pizza in New York now tastes better than in Naples, its birthplace. Seafood, especially mussels, once a standby of Neapolitan cuisine, ought to be shunned today because of severe pollution of the sea off the city. Espresso in Naples has remained the best in all of Italy, and that is very good indeed.

The celebrated Bay of Naples is still one of the world's great sights, and one of the places from which to take it in is Le Arcate. The restaurant, founded two decades ago by Aldo Izzo, who is still in charge, is on the Vomero Hill overlooking the bay and the teeming city. A meal at Le Arcate may be combined with a visit to the nearby Villa Floridiana, a park with a three-star panorama and a museum crammed with fine china and other art objects.

Le Arcate has a vast flower-adorned terrace. Dining is al fresco during the warm season, which begins early in Naples, and the service is good, as it is almost everywhere in the city. Italian honeymoon couples visiting Naples seem to like Le Arcate, and well-to-do Neapolitans take out-of-town guests there.

Pasta dishes, especially macaroni with four cheeses, are recommended. The four cheeses are mixed together and the dish is put into the oven for the cheeses to melt. Drink white Capri wine with your meal. The red house wine was found to be unsatisfactory during a recent visit.

Le Arcate is at Via Aniello Falcone 249. The phone number is 68-33-80. The restaurant is open daily except Tuesday from 1 to 3 P.M. and 7 to 10:30 P.M. A full lunch or dinner with wine will run between $8 and $10.

—*Paul Hofmann*

SCALOPPINA ALLA JACQUELINE

Based on the recipe of Le Arcate, Naples

RAGOUT SAUCE

1 pound soup bones with meat (beef or veal)
1 carrot, coarsely chopped
1 onion, coarsely chopped
1 rib celery, chopped
2 tablespoons butter
1 tablespoon tomato paste
¼ cup dry white wine
2 cups water
salt
black pepper

8 small new potatoes, or 4 large potatoes quartered
8 small white onions
½ cup thickly sliced carrots
½ cup fresh or frozen green peas
12 mushroom caps
4 4-ounce veal scallops, pounded thin
1 tablespoon flour
3 tablespoons butter
½ cup heavy cream
salt
black pepper

1. To make the ragout sauce brown the bones and vegetables in the butter in a heavy pot. Add the tomato paste, wine, and water and bring to a boil. Cover and simmer gently for 1½ hours. Season with salt and pepper and strain the sauce into a bowl. There should be about 2 cups. Set aside for later use.
2. Boil the potatoes, onion, and carrots in a little water until tender. Add the green peas and mushrooms and boil for an additional 2 minutes or until the peas are just cooked (fresh peas often take longer than frozen). Keep warm.
3. Flour the veal and shake off excess. In a skillet lightly brown the veal in butter. Remove the veal from the skillet, put in the cooked vegetables, place the veal on top of the vegetables, add 2 cups of the strained ragout sauce, and the heavy cream. Simmer gently for 3 to 4 minutes, until the sauce is slightly reduced and thickened. Place veal on a large warm platter and top it with the vegetables and sauce.

Yield: 2 servings

MACARONI WITH FOUR CHEESES
Based on the recipe of Le Arcate, Naples

2 cups ragout sauce (see preceding recipe)
1 pound macaroni
1½ cups grated parmesan cheese (4 ounces)
1 cup gruyère cheese cut in thin strips (4 ounces)
1 cup mild provolone cheese cut in thin strips (4 ounces)
1 cup Edam cheese cut in thin strips (4 ounces)

1. Make the ragout sauce, strain, and reserve.
2. Preheat the oven to 350 degrees.
3. Cook the macaroni al dente, or barely done, in lots of salted boiling water. Drain and place in a deep ovenproof dish. Add the ragout sauce and ½ cup grated parmesan cheese. Mix well.
4. Combine the remaining cheeses and arrange on top of the macaroni, spreading to cover. Bake for a few minutes, until the cheese melts and browns slightly. Serve at once on warm plates.

Yield: 4 to 6 servings

PALERMO

CAPRICE. Palermo, a city of three-quarters of a million people, has remarkably few good restaurants considering its size and importance as Sicily's capital, but one gastronomic bright spot is the Caprice. It is in Palermo's business center close to the Teatro Massimo, the opera house. Within walking distance are the cathedral and the Palace of the Normans, two of the city's most famous landmarks.

The atmosphere at the Caprice is clublike owing to its efficient service, immaculate linen, comfortable chairs, and decor of wood panels and mirrors. The clientele is mostly Sicilian with a sprinkling of mainland Italians. The restaurant's specialties are pasta dishes and seafood. (The Palermo fishing fleet sails out every night to work the sea with powerful lamps that attract fish, and Giovanni Torregrossa, the Caprice's owner, says he has a deal with some fishermen who bring directly to him every morning whatever they caught during the night.) Besides the pasta or seafood, you might want to try the *involtini alla siciliana,* veal rolled around a stuffing of ham, salami, cheese, bread, and other ingredients, then dipped in oil and bread crumbs and roasted over a charcoal grill.

The sweet tooth of the Sicilians explains the unusually vast variety of desserts at the Caprice. From a cart you can order two or three kinds of fresh pie, stewed, glazed, and candied fruits or the famous Sicilian *cassata,* a rich, delicious, creamy concoction whose base is candied fruit and cake. The espresso is good and strong.

For wine, order white or red Corvo, a heady product of the Mount Etna region of Sicily. Half a bottle is more than enough for me at lunch.

The Caprice is at 42 Via Cavour. The phone number is 24-03-89. It is open from noon to 4 P.M. and 7 to 11:30 P.M. every day except Monday from October 1 to June 15. A complete lunch or dinner with half a bottle of Corvo and espresso costs around $6.50.

—Paul Hofmann

RICE SALAD AURORA
Based on the recipe of the Caprice, Palermo

2 dozen clams in the shell
2 dozen mussels in the shell
1 pound small shrimp in the shell
3 cups water
6 tablespoons butter
1 cup chopped onions
2 cups raw white rice
3 cups seafood stock (see step 1), or chicken or beef stock (see pages 101 and 95), or canned chicken broth, or beef bouillon

AURORA SAUCE

1/4 cup mayonnaise
1/2 cup olive oil
1/4 cup ketchup
1 tablespoon brandy
1 tablespoon worcestershire sauce
2 tablespoons lemon juice
1/4 teaspoon paprika
salt
black pepper

1. Scrub and clean clams and mussels, removing the mussel beards. Bring the water to a boil in a saucepan, add the clams, mussels, and shrimp and cook at a simmer until the shrimp turn pink and the clams and mussels open. Lift out as they are cooked. Discard any clams and mussels that do not open. Strain the liquid and set aside for cooking the rice. There should be about 3 cups; add water if necessary.
2. In a saucepan heat the butter and sauté the onions until limp. Add the rice and toss to coat it with the butter. Add the liquid in which the shellfish cooked, or, if you prefer the rice less fishy, use the stock. Bring to a boil and boil 5 minutes to allow most of the liquid to be absorbed by the rice, cover pot, lower flame, and simmer 20 minutes for rice to cook. Cool the rice.
3. Meanwhile, make the aurora sauce by combining all its ingredients in a bowl. Shell the seafood.
4. To serve: In a large bowl mix together the cool cooked rice, the shellfish, and the aurora sauce, correct seasoning, and serve cold.

Yield: 4 servings

INVOLTINI ALLA SICILIANA
Based on the recipe of the Caprice, Palermo

STUFFING

½ cup chopped cooked ham
½ cup chopped Italian salami
¼ cup grated parmesan cheese
¼ cup chopped gruyère cheese
½ cup fine fresh bread crumbs
1 egg, beaten
1 tablespoon chopped parsley
salt
black pepper

1 pound veal cut into 8 thin slices, as square as possible
1 medium onion, cut into 4 slices
4 bay leaves soaked for 2 hours in water brought to a boil and then taken off
    heat
¼ cup olive oil
½ cup fine toasted bread crumbs

1. Make the stuffing in a bowl by combining all the stuffing ingredients.
2. Pound the veal slices very thin and place 2 tablespoons stuffing in the center of each slice. Roll up carefully, tucking in the sides. Secure with a toothpick.
3. Thread veal rolls on skewers, using 2 rolls per skewer and putting a slice of onion and a bay leaf in between the rolls.
4. Brush rolls with olive oil and sprinkle with bread crumbs to cover. Broil slowly, about 6 to 8 minutes on each side, until the veal is golden brown. Serve hot at once.

Yield: 2 servings

ROME

RISTORANTE NINO. This always-crowded place—just two L-shaped rooms—off the Piazza di Spagna is my favorite when food rather than profound or confidential talk is the main purpose of a meal. The tables are so close together that one inevitably picks up interesting snatches of the other patrons' conversations, mostly in Italian. Quite a lot of amusing or shocking things are said in such a way as to allow people all around to share in the fun.

Nino is good for lunch, possibly after a shopping expedition in the nearby Via Condotti with its elegant stores, and even better for dinner. The best time is after 9 P.M. when models from the high-fashion houses that are all over the area come in and go ravenously through their high-protein diets.

Nino's specialty is big Florentine—or T-bone—steaks roasted on a charcoal grill. The meat, all of it choicest cut, is brought to Rome from Tuscany, where Italy's best cattle are raised. Salads are never limp, and a vast selection of hors d'oeuvres is on display near the entrance. And rather exceptional for Rome, Nino's carafe wines are drinkable. The house red is actually a quite good, though unassuming, chianti.

The waiters don't speak or understand much English. If you need the bill for your tax or expense-account records, hold on to it because otherwise it is likely to be whisked away from you as soon as you pay.

Nino's owner is Anna Guarnacci, daughter of the late Gioacchino (Nino) Guarnacci, the founder. Her first cousin, Francesco Guarnacci, doubles as maître d' and chef.

Ristorante Nino is at 11 Via Borgognona. The phone number is 679-56-76. It is open daily except Sunday from 12:30 to 3 P.M. and 7:30 to 11 P.M. Steak is priced according to size at $3.50 a pound. It's a good idea to order a large steak for two. A complete lunch or dinner with wine and hors d'oeuvres or a pasta dish, dessert, and espresso costs about $8 a person.

—*Paul Hofmann*

ATOMIC HORS D'OEUVRES
Based on the recipe of Ristorante Nino, Rome

2 whole pigs' feet, about 1½ pounds each, cleaned and scrubbed
1 pound boneless lean pork shoulder
2 cloves garlic, minced
1 tablespoon dried rosemary
1 cup coarsely chopped parsley
3 cups thinly sliced red and/or green peppers
10–15 small sharp green Italian olives
¾ cup olive oil
⅓ cup wine vinegar
salt
black pepper

1. In a large pot place the pigs' feet, pork shoulder, garlic, rosemary, and enough water to cover. Bring to a boil, cover pot, and simmer for about 3 hours or until meat is tender but not falling apart. Lift out and cool.
2. Remove the meat from the pig's feet and discard the bones. Cut all the meat into long thin strips.
3. In a bowl toss together the meat, parsley, peppers, olives, olive oil, wine vinegar, salt, and pepper. Marinate 2 hours at room temperature before serving.

Yield: 4 to 6 servings

SAMBOSETO

CANTARELLI. An hour's drive from Milan, about two-thirds of the way toward Parma, you enter a region known as Emilia on the plains of the Po River. It is an area of lush farms celebrated for its *culatello*, or air-dried ham, its *vino frizzante*, the oldest natural sparkling wine, and its *parmigiano* cheese. In the heart of Emilia, in the tiny market village of Samboseto, three miles from Busseto, the birthplace of Verdi, there is a marvelous trattoria run by Peppino and Mirella Cantarelli where you can gorge on all the local products at a very reasonable price.

The restaurant is in what was a stable up to 160 years ago. Peppino's grandmother made the conversion when she went into the business of serving local farm workers around the turn of the century. Farm workers still come here to eat (a table is always reserved for them), but now the clientele also includes some of the most prominent people of Italy and Europe. Yet Cantarelli remains unspoiled.

It's a small restaurant, seating only 55 persons, which means you should reserve in advance. As much space is devoted to the kitchen as to the dining area. The walls are hung with colorful paintings by Udo Toniato, a local artist whose endeavors are more decorative than anything else. They provide a cheerful contrast to the immaculate white linen tablecloths, the dark green bottles of *aqua minerale*, the mellow hues of Mirella Cantarelli's incredibly fine food, and the garnet shade of the Scorzamara red wine, which puts any beaujolais to shame.

Peppino handles the wine and slices the *culatello* that almost everyone takes as a first course. He also manages the food shop that looks out on the main road. The Cantarellis' younger son, Fernando, helps serve the guests. Meanwhile, in the kitchen, where mixers and other machines are banned and the *mezza luna*, the crescent-shaped mincing knife of our grandmothers, occupies a place of honor, Mirella turns out mouth-watering preparations of the best that Emilia's farms, fields, streams, and orchards can provide. These include her *risotto primavera*, saffron rice surrounded by an inner ring of chicken livers sautéed with sage and rosemary and an outer ring of tiny peas cooked with butter and bacon. Among the desserts there is an almond cake, brown and crisp on the outside and topped with roasted almonds and sugar, whose goodness has to be tasted to be believed.

Cantarelli is on the main road of Samboseto. The phone number is

90133. It is closed Monday and for a month starting early in January. It serves lunch and dinner the rest of the year except during June and July, when it serves dinner only. A meal for two should come to around $15.

—*Clyde H. Farnsworth*

RISOTTO PRIMAVERA
Based on the recipe of Cantarelli, Samboseto

4 cups water
1 small onion, chopped
8 tablespoons (1 stick) unsalted butter
1 cup raw, untreated white rice (preferably short-grain Italian rice)
½ teaspoon saffron powder
½ cup grated parmesan cheese
½ cup diced bacon
2 cups small green peas
½ pound chicken livers, the larger pieces cut in half
¼ teaspoon dried rosemary
¼ teaspoon powdered sage
salt
black pepper

1. Bring the water to a boil. In another pot, sauté the onion until limp in 4 tablespoons butter, then add the rice and a pinch of salt, and stir to mix. Keeping the pot of rice over a low flame and keeping the pot of water boiling, add a spoonful or two of the boiling water to the rice, stirring continuously until the water is absorbed. Keep repeating this process, adding spoonsful of boiling water to the rice and stirring, until most or all of the water is used and the rice is cooked. The process should take about 30 minutes, and the cooked grains of rice should be a little gluey on the outside and have a firm, almost hard core.
2. Add the saffron and mix well with the rice. Add the parmesan cheese, stir to mix and keep warm on an asbestos mat over low heat.
3. Lightly brown the diced bacon in 1 tablespoon butter, add the peas, and cook until just tender. Keep warm.
4. In a skillet over medium heat, sauté the livers, rosemary, and sage in 3 tablespoons butter until lightly brown, turning once or twice, about 5 to 6 minutes. Season with salt and black pepper.
5. To serve: Place the rice in the middle of a platter, surround with a ring of livers, and an outer ring of peas and bacon.

Yield: 4 servings

VENICE

RISTORANTE LA MADONNA. The internationally known restaurants around St. Mark's Square are good but overrun by tourists throughout the travel season. They are also expensive. La Madonna is hard to find and patronized mostly by Venetians.

If you come from St. Mark's Square on foot—a 15-minute walk—you have to cross the Rialto Bridge, turn sharp left on the Grand Canal, and then go into the narrow Calle della Madonna on your right. You can also take the *vaporetto*, which is Venice's floating bus, to the Rialto stop, have a look at the Grand Canal from the bridge, and seek out the Calle della Madonna. The scouting effort is worth it.

The restaurant consists of a series of small rooms that tend to be crowded. As in many Italian places that cater to a local middle-class clientele and don't particularly care for tourists, the decor is utilitarian. The walls are whitewashed and the lights are bright. The service is quick.

La Madonna carries on its menu all the classic dishes of Venetian cuisine, including *fegato alla veneziana*—sliced calf's liver, Venetian style, with plenty of sliced cooked onions. It is served with a slab of polenta, the region's thick cornmeal mush.

A specialty of La Madonna is *seppioline alla veneziana*. This is a dish of small inky cuttlefish, specially prepared by La Madonna's chef, Remigio (Remi) Bortolin, who has been working for the restaurant for some 20 years. The *seppioline* don't taste of ink but have a tart flavor that is not unpleasant despite their somewhat leathery texture.

The wines to have are white Soave from Verona with the seafood and red Valpolicella from the Venetian mainland with the liver.

Ristorante La Madonna is at 594 Calle della Madonna. The phone number is 23-824. The place is open every day except Wednesday from noon to 3:30 P.M. and 7 to 10:30 P.M. A full lunch or dinner with wine, dessert and very good espresso should cost between $5 and $7 a person.

—Paul Hofmann

SEPPIOLINE ALLA VENEZIANA
Based on the recipe of Ristorante La Madonna, Venice

2 pounds small squid, cleaned, ink sacs removed, but the heads intact and the
  bodies cut into ½-inch bands
6 cloves garlic, minced
1 small onion, minced
½ cup olive oil
1 small tomato, seeded and chopped
2 bay leaves, finely crushed
dry white wine
salt

1. Cook squid in rapidly boiling salted water until they curl, about 2 minutes.
   Drain and place on a platter.
2. Quickly brown the garlic and onion in the olive oil and pour over the
   squid. Sprinkle the tomato and bay leaves on top, add a dash of white wine
   and salt, and serve at once.

Yield: 4 to 6 servings

SOLE FILLET ALLA REMI
Based on the recipe of Ristorante La Madonna, Venice

2 ½-pound sole fillets
1 dozen mussels or clams in the shell, cleaned
1 dozen small shrimp, shelled and deveined
¼ cup dry white wine
½ teaspoon lemon juice
½ cup water
salt
black pepper
3 tablespoons butter
1 tablespoon flour

1. Place the fish fillets in the center of a skillet and arrange the mussels or
   clams and shrimp around them. Add the wine, lemon juice, water, salt,
   and pepper and bring to a boil. Reduce heat and simmer until the fish is
   cooked and the mussels or clams open, about 10 minutes. Discard any
   that do not open.

(CONTINUED)

2. Remove the skillet from the heat. Drain the fish stock and reserve for the sauce. Take the mussels or clams out of their shells, and arrange around the fish. Keep warm.
3. In a small pan, melt the butter. Off heat add the flour and stir to a smooth paste. Strain the fish stock into the pan and return to the heat. Simmer, stirring, until the sauce becomes smooth and thickens. Pour the sauce over the fish in the skillet, heat a minute or two, then transfer to a platter, and serve.

Yield: 2 servings

SPAGHETTI WITH MUSSELS
Based on the recipe of Ristorante La Madonna, Venice

2–3 dozen mussels, scrubbed and debearded
2 cups boiling water
3 cloves garlic, minced
4 tablespoons olive oil
2 tablespoons chopped parsley
1 pound ripe tomatoes, peeled and chopped
salt
black pepper
½ pound spaghetti

1. Cook mussels in the boiling water until the shells open. Discard any that do not open. Remove the mussels and save the water. Take the mussels out of the shells and discard the shells.
2. In a saucepan sauté the garlic briefly in the olive oil. Add the parsley and tomatoes and simmer gently for 20 minutes. Add the shelled mussels, season with salt and pepper, and keep warm.
3. Cook the spaghetti in plenty of salted boiling water till barely done. Finish cooking the spaghetti in the pot of mussel water for extra flavor.
4. Drain the spaghetti and place it on a platter. Pour the sauce over it, and serve at once.

Yield: 2 servings

Japan

KYOTO

JUNIDANYA. Intimately involved in the most famous vendetta in Japanese history was Junidanya, or the Inn of the Twelve Steps. In 1701 a feudal lord was, in the eyes of his samurai warriors, unjustly forced to commit suicide. After his death 47 of his retainers gathered in Junidanya to plot revenge. They succeeded more than a year later, then committed suicide themselves and became heroes in the greatest of the Kabuki plays, *Chushingura.*

In Kyoto, the shrine- and temple-filled ancient capital of Japan, there is a traditional inn named for the original Junidanya. The guest takes his shoes off, sits on the tatami mats on the floor and eats with chopsticks. Around him is a decor of exquisite folk art—prints, pottery, utensils.

One of Junidanya's best dishes is *mizutaki,* which, as so often happens in Japan, is neither ancient nor Japanese. *Mizutaki,* which means to cook with water, is an adaptation of a northern Chinese dish imported after World War II. It is tender beef sliced razor thin, which the diner dips with his chopsticks into boiling water for a few seconds to cook, dabs into sesame-flavored soy sauce, and eats. Once a platter of beef has been consumed and the water has become a broth, vegetables and then noodles are cooked in it. Finally, the meal is washed down with the soup that has been made. Sake, the warm Japanese rice wine, is best with *mizutaki,* but beer is also good.

Junidanya is in the heart of the Gion district, the most famous *geisha* quarter in all Japan, which remains as it has been for centuries because Kyoto is one of the few Japanese cities that wasn't bombed during World War II. There are latticed teahouses along the Kamo River, a favorite place for strolling lovers. Tourists should walk Gion's narrow street either at 5 P.M. or between 10 and 11 P.M. to see the enchanting little *maiko,* the young apprentice *geisha,* in their fabulous kimonos and elaborately ornamented old-style hairdos, going by rickshaw to their assignments in various restaurants and teahouses. The Shinto shrine for *geisha* and *maiko,* called Yasaka, is near Junidanya. And within a few minutes' walk of the restaurant one may observe such traditional Japanese arts as No drama, Kabuki, and the tea ceremony.

The address of Junidanya is simply Hanamikoji, Gion. Although the restaurant has a legal street address too, it is complicated and there is no need to use it because every cab driver knows where Junidanya is. The phone number is 561-0213. A dinner costs upward of $20 a person, plus 10 percent tax and a 10 percent service charge, but there is no tipping. Sake is about $1.50 a half-pint. The place is open seven days a week from noon to 9:30 P.M., with orders stopping at 8 P.M.

—*Richard Halloran*

MIZUTAKI
Based on the recipe of Junidanya, Kyoto

2 pounds boneless sirloin or tenderloin steak, sliced razor thin
1 pound Chinese celery cabbage, cut into 2-inch pieces
½ pound spinach leaves
6 scallions, cut into 2-inch lengths
12 mushroom caps
2 medium onions, cut into ¼-inch slices
3 fresh bean curd squares, cut into 2-inch cubes
½ pound Japanese or Chinese noodles

DIPPING SAUCE

1½ cups Japanese soy sauce
3 tablespoons sugar
3 tablespoons sesame oil

6 cups water or chicken broth
a small sheet of dried kelp, rinsed (optional)
salt

1. Arrange the beef slices, cabbage, spinach, scallions, mushrooms, onions, and bean curd in separate rows or circles on one or two large platters.
2. Cook the noodles in plenty of boiling water, drain, and put in a bowl.
3. Make the dipping sauce by combining the soy sauce, sugar, and sesame oil. Divide into 6 individual dipping bowls. Arrange everything on the dinner table.
4. Place a tabletop burner or electric skillet in the center of the table. On the kitchen stove, using a large heatproof casserole or pot, bring to a boil the 6 cups of water with the kelp and a pinch of salt. Place the casserole on the table burner and maintain at a simmer all through the meal.
5. To eat the *mizutaki*, each guest dips a beef slice into the water to cook to the desired degree of doneness, then dips it into his bowl of sauce, and consumes it. When all the meat is eaten, the vegetables are eaten in the same manner. Finally the noodles are added to the rich broth that has been made and this noodle soup is ladled into individual bowls and served to each guest.

Yield: 6 servings

TOKYO

KUSHIHACHI. Eating places in Tokyo—and there must be a thousand good ones—come in all shapes and sizes. There are the formal *ryotei*, elegant Japanese-style restaurants to which foreigners customarily go only when invited by Japanese associates. There are Western-style restaurants ranging from Maxim's of Paris to McDonald hamburger stands. There are Asian restaurants serving all kinds of Chinese, Korean, Mongolian, Indonesian, and Indian foods. And then there are what might be called the specialty shops, each serving only one or two kinds of food—noodles, vegetables, grilled beef, breaded pork, raw sliced fish and rice, or the like. Kushihachi is one of these. Its specialty is *yakitori*, bits of chicken skewered on slivers of bamboo and cooked over an open charcoal fire.

Two kinds of *yakitori* are served: *shio-yaki*, in which the chicken is salted, sprinkled with wine, and grilled, and *tare-yaki*, in which the chicken is dipped into a soy-based sauce, grilled, dipped again, and grilled until done. With the delicious skewered bits you can have grilled mushrooms, perhaps a couple of other grilled vegetables, roasted clams, and green tea. Dessert is fresh fruit. With *yakitori* it's best to drink sake, the warm Japanese rice wine, but beer or *mizu-wari*, whiskey and water, can be ordered.

Kushihachi, which means "eight skewers," seats about a dozen persons around a counter, eight or ten more at Western-style tables, and four to six on the floor around a Japanese-style grill. The motif is Japanese, with sub-dued lamps decorated with ancient calligraphy, an old-fashioned utensil hung here and there, and a tiny rock garden outside the sliding glass doors. The atmosphere is quiet and relaxed.

Kushihachi is the sort of place that doesn't advertise much. One is taken there first by a friend, then one goes back on one's own. Luckily Kushihachi is easy to find, unlike many of the tiny restaurants sprinkled in alleys across this great, confusing city. It's near the Roppongi Crossing, which everyone in Tokyo knows, and it's on the third floor of a building above a Kentucky Fried Chicken shop, of all things.

The Roppongi—it means "six trees"—neighborhood offers a wide variety of restaurants besides Kushihachi, including Anne Dinken's kosher-style delicatessen, and many bars, but there are no historic sights or similar tourist attractions in the immediate vicinity. The area is a hang-out, however,

for with-it students, media people, entertainers, and other interesting speci-
mens of present-day Japanese.

The exact address of Kushihachi is Kajikawa-Seishido Building, 9-10
Roppongi 3-chome, Minato-ku. The phone number is 403-3060. The restaurant's hours are 5:30 P.M. to 3 A.M. on weekdays, 6 P.M. to midnight on Sunday. A satisfying meal of six skewers of chicken, three of vegetables, and a
bottle of first-class sake costs about $8, including a 10 percent tax. There
is no service charge and tipping is not customary, although it is courteous to
leave the silver from one's change.

—*Richard Halloran*

YAKITORI
Based on the recipe of Kushihachi, Tokyo

At Kushihachi only the thighs of fresh chickens are used for
yakitori meat, and the skewered morsels are grilled over a
fire made of very hard charcoal. The home cook, however,
can use breast meat, and if charcoal grilling is inconvenient,
the chicken bits can be put into an oven broiler.

MARINADE

¾ cup Japanese soy sauce
½ cup sweet sake or sweet sherry
3 tablespoons sugar
1 teaspoon grated fresh ginger

meat of 8 chicken thighs or 4 whole breasts, cut into 1-inch cubes

1. Prepare the marinade by combining all the ingredients in a shallow bowl.
2. Thread the chicken cubes on skewers and place in the marinade for 15 to
   20 minutes.
3. Prepare a charcoal fire or preheat the broiler. Broil the skewered chicken
   for about 2 minutes on one side. Dip the chicken into the marinade and
   broil it on the other side for about 2 minutes. Dip it into the sauce again
   and broil about 2 minutes more, or until cooked through and golden
   brown. Serve hot.

Yield: 4 servings

Korea

SEOUL

HAN-IL-GWAN. This restaurant, specializing in Korean food and patronized by Koreans, is one of the most popular eating places in the South Korean capital. You can dine at Western-style tables with chairs on the first floor, or you can take off your shoes and walk up one or two flights. Upstairs, on the hard vinyl-covered floor, you sit cross-legged on individual straw mats in summer and cushions the rest of the year while waitresses in traditional dress scurry from room to room carrying food on large trays. Han-Il-Gwan doesn't offer much in the way of decor, but what it lacks in this respect it usually makes up in atmosphere, for many of its patrons are local women, most of them traditionally dressed, who gather at the restaurant for monthly meetings of mutual savings clubs and chatter and laugh throughout the meal.

Han-Il-Gwan is a block from Insa-dong, better known to foreigners as Mary's Alley, which is lined with shops selling old Korean chests, paintings, and pottery. And not too far away are two of Seoul's top sightseeing attractions, the Changdok and Kyongbok palaces, where the kings of Korea lived in days gone by.

My favorite dishes at Han-Il-Gwan are *bulgogi*, which is marinated beef strips grilled over charcoal at the diner's table, and *bulkalbi*, barbecued ribs of beef, which are usually served already cooked but will be prepared at the table upon request. Both *bulgogi* and *bulkalbi* are served with rice or noodles, soup, and four vegetable side dishes, including *kimchi*, the spicy pickled Chinese cabbage or radish that is an essential part of every native Korean meal. Chopsticks and spoons are provided.

Prices are reasonable. *Bulgogi* costs about $1.50 a person; *bulkalbi* is about 85 cents a piece, with three pieces being sufficient for one person. Beer or *chongjong*, the Korean equivalent of sake, the Japanese rice wine, is served on request. A bottle of beer is around 90 cents, a glass of *chongjong* about 35 cents. A 5 percent tax will be added to your bill. Tipping is not required.

Han-Il-Gwan is at 119-1 Chongjin-dong. The phone numbers are 72-3077 and 72-3735. The place is open from 7 A.M. to 10 P.M. every day of the year except for the New Year holiday, January 1 and 2, and the Korean Thanksgiving Day, which falls on a different date in the fall every year.

Besides its main restaurant, Han-Il-Gwan has a branch at 2-50 Myong-dong, in a busy shopping district. Its phone numbers are 23-0258, 23-1609, and 23-9966. The branch is somewhat more modern than the main restaurant and closer to Seoul's major hotels, but it serves the same food and at the same prices. The days and hours of operation are also the same.

—Samuel Kim

BULGOGI
Based on the recipe of Han-Il-Gwan, Seoul

2 tablespoons white sesame seeds
2 pounds sirloin or tenderloin steak, sliced razor thin
2 tablespoons sugar
⅔ cup dark soy sauce
2 teaspoons minced garlic
⅔ cup finely chopped scallions
½ teaspoon black pepper
1 teaspoon MSG (optional)
1½ tablespoons sesame oil

1. Toast the sesame seeds by browning them in a dry skillet over low heat. Shake the pan often. Then crush the seeds in a blender, or in a bowl with a spoon.
2. In a bowl mix the beef slices and sugar well. Then add the soy sauce, garlic, scallions, sesame seeds, pepper, and MSG. Toss well, then add the sesame oil. Let stand about 30 minutes.
3. While the beef is marinating, start a charcoal fire in a hibachi or other small grill, or preheat a broiler. Grill or broil the beef, a little at a time, until golden brown outside and juicy within. Do not overcook. Eat the slices as soon as they are done. Extra soy sauce may be served on the side as a dip.

Yield: 4 servings

BULKALBI

Based on the recipe of Han-Il-Gwan, Seoul

2½ tablespoons white sesame seeds
4 pounds short ribs, cut into 3-inch pieces
5 tablespoons sugar
⅔ cup dark soy sauce
1 tablespoon minced garlic
⅔ cup finely chopped scallions
½ teaspoon black pepper
1 teaspoon MSG (optional)
2 tablespoons sesame oil

1. Toast the sesame seeds by browning them in a dry skillet over low heat. Shake the pan often. Then crush the seeds in a blender, or in a bowl with a spoon.
2. Trim the fat off the short ribs. Make deep gashes in the meat without cutting through to the bone.
3. Mix the ribs first with the sugar, then with the crushed sesame seeds and all remaining ingredients except the sesame oil. Combine well, then add the sesame oil and mix again. Let stand 1 hour or longer.
4. Prepare a charcoal fire or preheat a broiler. Grill the ribs slowly until the meat is brown on the outside and cooked through, about 12 minutes on each side. The ribs can also be cooked on a rack in a hot oven.

Yield: 4 to 6 servings

Liberia

MONROVIA

ROSELINE'S RESTAURANT. Six days a week at lunch and dinner the 120 seats of Roseline's Restaurant are filled. What fills them is home-style Liberian food and lots of good conversation. The conversation—humorous, business oriented, or political—is supplied by the establishment's steady customers: high and not-so-high government officials, businessmen, and intellectuals of both sexes and many nationalities. The food, including hot, spicy dishes that have close counterparts throughout West Africa, is supplied by Roseline's owner and hostess, Mrs. Roseline Porte, a pinch and dab cook who runs her modern kitchen on the basis of experience and instinct—or as she puts it, "just feeling."

Fifteen years ago Mrs. Porte, a pleasant, friendly woman, opened a "cook shop" in a small room that could serve, she says, "ten people at a time —ten small people." It was a success, and in 1962 she built her current restaurant. Here, amid air-conditioned and well-lighted but not opulent surroundings, a staff at 12 efficient waiters provides some of the best service to be found in Monrovia.

The food at Roseline's includes such typical products of the West African kitchen as jollof rice, palm butter, fufu, palava sauce, and dumboy. Jollof rice is boiled rice steeped in a spicy gravy full of some mixture of beef, chicken, pork, shrimp, or fish. Palm butter is palm oil cooked with beef, chicken, pork (pig's feet are a favorite here), fish, or a combination thereof to make a thick sauce that is served with rice. Fufu is an ash-colored starch that is made from fermented cassava, has the consistency of bread dough, and is eaten in lumps with sauces or soups. Palava sauce is a dish prepared with the cassava leaf, which is cut into shreds, cooked with a combination of meat, poultry, and fish and served with rice or fufu. Dumboy is the fresh cassava version of fufu; the cassava is boiled and pounded into an almost elastic paste that is served with meats, sauces, or soups.

Roseline's Restaurant, across from the new Post Office Building, is on Carey Street between Warren and McDonald streets. No matter where you start in Monrovia, it shouldn't cost much to get to Roseline's because a 25-cent taxi ride will take one almost anyplace downtown and 50 cents is about the top fare anywhere in this small but increasingly busy capital city of Liberia, a nation unusual in West Africa in that it has been independent ever since 1847, just a quarter-century after some freed American slaves first settled near here. (Monrovia is named for an American President, James Monroe.) Roseline's is open Monday through Saturday for lunch and dinner and is closed Sunday. The phone number is 22513, and although official and private luncheons are frequently held at Roseline's, couples do not normally need to make reservations in advance. The price of typical West African dishes runs from $1 to $2.

—Thomas A. Johnson

JOLLOF RICE
Based on the recipe of Roseline's Restaurant, Monrovia

2 cups vegetable oil
¾ pound beef, cut into 1-inch cubes
¾ pound pork, cut into 1-inch cubes
¾ pound chicken, cut into small pieces
¾ pound peeled shrimp
2 large onions, finely chopped
¼ cup tomato paste
¼ cup sliced and seeded hot red peppers or 2 tablespoons hot red-pepper sauce (use less if a milder dish is preferred)
1 cup water
1 cup beef stock (see page 95) or canned beef bouillon
1 cup green peas
2 cups raw untreated rice boiled for 20 minutes
salt
black pepper

1. Heat the oil in a deep saucepan until it barely smokes. Fry the beef and pork for 5 to 8 minutes, until brown. Remove to a large pot or casserole

and set aside. Then fry the chicken and shrimp for 5 minutes. Remove and set aside with the beef and pork. Fry the onions until brown. Add to the meat mixture.

2. Add the tomato paste, water, red pepper, and beef stock to the meat and onion mixture. Simmer fast for 40 mintues.
3. Add the green peas and simmer gently for 10 minutes.
4. Add the half-boiled rice, which will soak up most of the liquid. Stir gently. Lower heat and simmer gently for another 10 minutes, or until the rice is fully cooked.
5. Season with salt and pepper to taste. Serve immediately.

Yield: 6 to 8 servings

Mexico

CUERNAVACA

LAS MAÑANITAS. If you want Mexican food in a lovely *ambiente*, come to Cuernavaca and try Las Mañanitas. Cuernavaca is only 47 miles south of Mexico City, but it is some 3,000 feet lower, which makes it subtropical. A fine road connects the two, and the drive has the advantage of getting you away from that horrible Mexico City smog.

Las Mañanitas tends to be crowded on weekends, but during the week you can sit in a lush garden among a lot of friendly white and green peacocks, flamingos, and African crested cranes. The birds will saunter by your table and you can feed them with peanuts supplied by the management while you sip a drink. If you like rum punch, incidentally, this is one of the best places in Mexico to order it.

Las Mañanitas is not a pure Mexican restaurant: It offers U.S.-style beefsteaks and other dishes not Mexican. But they are good. If you are like me, however, and enjoy well-prepared Mexican food, the spicy pork *adobo* in a red sauce made of several kinds of *chiles* is notable. Chef Manuel Quinto, who has been with Las Mañanitas since Robert Krause, an American, opened it almost 20 years ago, sees to that. Of the appetizers, I would recommend either the *seviche*, which is raw bits of the local cod called sierra marinated in lime juice and served with a tangy sauce, or the hot eels in garlic sauce, offered up in delicate slivers seasoned with *chile ancho*. But of all the dishes that Las Mañanitas prepares, it is the *chiles rellenos* that are really fantastic. They are deep-fried peppers stuffed with cheese and served with an onion-flavored cream sauce. Don't miss them.

One last thing about Las Mañanitas. When you order your drinks at the little tables near the strolling birds, tell the waiter when you think you would like to eat. If you want time for two drinks, say so and your meal will be ready when you are. Then the waiter will call you up to a veranda overlooking the garden for the feast. Incidentally, for dessert try the black bottom pie. Believe it or not, it's a house specialty.

Before dining at Las Mañanitas or after the management gives you your complimentary Kahlúa, you might be tempted to explore Cuernavaca, which was a favorite watering spot of that kindly gentleman Hernán Cortés, who came here, apparently, when he wearied of watching his *conquistadores* plunder and bully the Aztecs. He built a palace, which still stands. Later in history even the ill-fated Maximilian and Carlotta liked Cuernavaca for its climate. Aside from old churches and the palace, which you may or may not want to see depending on how many you've seen before and how tired you are, Cuernavaca is simply a lovely little city with nothing in particular to offer except the increasingly rare privilege of breathing air that isn't too polluted. You can drive to any neighborhood where the flowers seem especially beautiful and just walk around.

Of course, if you want to, you can buy some overpriced merchandise in two shops located near Las Mañanitas, but for me the best part of Cuernavaca are those sections away from the middle of town where the air is sweet, the sky is blue, and the sun warms you right down to the marrow. There's no Chartres to prowl through here, no Prado, nothing to make you feel guilty if you've missed it. All you have to do is to enjoy yourself.

Las Mañanitas is at Ricardo Linares 107. The phone number is 2-46-46. A la carte entrées fall mainly in the $4 range. The restaurant is open seven days a week and serves lunch from 1 to 5 P.M., dinner from 7 to 11 P.M. The garden opens at noon.

—Richard Severo

SEVICHE
Based on the recipe of Las Mañanitas, Cuernavaca

2 pounds fillet of sierra or any other firm white-flesh fish

MARINADE

2 cups fresh lime juice
5 tablespoons salt

(CONTINUED)

SAUCE

3 cups tomato juice
3 tablespoons canned chopped jalapeño peppers (if unavailable, substitute
    Tabasco or Louisiana hot pepper sauce to taste)
2 medium tomatoes, chopped
1 medium onion, chopped
4 tablespoons white wine
4 tablespoons olive oil
10 green olives
½ teaspoon Maggi seasoning, or ¼ teaspoon soy sauce
½ teaspoon worcestershire sauce
1 teaspoon salt
1 teaspoon dried oregano

1. Cut the fish into bite-size pieces and marinate in the lime juice and salt
   for about 2 hours.
2. To make the sauce, mix the tomato juice with the chopped jalapeño
   peppers and add the chopped tomatoes and onion. Then add the white
   wine, olive oil, olives, Maggi seasoning, worcestershire sauce, salt, and
   oregano. Mix well. Set aside.
3. Wash the marinated fish chunks thoroughly in cold water. Drain and
   place them in the sauce.
4. Chill well and serve in cups or small bowls.

Yield: 8 to 10 appetizer servings

CHILES RELLENOS DE QUESO
Based on the recipe of Las Mañanitas, Cuernavaca

10 green poblano chiles (if unavailable, substitute bell peppers and add ½
    teaspoon ground red pepper or cayenne to the sauce. Bell peppers,
    however, cannot match the piquant poblano flavor.)
salt
black pepper
vegetable oil
1 pound Manchego cheese (if unavailable, substitute Monterey Jack or similar
    cheese) cut into wedges slightly smaller than the chiles
flour
3 eggs, separated

SAUCE

1 medium onion, sliced
3 tablespoons butter
3 tablespoons sifted flour
4 cups heavy cream

1. Dry the chiles with paper towels. Salt and pepper them. Heat the oil in a deep, heavy skillet. When it is very hot, drop in the chiles and fry them very quickly until blistered. Take them out and drain them on paper toweling. Allow them to cool.
2. Peel off the thin, papery skin; slit each chile lengthwise and remove the stem, seeds, and veins. Stuff each chile with a wedge of cheese.
3. Roll the stuffed chiles in flour, coating them well.
4. Beat the egg whites until stiff. Lightly beat the yolks separately. Fold the yolks into the beaten whites. Dip the floured chiles in the egg mixture.
5. Deep fry the chiles rapidly until golden brown. Drain them on paper towels.
6. Prepare the sauce as follows: Sauté the onion in the butter until lightly golden. Add the sifted flour. Mix well and brown a bit. Remove from the heat and add the cream slowly. Mix well. Return to low heat and cook until the sauce thickens and begins to boil. Add salt and pepper to taste.
7. Put the fried chiles into the sauce for reheating just before serving.

Yield: 4 to 5 servings

MEXICO CITY

LA PERGOLA. In Mexico City, as in New York, good Mexican restaurants are hard to find. Restaurant men here tend to deprecate their own cuisine, partly in the belief that it is too spicy for foreign tastes and partly because some newly affluent Mexicans seem to want to disassociate themselves from native cooking, seeking out instead the so-called international restaurants that frequently offer pseudo-French fare. Moreover, the tourist, contrary to what he might do in Paris or Rome, should not seek out little cafes or family-run restaurants in Mexico. Those small out-of-the-way places are prime sources of amebic dysentery and typhoid.

In Mexico City my favorite restaurant, La Pergola, is not Mexican but Italian. I was introduced to it by Mexican friends who think it is really good and they are right. The owners are the family Tavano who are, praise God, from the Abruzzi section of central Italy, the section that has given Rome so many of its good restaurants because exporting chefs is a tradition in Abruzzi. La Pergola's homemade pasta, and especially the fettucine, is comparable to authentic Roman fare. (I should point out that I was raised on homemade pasta and have spent a great deal of time in Italy.) My favorite dish at La Pergola is the fettucine specialty called *paglia e fieno ciociara*. It is always served al dente, piping hot, in a red sauce with endless slivers of tender chicken. The pizza is also very good.

One enters La Pergola by pulling open a heavy wooden door and stepping into a place of white stucco walls and little nooks and corners. On the walls are framed antique maps and prints of Italy, arranged not by a decorator but by the owners, who say they wanted La Pergola to have a "typically Italian" ambience. The service is more than adequate by Mexican standards, although one should expect a leisurely meal. Remember, the pasta is always cooked to order and good pasta takes time. Also, you always have to ask for the check at La Pergola—they'll never bring it otherwise. Unlike restaurants in New York, you never feel there's any pressure on you to leave when the meal is over. That's a hazard if you work in Mexico City and have something to do in the afternoon.

La Pergola is in Mexico City's fashionable Zona Rosa (Pink Zone) at the corner of Londres and Genova. It is open from 1 P.M. to 1 A.M. every day. The phone number is 5-11-30-49. A complete meal, including a drink beforehand and 10 percent tip, but not wine, should be less than $10. Caution: Before ordering Italian or French wine with a meal, ask what it costs. Mexicans slap a horrible tax on imported wine to protect their own wine industry. Mexican wines are not distinguished, but a white wine, Santo Tomas Chenin Blanc, available from March to November, is passable as a table wine. If you insist on champagne with your meal anywhere in Mexico, be prepared to pay from $35 to $50 a bottle for it. Don't say you weren't warned.

You ought to be warned, too, about the altitude of Mexico City, which is well over 7,000 feet. Wherever you choose to eat, you may have a stuffy feeling after a few days and conclude you have indigestion. You really haven't, or at least you can blame it on the high altitude rather than the cook. The altitude tends to slow the digestive process of many (not all) people and so you may find yourself wanting to eat only twice a day. If you get that feeling, have your big meal around 2:30 P.M. as so many Mexicans do. Also, until you get used to the high altitude, you may find that alcoholic beverages work much faster on you in Mexico City than they do at sea level. In short, exercise a little moderation your first few days in town.

Before or after a meal at La Pergola, you can do a bit of shopping or people-watching in the Zona Rosa, which is noted for both. Gucci is there, and shops full of Mexican silver and European and American-style clothes. There are also lots of little sidewalk cafes where you can have a coffee and observe the passing scene.

—Richard Severo

PAGLIA E FIENO CIOCIARA
Based on the recipe of La Pergola, Mexico City

¼ medium onion, thinly sliced
2 green peppers cut into julienne
2 red peppers cut into julienne
½ cup olive oil
1 pound raw chicken cut into julienne
3 bay leaves
½ cup dry white wine
3 tomatoes, peeled and finely chopped
black pepper
2 pounds green and white fettucine (thinnest variety)
grated parmesan cheese

1. Sauté the onion and the peppers in the oil for 10 to 12 minutes, stirring frequently.

2. Add the chicken, bay leaves, white wine, tomatoes, and black pepper. Simmer, partially covered, for about 45 minutes.
3. Meanwhile, cook the fettucine according to package directions until they are al dente. They should not be overcooked.
4. Drain the fettucine, place on a large platter, and pour the chicken mixture over. Sprinkle liberally with the parmesan cheese, mix, and serve.

Yield: 6 servings

PIZZA À LA PERGOLA
Based on the recipe of La Pergola, Mexico City

CRUST

3 cups flour
1½ ounces dry-active yeast
4 tablespoons olive oil
4 tablespoons warm milk
¼ pound potatoes, mashed
salt
black pepper

TOPPING

½ pound tomatoes, peeled and chopped
2 cloves garlic, crushed
3 sprigs parsley, minced
1 teaspoon dried basil
12 ounces mozzarella cheese, thinly sliced
2 green peppers, chopped
¼ cup chopped mushrooms
1 pound Italian salami, sliced
12 anchovy fillets, whole or cut
1 tablespoon olive oil

1. Mix all crust ingredients in a bowl and let stand in a warm place. When the dough has risen, in about 30 minutes, divide it into 6 parts. Roll each part into a ball and let stand for another 30 minutes.
2. Knead each ball and roll it out on a lightly floured board into a disk about ⅛ inch thick. Place the disks on a greased baking sheet.

3. Preheat the oven to 475 degrees.
4. Mix the tomatoes with the garlic, parsley, and basil and spread on the pizzas. Cover with the mozzarella. Then top with the green peppers, mushrooms, salami, and anchovies. Sprinkle with olive oil.
5. Bake for 10 to 12 minutes. Exact time depends on the thickness of the crust. Serve hot.

Yield: 6 servings

Morocco

MARRAKESH

LA MAISON ARABE. Marrakesh, beautifully situated in the foothills of the Grand Atlas, was a great favorite of Winston Churchill's, and today this city in central Morocco is one of the "in" places. It was from here in earlier times that the caravans left for the Sahara and Timbuktu, often to bring back slaves.

The best restaurant in Marrakesh is La Maison Arabe, and by consensus it is the best in all of Morocco. Meals are served by appointment only, and the owner, Suzie Larochette, likes to have 48 hours notice. She can, however, often manage with 24.

Besides making your appointment in advance, it is best to go to La Maison Arabe in a party of at least four. The reason is that Mlle. Larochette sometimes does not think it worthwhile to make masterpieces for one or two persons.

La Maison Arabe is small and intimate, seating 20 persons at most. It is in a typical old city house and the decor and furnishings are luxuriously Moorish. There is no music. Note that Marrakesh taxi drivers have a habit of taking tourists to other restaurants, brash and noisy places with music and dancing, so if you have made arrangements with Mlle. Larochette, be sure to ask for La Maison Arabe opposite the Bab Doukkala Mosque in Derb el Ferrane. Derb el Ferrane is a little alley off the Rue R'Mila that runs from the Koutoubia Mosque to the Bab Doukkala Mosque.

Mlle. Larochette has been running La Maison Arabe since 1946. She does all the cooking, which she learned from Khadija, cook in the harem of the late Pasha of Marrakesh, Si Thami El Glaoui. A four-course meal can include *bastila*, fish, *tajine*, and *couscous*, and it is best to fast the whole day before. *Bastila* is a flaky pigeon pie, *couscous* is the staple Moroccan dish of steamed mutton or chicken and vegetables on a bed of semolina, and as for *tajine*, it's a stew of which there are many varieties, nearly all of them combining meat or poultry with some such ingredients as prunes, quince, pickled lemons, oranges, olives, almonds, etc. The name comes from *tajine slaoui*, a cooking pot with a conical cover in which the stew is made. Ask Mlle. Larochette (she speaks English) to do a *tajine msir zitun* (chicken with pickled lemons and olives) in her "special way." For newcomers to Moroccan cuisine, it is best to leave the whole meal to her.

La Maison Arabe is within an easy walk of many of Marrakesh's sights. A guide should be retained, if only to keep the other guides away, and one can be had for the whole day for about $2.50. Nearby are the Saadian Tombs, an architectural ensemble that is one of the few relics of Marrakesh's Golden Age under the Saadian Sultans of the sixteenth century. Also close at hand is the nineteenth-century Royal Palace, noted for its interior decoration and Andalusian-style patios and gardens. Close, too, is the Djemaa El Fna (Meeting Place of the Dead), the liveliest piece of real estate in Morocco, especially in the evenings when the large open space is thronged with dancers, singers, acrobats, snake charmers, storytellers, etc. Off the Djemaa El Fna are the *souks*, or covered alleys where the bazaars are located.

The address of La Maison Arabe is 30 Derb el Ferrane, 67 Rue R'Mila. The phone number is 226-04. The place is open in the evenings only, from 8:30 onward, and it usually closes altogether in July and August. A meal costs about $12 a person, and this includes a service charge, although the waiters naturally are always glad to receive a little something extra. Wine (about $3 or $4 a bottle) is additional.

—*Stephen Hughes*

CHICKEN WITH OLIVES AND PICKLED LEMONS
Based on the recipe of La Maison Arabe, Marrakesh

1 3-pound chicken, quartered
4 tablespoons olive oil
1 cup chopped onions
2 teaspoons paprika or to taste
1 teaspoon ground ginger
1/2 teaspoon turmeric
salt
black pepper
1 lemon, quartered
1 cup water
24 small green olives
2 pickled lemons, quartered (see note), or 2 fresh lemons, quartered

1. In a large heavy frying pan, brown the chicken quarters in the olive oil. Remove the chicken to a plate.
2. Put the onions in the pan and sauté until brown, about 10 minutes, but do not burn the onions. Stir in the paprika, ginger, turmeric, salt, and pepper. Add the quartered lemon and the chicken. Add the water and bring to a boil. Cover and simmer for 30 minutes, or until the chicken is tender.
3. Add green olives and place the pickled (or fresh) lemon quarters on each piece of chicken. Cover and simmer 5 minutes more until heated through. Serve on warm plates.

Yield: 4 servings

NOTE: To pickle lemons, make 4 longitudinal incisions in each lemon and force salt inside, closing the incisions over the salt. Place the lemons in a jar of salt water (as salty as sea water), cover, and let stand for 2 weeks. Drain lemons for 30 minutes before using.

RABAT

DIFFA ROOM. In the older part of the Hotel de la Tour Hassan here in the capital of Morocco, next to the bar on the second floor, is the Diffa Room, reputed to be the best hotel restaurant in the country for Moroccan food. Almost always it lives up to its reputation.

The range of dishes is very wide. A specialty of the house is *bastila* (in French, *pastilla*), the famous Moroccan pigeon pie, a complex creation of flaky pastry, broiled pigeon flesh, and a stuffing of eggs, parsley, onions, and spices, the whole sprinkled with cinnamon and confectioners' sugar, and served hot. Normally a *bastila* is about two feet in diameter and serves six to eight people seated around the same circular table, but the Diffa Room serves single-portion pies. Actually, these small pies are enough for two people if you are going to eat another dish, as Moroccans usually do.

Instead of *bastila*, if you prefer, you could try *harira*, a thick soup made with lamb and eggs, or *brochettes*, meat on skewers. For your main course have a *tajine*, a stew made with fruit and either meat or poultry, or else *couscous*, the Moroccan staple dish of steamed mutton or chicken with vegetables on semolina. Excellent sea bass is also served.

For dessert one usually takes fruit, nuts, or pastries. A specialty of the house is *karb r-zel* (gazelle horns), a crescent-shaped pastry stuffed with almond paste.

The Diffa Room seats about 50 persons and is decorated in traditional Hispano-Moorish style, with carved and painted ceilings, sculptured stucco, and mosaics. The furnishings are low circular tables and a few deep armchairs, but mainly divans with brocade cushions. In the center of the carpeted dining area is the traditional Moroccan tea set, from which digestive green tea flavored with fresh mint is dispensed. The manager of the Diffa Room, Mohamed Filali, speaks English.

The Hotel de la Tour Hassan, which houses the Diffa Room, is named for the unfinished minaret of a ruined twelfth-century mosque: the Tour Hassan. The minaret, similar to the celebrated Giralda in Seville and a vantage point for panoramic views of Rabat and its environs, is within easy walking distance of the hotel. Next to the minaret is the new Royal Mausoleum, also open to the public and worth visiting because of its sumptuous interior decoration.

From the 140-foot summit of the Tour Hassan can be seen the twelfth-century Oudayas Kasbah, a fortress on a bluff overlooking the Atlantic; the medina, or old city; the mellah, or former Jewish quarter; the city of Salé on the other bank of the Bou Regreg (Father of Frogs) River, and the Roman ruins of Chellah. After lunch in the Diffa Room it is pleasant to ride over to the Oudayas Kasbah and have mint tea and pastries in the Moorish cafe in its gardens on a terrace with another grand view.

The address of the Diffa Room is Hotel de la Tour Hassan, Avenue Annegai. The phone number is 214-01. The restaurant is open every day from noon to 3 P.M. and 7 to 11 P.M. A three-course meal averages about $12 a person with wine and service charge, but the waiters are always grateful to get a little extra.

—Stephen Hughes

HARIRA
Based on the recipe of the Diffa Room, Rabat

This soup, a Moroccan specialty, includes raw eggs that are beaten and added just before serving. The eggs impart a stringy appearance that is typical of harira.

½ pound lean lamb, cut into 1-inch-long fine strips
2 tablespoons olive oil
½ teaspoon ground ginger
¼ teaspoon turmeric
½ cup chopped onions
2 medium tomatoes, cubed
1 cup cooked or canned chickpeas, drained
2 tablespoons chopped coriander sprigs (also called Chinese parsley or cilantro) or ½ teaspoon dried coriander seed
2 quarts water (approximately)
salt
black pepper
2 eggs, beaten
1 tablespoon lemon juice
ground cinnamon

1. In a heavy pot brown the lamb in hot oil with the ginger and turmeric. Add the onions, tomatoes, chickpeas, coriander, water, salt, and pepper. Bring to a boil, cover the pot, and simmer 45 minutes to 1 hour or until the meat is tender.

2. Remove from heat. Dribble in the beaten eggs while stirring the soup. Add the lemon juice and a sprinkling of cinnamon. Serve hot in bowls.

Yield: 6 to 8 servings

BAKED SEA BASS WITH CUMIN PASTE
Based on the recipe of the Diffa Room, Rabat

1 3-pound sea bass, with head and tail intact, cleaned and ready for cooking
1 tablespoon salt
½ cup olive oil
½ cup finely chopped parsley
1 teaspoon minced garlic
2 tablespoons paprika or to taste
2 tablespoons ground cumin
salt
black pepper
lemon wedges

1. Preheat the oven to 400 degrees.
2. Rub the fish inside and out with the salt and let stand for 15 minutes. Rinse in cold water and pat dry.
3. In a bowl make a paste of the olive oil, parsley, garlic, paprika, cumin, salt, and pepper. Spread this evenly over the fish, inside and out, except for the head.
4. Place the fish in an earthenware baking dish with a tight-fitting lid, or seal in aluminum foil and place on a baking sheet. Bake for 40 minutes or until flesh feels firm. Do not overcook. Serve on a warm platter garnished with lemon wedges.

Yield: 4 servings

Nepal

KATMANDU

THE YAK AND YETI. For many people Katmandu, capital city of the mountainous Central Asian country of Nepal, conjures up visions only of Everest and the Himalayas, Sherpas, Gurkhas, and hippies. But for those in the know the real tourist attraction here is Boris Nicolevitch Lissanevitch and his fabled restaurant, the Yak and Yeti.

An erstwhile dancer with Diaghilev's Ballet Russe, Boris, as he is known to everybody who is anybody in Katmandu, was running a club called The 300 in Calcutta, India, in 1951 when he was induced to come here by King Tribhuvana, then Nepal's monarch, to run Nepal's first deluxe hotel.

Kings and hotels come and go, but Boris, now in his mid-sixties, lingers on. In a ruthlessly poor city dotted with decaying temples, where streets are filled with cows, chickens, Japanese taxis, and rickshaws, the Yak and Yeti is a must for the members of the diplomatic corps stationed here as well as the more affluent tourists. Its cozy arcaded red brick chimney lounge and high-camp dining room and ballroom (complete with wonderful primitive murals by the wife of a one-time British ambassador) are housed on the first floor of a rambling old royal palace.

The Yak and Yeti's very international cuisine ranges from ham and eggs with fried potatoes to mixed shashlik with Persian rice to sweet and sour pork. The smoked *becti*, a fish flown in from the Bay of Bengal and smoked over aromatic herbs just before you eat it, is exquisite. And the Ukrainian borsch, a soup made with rich stock, beets, cabbage, and other vegetables and garnished with sour cream, finely chopped scallions, and dill, can be like something you wish your mother could have made. If Boris isn't around, his knowledgeable maître d'hôtel, Ashok Sharma, can fill you in on the vagaries of the daily menu, local customs, or Nepali politics.

The Yak and Yeti is in the Lal Durbar (Red Palace). The phone number is 11611. It opens at 11 A.M. every day and closes at 11 P.M. except on Friday, when it stays open until 2 or 3 in the morning. A dinner for two without liquor or tips should come to something around $10 (very expensive for Katmandu). Neither *yak* (the Himalayan bovine) nor *yeti* (the Abominable Snowman) is on the menu.

—Judith Weinraub

UKRAINIAN BORSCH
Based on the recipe of the Yak and Yeti, Katmandu

*According to Ashok Sharma, the maître d'hôtel of the Yak
and Yeti, the ingredients of a good borsch vary with the
seasons. The two essential vegetables are beets and cabbage,
and they are used in greater proportion in winter than in
summer. Conversely, in summer there are more tomatoes
in the soup than in winter. Other vegetables that can be
used in addition to those listed below are turnips and leeks.*

3 pounds soup bones with meat (beef or a combination of veal and chicken)
2 quarts water
2 medium onions, quartered
4 tablespoons butter (approximately)
2 cups shredded cabbage (red or white or a combination)
4 medium beets, peeled and sliced
2 carrots, sliced
2 large potatoes, cut into chunks
2 ribs celery, sliced
2 large tomatoes, quartered
salt
black pepper

GARNISHES

sour cream
finely chopped scallions
chopped dill (optional)

1. In a large pot, simmer the bones and water, partially covered, for 2 hours. Remove meat from bones, return meat to broth and discard bones. Skim the fat from the broth.
2. Sauté the onions in butter and add to the broth together with the cabbage, beets, carrots, potatoes, celery, and tomatoes. Cover and simmer very gently for about 2 hours. Season with salt and pepper.
3. To serve: ladle the soup with bits of meat and pieces of vegetables into large soup bowls. Top with sour cream, chopped scallions and, if available, some chopped dill.

Yield: 6 to 8 servings

The Netherlands

AMSTERDAM

BISTRO KLEIN PAARDENBURG. A ten-minute drive at sunset along the dreamy Amstel River creates the perfect mood for a superb dinner at the Bistro Klein Paardenburg, my favorite restaurant. You'll find it near Amsterdam in the village of Ouderkerk, a place with an air of times gone by. The restaurant itself is in a 300-year-old building and is still paneled with the original wood in typical Dutch style.

The secret of owner Paul Fagel's success in Amsterdam's gastronomic circles is simple—superb meat and fish, the choicest of fresh vegetables, and expert preparation. My favorite dish—it's Fagel's as well, incidentally—is *coquilles St. Jacques au vermouth*, a delicate concoction of bay scallops poached in Noilly Prat and covered with a sauce made of butter, cream, salt, pepper, and chopped parsley. Another noted specialty is rack of lamb rubbed with Provençal herbs and garlic and served with cheese-topped scalloped potatoes.

As befits a restaurant in a 300-year-old building, the Bistro Klein Paardenburg is old-fashioned. It's adorned with aging posters and various family portraits of the Fagels and their in-laws. The service is excellent. There are only eight tables and the place has so many patrons that reservations three or four days in advance are highly recommended, although sometimes, if you show up without having called or written ahead, Fagel and his staff will be able to seat you around an old billiard table.

The easiest way to get to the Bistro Klein Paardenburg by car is to follow the Amstel River, which flows through Amsterdam, out to Ouderkerk. The road running along the river is called Amsteldejk. Bus service is available from the Amstel Station in downtown Amsterdam—take the Maarse-Kroon Line bus marked "Ouderkerk." In summer it is possible to get out to the restaurant by boat, which leaves once a day from Weringschans, again in downtown Amsterdam. (Have your hotel check time and details for you.) Once you are in Ouderkerk you might stroll about the village. If you take a five-minute walk on the opposite bank of the Amstel from the Bistro Klein Paardenburg you will come upon a beautiful old Sephardic Jewish cemetery.

The address of the Bistro Klein Paardenburg is Amstelzijde 59, Ouderkerk aan de Amstel. The phone number is (02963) 13-15. The place is open Tuesday through Saturday for lunch and dinner. A meal with aperitif, wine, coffee, and service charge will cost around $12 per person.

—*Wim Van Der Meulen*

COQUILLES ST. JACQUES AU VERMOUTH
Based on the recipe of the Bistro Klein Paardenburg, Ouderkerk

½ pound bay scallops
1 tablespoon dry vermouth, preferably Noilly Prat
¼ cup heavy cream
4 tablespoons butter, softened
salt
white pepper
chopped parsley

1. Poach the scallops in the vermouth until cooked through. They will release liquid. Transfer the scallops to a warm serving dish, leaving the liquid in the saucepan.
2. Boil liquid until it is reduced to ¼ original volume, then add cream and reduce again until sauce starts to caramelize. Take saucepan off heat, stir in softened butter, and season with salt and pepper.
3. Pour the sauce over the scallops, sprinkle with the chopped parsley, and serve. Or if you have scallop shells, add the scallops to the sauce in the pan, heat briefly, spoon into the shells, sprinkle with the parsley and serve.

Yield: 2 appetizer servings

RACK OF LAMB WITH HERBS
Based on the recipe of the Bistro Klein Paardenburg, Ouderkerk

1 tablespoon chopped parsley
¼ teaspoon each dried thyme, rosemary, marjoram, and savory
salt
black pepper
1 pound well-trimmed rack of lamb (about 4 to 5 ribs)
2 cloves garlic, halved
1 tablespoon olive oil

1. Preheat the oven to 350 degrees.
2. In a small bowl combine the parsley, dried herbs, salt, and pepper.
3. Rub the rack of lamb with the garlic and then with the parsley and herb mixture.
4. Heat the olive oil in a skillet and brown the lamb in it on both sides.
5. Place the lamb in a shallow ovenproof dish and roast it in the oven for about 25 minutes. When it is served, the lamb should be pink inside.

Yield: 2 servings

DORRIUS RESTAURANT. In Amsterdam, which is no eater's paradise to begin with, one of the scarcest commodities is traditional Dutch food. There are plenty of Indonesian and French restaurants in this large, lively city with its canals, bridges, medieval houses, and art treasures, but the plain, heavy stews and fish dishes "like mother used to make" are hard to come by. "Our food's just not exciting," complains one Dutchman. "Besides it's so heavy you can eat it only in winter."

In the heart of old Amsterdam is a restaurant that defies this attitude and serves a variety of dishes that seem to come straight from "Aaltje's [the old lady's] frying pan." It is the Dorrius, which was founded in 1890. With its spacious, comfortable dining rooms, it draws both Dutchmen and foreigners who don't mind paying a little more than average Amsterdam prices for a chance to feast on a few of the many specialties. The restaurant is at the edge of one of Amsterdam's best shopping districts, and along the Spuistraat, on which it is located, are many lively old Dutch taverns, including the well-patronized Hoppe.

During the summer the Dorrius offers a large selection of Dutch fish specialties and grilled meats. For starters the smoked Ijsselmeer eel is excellent, and there is also cheese soufflé and home-style pâté. For a main dish try the sole in a thick cream sauce or the sea bass covered with grated cheese and leek rings. If you prefer meat, the *kalfoester* is an excellent grilled chunk of veal, and at least one kind of hunter's stew is available.

In the colder months the menu changes to make room for the real house specialties. Winter seafood includes *stokvisch*, a Norwegian dried fish boiled and served with rice and herbs. There is the traditional pea soup served with boiled bacon and rye bread. There are also numerous stews based on beef, sauerkraut, and cabbage, and there is the *Hutspot*—boiled beef on top of mashed potatoes and carrots. With most heavy dishes the good Dutch beer goes fine. With the lighter fare sturdy house bordeaux wines are available. And if you start your meal with a herring or mackerel appetizer, you might want to try an unusual Dutch liqueur called *Schelvispekel* (literally: haddock pickling juice). It has a soft spicyness that comes close to a well-seasoned eggnog.

The Dorrius, which has two entrances, is at Spuistraat 285–295 or Nieuwe Zijds Voorburgwal 336–342, depending on which entrance you choose. The phone number is 23-56-75. The place is open from noon to 10 P.M. every day except Sunday and Christmas. A full meal with wine, dessert and tip should run from about $8 to $10 per person.

—Paul D. Kemezis

SPLIT PEA SOUP
Based on the recipe of the Dorrius, Amsterdam

½ pound lean bacon
2 quarts water
1 pound quick-cooking dried split peas
1½ cups white part of leeks, cut into ½-inch rounds
1 cup chopped celery
1 medium onion, sliced
salt
black pepper

1. Put the bacon and water in a large pot and bring to a boil. Let boil for a few minutes, then remove the bacon and skim off the scum from the water.
2. Put the peas into the same water in which the bacon was boiled, bring to a boil again, partially cover the pot, and cook at a high simmer for about 1½ hours.

3. In a small amount of salted water in another pot, boil the leeks, celery, and onion until tender.
4. Drain the vegetables, add them to the pea soup, salt the soup to taste, pepper it liberally, and serve. (If a little thinner soup is preferred, stir in a small amount of water in which the vegetables cooked, and simmer to blend before serving.)

Yield: 8 servings

HUTSPOT
Based on the recipe of the Dorrius, Amsterdam

2 pounds brisket of beef
8 black peppercorns
1 bay leaf
2 cloves
1 pound potatoes
1½ pounds carrots, each cut into 4 pieces
1–1½ cups finely chopped onions
prepared grated horseradish

1. Place the brisket in a heavy skillet or saucepan with a cover. The pan should be just large enough to contain the meat. Pour in enough boiling salted water to barely cover the brisket. Add the peppercorns, bay leaf, and cloves; partially cover and gently simmer for 3 to 4 hours, or until the meat is tender, skimming off any scum from the surface of the liquid.
2. About 30 minutes before the dish will be served, boil the potatoes. In a separate saucepan boil the carrots and chopped onion together.
3. Mash the potatoes and place them on a serving platter. Drain the carrots and onion and place them on top of the mashed potatoes. Place the boiled beef over all and serve with the horseradish as accompaniment.

Yield: 4 servings

New Zealand

WELLINGTON

THE COACHMAN. Des Britten, who demonstrates cookery in prime time on New Zealand television, opened his own restaurant in 1966, in order, he relates, "to get away from the french fries and frozen peas" so commonly served in standard New Zealand restaurants. Within a year the place was booming, and still is. Since it seats only 45, it is always completely booked for dinner by late morning—and sometimes even days ahead. There is usually plently of room at lunch, however, for the executive types in the clientele eat their midday meal closer to their offices and the younger and less affluent customers lunch at milk bars to save up for a Saturday night splurge at the Coachman.

One finds the restaurant one flight up in a small building on a street of undistinguished shops and less recommendable eating places a little out of the main business section of this gusty capital, deservedly known as "windy Wellington." The square room, with a semicircular bar at one end, is dimly lighted. Closed window curtains hide the view of the street, which wouldn't be very interesting anyway. The decor is quiet, the handsomely turned out waiters courteous and efficient.

A favorite dish to begin with is *delice Lorraine*, a creamy grilled crêpe with ham and cheese filling, named for the young proprietor's wife, who is the restaurant's hostess in the evening. The scallops sauté, done with a delicately flavored sauce, are special. So is the sole stuffed with seafood. The menu also includes such New Zealand specialties as lamb and crayfish, but

Mr. Britten avoids a local food cliché, the thick meringue confection called a Pavlova, "because you get it in so many homes."

The Coachman is at 46 Courtnay Place. The telephone number is 558-200 (telephone dials in New Zealand have the figures running clockwise instead of counter-clockwise, as in the United States, which causes Americans to call wrong numbers frequently). The restaurant is open for lunch from noon to 2:30 P.M. Tuesday through Friday, and for dinner from 6 to 11 P.M. Monday through Saturday. Mr. Britten says the average diner spends about $11.50 to $14. This amount includes wine, with imports from Australia preferable to the slightly cheaper New Zealand brands.

—Robert Trumbull

DELICE LORRAINE
Based on the recipe of the Coachman, Wellington

CRÊPES

2 cups sifted all-purpose flour
1 teaspoon sugar
¼ teaspoon salt
4 eggs
1 cup milk
1 cup water
2 tablespoons melted butter
½ cup clarified butter (see note on page 35)

FILLING AND GARNISH

3 cups heavy cream
2 cups chopped cooked ham
4 cups grated sharp cheddar cheese
2 tablespoons chopped parsley

1. To make the crêpes, sift flour into a mixing bowl, add salt and sugar. Make a well in the center and add the eggs. Beat to mix the eggs with the flour while slowly pouring in the milk and water. Mix to a smooth batter. Add 2 tablespoons melted butter and strain through a sieve to smooth out the lumps. Let the batter stand for 2 hours to insure lightness.
2. Brush a 6- to 7-inch skillet or crêpe pan with clarified butter and heat to smoking. Remove pan from heat and pour 3 to 4 tablespoons batter into

it, tilting pan in all directions so that batter thinly and evenly covers bottom. Return pan to heat and cook the crêpe just under 1 minute on each side. Slide the crêpe onto a plate and keep warm while you cook the rest of the crêpes, brushing the skillet with clarified butter each time. Batter will yield about 12 crêpes.

3. Preheat the oven to 375 degrees.
4. Fill the crêpes, one by one, as follows: Moisten the side of the crêpe that will take the filling with a little cream. Place 2 tablespoons chopped ham and 2 tablespoons grated cheese down the center, then add 1 tablespoon of cream. Roll up the crêpe.
5. Place the crêpes in a single layer in a shallow ovenproof serving dish. Pour the remaining cream on top, then sprinkle with the remaining grated cheese. Put in the hot oven until light brown and bubbly. Sprinkle with parsley and serve immediately.

Yield: 4 servings

Nigeria

LAGOS

CRIMSON ARCADE. In 1972 Mrs. Gladys Olufemi-Akindeinde had an idea. It was that a restaurant would do well in this West African country and former British colony if it served both African and European food and had a good location. She was right. Today her successful Crimson Arcade restaurant stands at a major suburban crossroads outside Lagos and not far from Ikeja International Airport. Through it, seven days a week, stream satisfied breakfast, lunch, snack, and dinner customers.

There are no frills at the Arcade, which, though in Nigeria, looks very much like the restaurants you've seen in a thousand and one Holiday Inns or Howard Johnsons back home. The place is modern, functional, well lighted and air conditioned. The waiters are uniformed. The diners and snackers are not only foreign businessmen and other travelers but also office and factory workers in this booming, expanding suburb of booming, bustling Lagos.

Mrs. Olufemi-Akindeinde, a trained caterer who studied her craft at a technical college in England, notes that traditional African starchy yam- and cassava-based meals with meat or vegetables sauces are far more popular with her African clientele than European foods. When Europeans or Americans experiment with African cooking, however, they are apt to try one of the Crimson Arcade's meat or fish stews. The African cooking at the Crimson Arcade is of high caliber and the kitchen is scrupulously clean.

The Crimson Arcade is located at the Ikeja Airport Roundabout, half a mile from the airport and 17 miles from Lagos. The cheapest way to get to the restaurant from town is to take the airport limousine, which costs $3. The limousine will stop at the Crimson Arcade on request. To return to town have the restaurant call you a cab and take it the short distance to the airport, then ride the airport limousine back to Lagos, again for $3. If you are going to the Crimson Arcade in a party of three or four, it would pay you to take a cab all the way out from Lagos and back, which will cost about $9 each way.

The Crimson Arcade is open every day of the week from 8 o'clock in the morning until 10 at night. The phone number is 342-33. Lunch can run from something over a dollar to $3 or more a person, and dinner from upwards of $2 to $4 or more.

—Thomas A. Johnson

MEAT AND VEGETABLE STEW
Based on the recipe of the Crimson Arcade, Lagos

*This is a very popular basic stew that has many variations
and lends itself to experimentation, according to Mrs. Gladys
Olufemi-Akindeinde of the Crimson Arcade. As with most
African meals, it is usually eaten with or served on a bed of
starchy staple food, such as rice, semolina, potatoes, cornmeal, or the African cassava-based starches like fufu. Some
of the starches are seasoned with butter or tomatoes before
the stew is ladled on.*

1 pound beef or other meat or combination of meats
1 cup water
1 large onion, chopped
½ cup sliced tomatoes
½ cup sliced green pepper
½ cup palm oil or vegetable oil
½ cup cut-up green vegetables (spinach, mustard greens, etc.)
salt
black pepper

1. Cut the meat into 8 pieces. Put the pieces in a large pot. Add the water and onion. Cover the pot and let simmer for 20 minutes or until the meat is tender.
2. Add the tomatoes, green pepper, and oil. Cover and simmer over low heat for 10 minutes or until the green pepper is tender.

3. Add the green vegetables to the mixture. Simmer, covered, for 20 minutes. If there is too much liquid, remove lid and boil until some of the liquid evaporates.

Yield: 4 servings when ladled over starchy vegetable

MRS. GLADYS OLUFEMI-AKINDEINDE'S YORUBA FISH STEW
Based on the recipe of the Crimson Arcade, Lagos

1½–2 pounds red snapper, striped bass, or bluefish cut into thin slices
salt
dried thyme
¼ cup crushed red pepper (more or less, depending on desired degree of hotness)
6 ounces (1 small can) tomato paste
1 medium onion, chopped
4 cups water
¼ cup peanut oil
1 chicken bouillon cube

1. Wash and drain the fish. Season with salt and a pinch of thyme. Set aside.
2. In a large pot put the crushed red peppers, tomato paste, onion, and water. Cook together for about 10 minutes over medium heat.
3. Add the peanut oil and the bouillon cube. Let the mixture simmer gently for 15 minutes over medium heat.
4. Put the fish slices into the simmering mixture and cover the pot. Cook for about 10 minutes. Serve piping hot.

Yield: 4 servings

Norway

OSLO

BRISTOL GRILL ROOM. Among the first-class restaurants in Oslo, my favorite is the Grill Room of the Bristol Hotel. Its oak-paneled walls and open-fireplacelike grill create an atmosphere of relaxation and expectation. One enters and is immediately prepared for culinary pleasure.

There are no disturbing elements in this place, no dancing, no singing, no music. For these you must look elsewhere in Norway's capital. Here patrons are accorded the privilege of enjoying an excellent meal in peace, a conversation can be carried on in a normal voice, and shouting is not required to attract the attention of the waiters. Besides giving excellent service, the Bristol's waiters pride themselves on offering reliable guidance to guests in doubt about what dishes to order.

Meat or fish, or both? My own choice is uncomplicated: dill-cured salmon, a specialty with a great reputation (but no greater than it deserves). As prepared by award-winning chef Finn Weirum, it is mild and mellow, rich in flavor and spiced with a mustard sauce that brings out its maximum goodness. Even Americans firmly wedded to steak and potatoes, it is reported, smile as they savor this dish in the Bristol Grill Room. It is served either as a main course accompanied by creamed potatoes or as an appetizer.

The Bristol Hotel is centrally located at 7 Kristian 4 Gate, a quiet street in an area of interesting shops. The phone number is 41-58-40. The Grill Room is open from noon to 11:30 P.M. Prices vary from about $5 for lunch to $13 or more for a full dinner with wine. The dill-cured salmon is about

$9 as a main course at dinner, $5 as an appetizer. A service charge is included in the bill, but leaving a small tip will not be regarded as an offense.

—*Olav Maaland*

DILL-CURED SALMON
Based on the recipe of the Bristol Grill Room, Oslo

1 7–8 pound salmon (see step 1)
3 tablespoons crushed white peppercorns
¼ cup coarse (kosher) salt
⅓ cup sugar
2 cups coarsely chopped fresh dill

MUSTARD SAUCE

½ cup prepared brown mustard
2 teaspoons dry mustard
⅔ cups finely chopped fresh dill
⅓ cup sugar
¼ cup white vinegar
white pepper
⅔ cup vegetable oil

1. Ask your fish dealer to chop off the head and tail of the salmon and split the body lengthwise into 2 fillets with the skin attached. Remove the backbone and any small bones.
2. Combine the crushed peppercorns, salt, sugar, and dill.
3. Place the fillets, skin down, on a stainless steel or glass platter or tray. Sprinkle with the peppercorn mixture. Cover with foil and place a large plate on top as a weight. Refrigerate to cure. After 18 hours turn the fillets over, then cover and weight again and leave in the refrigerator to cure for another 18 hours.
4. To prepare the mustard sauce, combine the mustards, dill, sugar, vinegar, and pepper. Add the oil and beat with a wire whisk to a smooth consistency.
5. To serve, place the salmon fillets, skin side down, on a carving board and scrape away the peppercorn and dill. Slice thinly, leaving the skin behind as you detach each piece. Serve with the mustard sauce.

Yield: 10 servings

Panama

PANAMA CITY

PANAMA SEÑORIAL. Because Panama is situated at one of the crossroads of the world, the country's restaurants are as varied as its 1.5 million people. What makes the Panama Señorial so popular with natives and foreigners alike is its broad menu based on local seafood and beef, both of which have become major exports because of their superb quality. Another reason for the restaurant's success is the pleasant Spanish manor house atmosphere that pervades the various indoor and outdoor dining areas and bars.

The Señorial's chefs are familiar with the tastes of their polyglot clientele, so one need not hesitate to request favorite dishes. One delicious and popular specialty is *delicias de pescador* (fisherman's delights), a platter of scallops sautéed with sherry, broiled lobster in the shell and broiled corvina, a basslike fish, the whole served with lemon wedges, broiled tomato halves, fresh string beans, and parsleyed new potatoes.

Such is the popularity of the Panama Señorial with local patrons that it is open Sunday only for private parties and fiestas. If you have friends in Panama and are fortunate enough to be invited to a Sunday affair at the Señorial, you will see traditional family gatherings at long tables. Out of the sight and hearing of most foreigners and strangers, the food and the music become simpler and more Panamanian than during the rest of the week, voices and laughter grow louder and the patrons, usually bound together by strong family ties, lose much of their customary formality. Even the waiters unbend and seem to become part of the *familia*.

If you can't get invited to the Panama Señorial on a Sunday, it is well worth going there on your own any other day of the week, for the restaurant is open to the general public Monday through Thursday from 11 A.M. to midnight and Friday and Saturday from 11 A.M. to 1 A.M. Entertainment is international and offered from 7 P.M. on. The host is Saul Mosquera and he keeps a sharp eye on the food and service.

The Panama Señorial is at 51st Street, corner of Ricardo Arias Street, in the Campo Alegre district of Panama City. The phone numbers are 64-3595 or 23-7743 or 23-0277 or 23-5733. A dinner, without drinks, should run about $8 a person.

—H. J. Maidenberg

DELICIAS DE PESCADOR
Based on the recipe of the Panama Señorial, Panama City

At the Panama Señorial the fish used in this mixed seafood platter—the name means "Fisherman's Delights"—is corvina, but striped bass makes a fine substitute.

1 pound bay scallops
8–10 tablespoons butter
¼ cup dry sherry
1 pound fillets of corvina or striped bass
2 1½-pound lobsters, split and cleaned (see note)

1. Sauté the scallops in 3 or 4 tablespoons butter until they turn an opaque white. Add the sherry and stir. Reheat just before adding to the rest of the dish.
2. Brush the fish fillets with butter, place them under a preheated broiler, skin side down, and broil them about 5 minutes, or until the flesh is white throughout and the tops are golden.
3. Brush the split lobsters with butter and place them under a preheated broiler. Broil until the meat is browned on top and white all the way through, about 10 minutes.
4. Place the fish fillets on a large serving platter, top them with the scallops

in their sherry sauce, and surround them with the lobster halves. Serve with lemon wedges, broiled tomato halves, fresh string beans, and new potatoes tossed in butter and chopped parsley.

Yield: 4 servings

NOTE: Prepare the lobsters as follows before cooking (or ask your fish dealer to do it if you are going to cook them right away): Insert a sharp knife into the back between the body and tail shells, severing the spinal cord and killing the lobster. Place the lobster on its back and split it in two. Remove the stomach sac near the head, the intestinal tube that runs from stomach to tail, and the spongy lung tissue.

Paraguay

ASUNCIÓN

HERMITAGE. When Paraguayans say they are going to have soup, they mean they are sitting down to steak, french fried potatoes, salad, beer, and thick black coffee—in fact, anything but soup. In this South American land of understatement a *sopa*, or soup, is just a euphemism for a meal.

Basically Paraguay is a poor land, one whose major industry is the raising and processing of cattle. Consequently this is steak-and-potatoes country. And as often as not the meat is roasted over quebracho wood, which imparts a distinctive smoky taste and a smell that is unequaled.

Though the quebracho tree takes upward of 100 years to mature to commercial height and few if any have been planted, the Hermitage, happily, has plenty of quebracho wood on which to roast its beef. In typical Paraguayan fashion a side dish of manioc meal is provided so that diners may dip their juicy meat into it. Paraguayans like their beef rare; those who don't should quickly inform the waiter.

The Hermitage is typically unpretentious as Paraguayans tend to suspect elegant eating places. Paraguayan restaurants, in fact, are social centers for poorer people unable to entertain at home, and it is quite common on hot summer nights for owners to set out tables not only on the sidewalk in front of their places but in the road as well. This often gives foreigners the erroneous impression that the restaurants are being evicted from their premises.

It is unlikely, however, that Rigoberto Ramirez, the owner of the Hermitage, will ever see his restaurant evicted. Not only does his "soup" bring in the customers but so do his groups of harp players (the harp is the national instrument) and singers of sad Paraguayan music.

The Hermitage is at 15 de Agosto, No. 1A and 2A, and the phone number is 41-001. The restaurant is open every day from noon to 2:30 P.M. and 8 P.M. to 1 A.M. A dinner with beer costs about $6 a person and includes the price of the nightly show.

Foreigners should be reminded that most Paraguayans speak Guarani as well as Spanish and that a polite conversation in that indigenous language often sounds as if those speaking it were arguing in Chinese.

—*H. J. Maidenberg*

Peru

LIMA

TAMBO DE ORO. This restaurant—the name means "Inn of Gold"—is truly one of the delights of Lima. Its Swiss-French-Peruvian cuisine is unsurpassed on the west coast of South America.

Because Lima is a great seafood center, the large menu includes such Peruvian specialties as Andean smoked salmon or trout, fish soups and stews (the latter served over beds of crisp local rice), sea bass in its own broth, and other unforgettable dishes. Of course, no one going to Lima should ever pass up *conchitas à la parmigiana*—certainly not at the Tambo. This typical Peruvian appetizer consists of local scallops served just as a light coat of parmesan cheese melts under the fire. Another taste awakener is the famous Peruvian *seviche*—raw marinated fish bits. Foreigners are hereby warned that the *seviche* is often hot, and it is wise to have the Tambo's delicious mineral water with it or a bottle of one of Peru's fine beers. It would be a pity to wash down the *seviche* with any of the Tambo's fine Chilean or French wines.

Jean Pierre Piaget is the Tambo's manager and maître d'. He is the son of Roget, the Swiss-born restaurateur who was paid by Braniff Airways to close his famous Pavillon and open the Tambo some years ago. The elder Mr. Piaget now operates a new Mexican restaurant for the airline.

Being Swiss, Jean Pierre takes pains with the fondues while diplomatically insinuating standard French and other Continental dishes onto his menu. As a gesture to North Americans, he serves rather large drinks—and equally big steaks and roast beef when he can find good meat on his early morning shopping rounds. One measure of the loyalty of Tambo's customers is that they often volunteer to bring back herbs, spices, and other ingredients that are hard to obtain because of Peru's stringent import controls.

The Tambo's food is only part of the experience of dining there, however. The restaurant is situated in a reconstructed former town house that was built in colonial times. An arcade houses handicraft shops and the courtyard fountain pours water over wrought iron sculpture by Victor Delfin, whose shop is on the premises.

The service at Tambo, even by Peruvian standards, is attentive to a fault. During the evening, strolling players sing Spanish and Peruvian songs as they wander through the various dining rooms. The furniture, particularly the ornate mirrors, was taken from antique shops or old mansions razed to widen Lima's narrow downtown streets.

The Tambo de Oro is at Belen 1066, only a block away from Plaza San Martin, the hotel and shopping center. The phone number is 31-00-46. The restaurant opens at noon Monday through Saturday for the usual three-hour lunch period favored by government officials and businessmen. It reopens again at 7 P.M. and stays open until midnight. It is closed Sunday. Lunch or dinner, including cocktails, should run about $10 a person. Although Peruvian restaurant bills include service and tax charges amounting to 26 percent, an additional 10 percent tip is customary.

—*H. J. Maidenberg*

ARTICHOKE BOTTOMS TAMBO DE ORO
Based on the recipe of the Tambo de Oro, Lima

¾ cup seasoned hollandaise sauce (recipe below)
4 tablespoons butter
2 tablespoons minced onion
2 bay leaves
12 artichoke bottoms, canned or fresh (to prepare fresh artichoke bottoms, see
        page 156)
salt
white pepper
1 clove garlic, minced
1 pound cooked shrimp, each cut into 4 pieces if jumbo size or halved if large
        or medium
2 tablespoons dry white wine
1 tablespoon chopped parsley
1 teaspoon worcestershire sauce
parsley sprigs

1. Prepare the seasoned hollandaise sauce and set aside.
2. Melt 2 tablespoons butter in a large skillet and add 1 tablespoon minced onion and 1 bay leaf. Add the artichoke bottoms and sauté gently for a few minutes to heat through. (If using fresh artichoke bottoms, sauté until they turn yellowish.) Turn the bottoms once in the butter while sautéing or else brush the tops with butter. Season with salt and pepper and transfer to an ovenproof dish.
3. In the same skillet in which the artichoke hearts were sautéed, melt the remaining 2 tablespoons butter, add the remaining tablespoon minced onion, and the garlic. Add the cooked shrimp and sauté gently, turning them in the pan, for 2 to 3 minutes. Add the wine, parsley, and worcestershire sauce. Stir to blend and cook for 2 minutes.
4. Preheat the oven to 450 degrees or the broiler to hot.
5. Divide the shrimp into 12 equal portions and place a portion on each of the artichoke bottoms along with the butter and wine sauce from the skillet.
6. Spoon the seasoned hollandaise sauce over the shrimp.
7. Bake in the oven or put under a broiler until the hollandaise sauce is golden brown. Garnish with parsley sprigs. Serve immediately.

Yield: 3 to 4 servings

SEASONED HOLLANDAISE SAUCE

8 tablespoons (1 stick) butter, softened
2 egg yolks
1 tablespoon lemon juice
2 tablespoons hot water
1 tablespoon chopped parsley
1 tablespoon dry white wine
1 teaspoon worcestershire sauce
salt
white pepper

1. In the bottom of a double broiler bring some water almost to a boil, then turn the heat very low so that the water stays hot but never boils or even simmers.
2. In the top of the double boiler, off the heat, put in half the softened butter, then the egg yolks and lemon juice. Place the top part of the double boiler in the bottom part over very low heat and stir constantly until the butter is melted. Add the rest of the butter and stir until melted. Add

2 tablespoons hot water from the bottom of the double boiler and stir until the sauce thickens. All during this operation it is important that the water never be allowed to boil or the sauce will curdle. Any time you feel the water may be getting too hot, simply remove the whole double boiler from the heat temporarily while continuing to stir. When the sauce has thickened, add the parsley, dry white wine, worcestershire sauce, salt, and pepper. Stir to blend.

Yield: about 3/4 cup

The Philippines

MANILA

SULO RESTAURANT. Ten minutes from central Manila by taxi is Makati, a well-planned suburb of lovely homes and sleek office buildings. At its heart is the Makati Commercial Center, a complex of hotels, shops, nightclubs, and restaurants. One of the restaurants is the Sulo, which more than any other local eating place captures the Philippine mood through its cuisine, decor, and service. That mood is one of cultural diversity, friendliness, and adventure.

As befits its name, which means "torch," the Sulo occupies a bungalow-shaped building around which blaze oil torches. Under the peaked Malayan roof is the Chinese Room, where we occasionally take our children for Sunday dinner. In addition, there are four main dining rooms—the Tambourine, the Rajah Room, the Vinta Grille, and the Diwata Room.

The Tambourine, named for a filigree necklace worn with a traditional costume, seats 90 guests against a background of carved wood paneling. The Rajah Room, whose subdued red ceiling lamps cast shadows on a Moslem brass decor, including a brass mural of a chieftain and his retinue, seats 180. The Vinta Grille, the most formal of the rooms, has heavy wooden furniture and luminous shell table lamps and also seats 90. And then there is the Diwata Room, whose name means "nymph." It is a big, festive place enlivened with multicolored bunting, decorated grass huts, and nightly performances by a folk dance troupe, and it seats 500 people—that's right, 500. Besides all the foregoing rooms, the Sulo also has a coffee shop.

The clientele of the Sulo includes more Filipinos than tourists. It is where the Rotary, Lions, and Kiwanis clubs hold their regular luncheon meetings. Wealthy and middle-class Filipinos patronize the dining rooms and dating teenagers hang out in the coffee shop. Formal dress is out; business suits, dressy casuals, or native costumes are preferred. The service is in keeping with the national character—not stiffly efficient but attentive in a relaxed way.

The cuisine encompasses both standard Western fare and indigenous dishes expertly prepared by the Sulo's cooks, some of whom were trained by the restaurant's first owner-managers, Mr. and Mrs. Modesto Enriquez, and all of whom are now supervised by their daughter, Linda Enriquez-Panlilio. Among the specialties is *kari-kari*, a stew of calf's knuckles thickened with ground peanuts. Seafood dishes include shrimp boiled in coconut milk and fish steamed in a banana leaf wrapping. A favorite of both Filipinos and tourists is *adobo*, which can be prepared with meat, poultry, shrimp, or even vegetables alone.

The Sulo's address is Makati Commercial Center, Makati, and a cab ride from Manila should cost less than $1. The phone number is 88-19-16. The place is open from 7 o'clock in the morning until 11 at night, and a dinner, depending on the dishes chosen, should run from about $3 to $7 a person, exclusive of cocktails and wines (generally under $1 a glass). In addition, there is a 10 percent service charge and it is customary to leave a small tip besides. The prices are the same in all the rooms except the Diwata, which adds a charge (less than $2) for the hour-long folk dance show. Before or after a meal in the Sulo, tourists can browse in the Makati Center's antique shops, buy Philippine embroideries, or take in exhibits at several small galleries.

—*Alice Villadolid*

KARI-KARI
Based on the recipe of the Sulo Restaurant, Manila

*At the Sulo this dish is prepared with banana heart and
served with Philippine anchovy sauce. Both the banana heart
and the anchovy sauce can be purchased in some Philippine
and Chinese groceries in the United States. If unavailable,
they may be omitted.*

3 pounds calf's knuckles or feet
1 pound beef tripe, soaked, cleaned, and cut into 2-inch pieces
5 cloves garlic, minced

2 medium onions, quartered
¼ cup lard or vegetable oil
½ pound green beans, trimmed and cut into 2-inch pieces
1 small banana heart, quartered (optional)
1 pound (2 small) eggplant, sliced
2 cups water
salt
black pepper
¼ cup ground peanuts (peanut butter may be substituted)
red food coloring
Philippine anchovy sauce (optional)

1. In a large pot place the calf's knuckles and tripe, cover with water, and bring to a boil. Cover the pot and simmer about 2 to 3 hours or until the meat is tender. Lift out the knuckles and tripe, separate the meat from the bones, discard the bones, cut all the meat into 2-inch pieces. Set aside.
2. In a heavy casserole, brown the garlic and onions in the lard, add the meat, beans, banana heart, eggplant slices, water, salt, and pepper. Bring to a boil. Cover and simmer 10 to 15 minutes or until vegetables are tender.
3. Stirring constantly to avoid sticking, add the ground peanuts to thicken sauce. Bring to a simmer, correct seasoning, and add a dash of red food coloring. With the dish, if available, serve Philippine anchovy sauce sizzled in hot lard or oil.

Yield: 4 to 6 servings

CHICKEN ADOBO
Based on the recipe of the Sulo Restaurant, Manila

6 cloves garlic, minced
6 black peppercorns
2 bay leaves
½ cup white vinegar
2 tablespoons dark soy sauce
salt
1 2½–3-pound chicken, cut into serving pieces
oil for frying

1. In a large skillet with a cover, bring to a simmer the garlic, peppercorns, bay leaves, vinegar, soy sauce, and salt. Add the chicken pieces, stirring

to coat them with the sauce. Bring again to a simmer. Cover and simmer for about 30 minutes or until the chicken is cooked, basting once or twice with the liquid in the skillet. Remove the chicken to a plate, skim the fat from the sauce in the skillet, and keep the sauce warm.

2. In a large frying pan brown the chicken pieces in a thin film of oil. Arrange the browned pieces on a platter and pour the sauce over them. Serve hot with plain white rice.

Yield: 4 servings

Poland

CRACOW

WIERZYNEK RESTAURANT. Cracow, the most attractive city in Poland, has the country's finest restaurant. The Wierzynek stands behind massive wrought-iron gates at a corner of the Old Town Square. The foyer contains a display case of hors d'oeuvres—cold cuts, duck in malaga sauce, jellied trout, smoked eel, salmon. The dining rooms, up an ornate red-carpeted staircase, are decorated with armor and other reminders (huge functioning tile stoves, for example) of the time when Cracow was the capital of the Kingdom of Poland.

Try Wierzynek's carp "Jewish style" as a first course (there's also carp "Polish style") followed by a clear borsch with dumplings and then rolled beef stuffed with mushrooms. Most of the restaurant's dishes are delicious, although you can skip the specialty à la Wierzynek, an unimaginative beef and veal dish heaped on a mound of french fries.

The Wierzynek's address is simply Old Town Square and it is in the heart of the historical city near such medieval showplaces as the Cloth Hall and the monumental gothic Church of St. Mary with its magnificent carved wooden altarpieces by Viet Stoss. The restaurant is open seven days a week, all year round, from 1 P.M. to midnight. The phone number is 56507. A meal, with vodka or a half bottle of wine, should cost in the neighborhood of $8 a person.

—*James Feron*

233

CARP, JEWISH STYLE
Based on the recipe of the Wierzynek Restaurant, Cracow

1 4–5 pound carp, dressed and well rinsed
2 large onions, chopped
½ cup raisins
½ cup slivered almonds
1 teaspoon salt
white pepper
2 tablespoons sugar
1 envelope (tablespoon) unflavored gelatin, softened in a little water

1. In a pot large enough to contain the carp, bring about 3 quarts of water to a boil. Add the chopped onions and let boil for a few minutes.
2. Rinse the carp well and wrap it in cheesecloth to make it easier to remove when cooked. Place the carp in the boiling water, bring back to the boil, reduce the heat, and let the carp simmer very gently for 30 minutes.
3. Remove the carp. To the water in the pot add the raisins, almonds, salt, pepper, sugar, and softened gelatin. Bring to a boil and reduce the volume of the liquid to less than half.
4. Remove the carp from the cheesecloth, cut it into serving pieces, and place the pieces in a serving dish deep enough so that the carp can be covered with the liquid. Pour the liquid over the carp, let cool, then place in the refrigerator. When the dish has chilled and the sauce has turned into a firm jelly, the carp is ready to serve.

Yield: 6 to 8 appetizer servings

WARSAW

BASZTA. This restaurant existed before the Second World War and reopened in 1962 under the same family management. It occupies a villa across the road from its original site. The villa, a 15-minute drive from the center of town, resembles an American country inn except that peacocks stroll around the courtyard among the parked foreign cars, the vehicles with diplomatic plates and the automobiles of Polish officials and other members of Warsaw's elite.

The rooms at the Baszta, connected by flights of stairs, are relatively small, but some of the larger ones have tables or booths that can accommodate parties of six or eight. The menu is in Polish, but English-speaking waiters can be found. A violin trio wanders about, offering everything from waltzes, polkas, and tangos for the general clientele to nostalgic partisan songs for inebriated functionaries.

Occasionally the Baszta offers smoked salmon, which is good with the strong Zubrowka vodka. The restaurant's fish dishes are usually fine. The crayfish, served hot or cold, is cooked Polish style, which means it is dropped into boiling water flavored with salt and dill. But the most highly recommended dish comes not from the sea but from the sky. It is wild duck and it is marinated for two days, baked with thin slices of bacon, and served with baked potatoes and whole peeled fresh apples filled with cranberry jam. Another interesting dish is one in which venison is combined with pork fat, onions, fresh cabbage, sauerkraut, prunes, apples, mushrooms, pimientos, and various seasonings, stewed for 15 hours (that's right, 15 hours), and served with the addition of thin slices of Polish sausage and the usual accompaniment of well-chilled vodka.

The Baszta is on Highway 121. Its phone number is 43-06-96. If you go by cab from Warsaw, the ride should cost about $2 and the restaurant can call a taxi for the return trip. The Baszta is open seven days a week, all year round, from 1 P.M. until the early hours of the morning, usually closing around 2 A.M. A meal will run about $10 a person with caviar and wine.

—*James Feron*

BIGOS
Based on the recipe of Baszta, Warsaw

*As prepared at the Baszta, this Polish hunter's stew cooks for
a total of 15 hours. It is usually served with rye bread and
well-chilled vodka.*

2 pounds venison, or a mixture of beef, pork, and lamb, or 1½ pounds cooked
    leftover meats as above
2 tablespoons butter
salt
black pepper
1 pound pork fat, cubed
1 pound onions, diced
2 pounds cabbage, finely sliced
1½ pounds sauerkraut, drained
½ pound pitted prunes, soaked in water for several hours
1 ounce dried mushrooms
2 tablespoons tomato paste
4 sour apples, peeled and sliced
2 bay leaves
3 pimientos, sliced
4 dried juniper berries
1 clove garlic, sliced
sugar
paprika
1 pound Polish sausage

1. If the meat is uncooked, brown it in the butter over high heat and season
   with salt and pepper. Then add 3 to 4 tablespoons cubed pork fat and
   braise or bake the meat, covered, at low heat for about an hour. (If leftover cooked meat is being used, omit this step.) Cut the meat into 1½- to
   2-inch cubes.
2. In a skillet, melt the remainder of the pork fat cubes over low heat until
   rendered; remove the cracklings. Add the diced onions and sauté them
   until tender.
3. In a very large pot combine the sliced cabbage, sauerkraut, melted pork
   fat, and onions. Mix in the prunes, mushrooms, tomato paste, sliced
   apples, and the cubed meat. Then mix in the bay leaves, pimientos, juniper
   berries, and garlic.
4. Cook, covered, in a 275-degree oven or over very low heat on top of the
   stove for a total of 15 hours. The cooking should be done in stages as
   follows: Let cook for several hours, then remove from heat, cool (can be
   placed in refrigerator overnight), and cook again for several hours. Stir

occasionally to make sure the stew does not stick to the bottom of the pot. After the first few hours the cabbage will have cooked down and the stew can be transferred to a smaller, more convenient pot or ovenproof casserole. Once or twice, when the stew is removed from the heat to cool, spoon off as much of the liquid as you can, chill it separately in the refrigerator, skim off the fat that congeals on the surface and return the skimmed liquid to the stew.

5. When the stew has cooked for a total of 15 hours (excluding cooling time), season it to taste with salt, pepper, sugar, and paprika. Cut the Polish sausage into slices ⅛ inch thick and add to the stew. Raise the heat either on top of the stove or in the oven and bring the *bigos* to a boil. It is now ready to serve, or it can be stored in the refrigerator for up to a week and reheated just before serving.

Yield: 8 servings

Portugal

LISBON

AVIZ. This restaurant is elegant, it also serves good food, and so it is a favorite at lunchtime with Portuguese businessmen, who like to combine eating with wheeling and dealing. At night the clientele includes more tourists than in the daytime, at least the kind of tourists who don't have to worry too much about every escudo they spend. Prices are high for Lisbon, but eminently reasonable by New York standards.

In general, one eats well in this city, but in few places can one do so as comfortably as in Aviz. To get to it one goes through a rather anonymous-looking door in the central business part of town, then up a flight of steps whose decor is reminiscent of the turn of the century, when living was supposed to have been more gracious. And gracious living is the overwhelming impression Aviz conveys as soon as one enters.

The premises used to be a factory loft until the restaurant was established a decade ago with fixtures and personnel from the old Aviz Hotel, which is now part of Lisbon's past. The three dining rooms can seat 90, but Tony Ruggeroni, a Portuguese with a British accent who runs the place as a hobby ("a profitable hobby," he says), limits the number of patrons seated to 75 at any one time. More than that slows down the service, and at Aviz good service comes along with the good food.

Waiting in the bar for one's table is not hard to take, thanks to dark wood paneling, black leather banquettes, and the expertise of Tony Fadda, the barman and one of Ruggeroni's associates. Green silk damask on the walls and elaborate brass lighting fixtures heighten the turn-of-the-century feel of the dining area. The round tables are generous in size and so are the high cane-backed chairs with velvet cushions.

The large menu, changed every two days, is in French, except for the Portuguese dishes, which are listed in Portuguese. Aviz, which has its own smokehouse, offers an unusual plate of smoked duck, turkey, and lamb seasoned with lemon and pepper. The Portuguese also do original things with codfish, pork, and seafood and this restaurant is no exception. One highly praised dish is the fried pork with clams. Wines may not be up to French standards but are highly drinkable.

The address of Aviz is Rua Serpa Pinta 12-B. The phone number is 328391. One should figure on spending about $10 a person with wine and tips but not pre- or post-dinner drinks. Meals are served from 1 to 3 P.M. and 8 to 11 P.M.

—Henry Giniger

FRIED PORK WITH CLAMS
Based on the recipe of Aviz, Lisbon

MARINADE

2 cups dry white wine
1 tablespoon paprika
2 cloves garlic, mashed
2 bay leaves
1 teaspoon salt
2 teaspoons black pepper

2 pounds fillet of pork, cut into ½-inch cubes
2 tablespoons lard
2 dozen clams in the shell, washed and scrubbed
3 tablespoons chopped parsley

1. Combine all the marinade ingredients in a nonmetallic bowl. Add the cubed pork and allow to marinate for at least 6 hours.
2. Remove the pork from the marinade and reserve the marinade. Pat the pork completely dry with cloth or paper towels. If the pork is not dry it will not brown properly.
3. In a very large heavy skillet with a cover, melt the lard over the highest possible heat until it smokes, toss in the pork cubes and brown well. The

high heat is essential, for otherwise the pork will sweat and turn gray rather than brown.

4. When the pork is well browned, pour the marinade over it and bring to a boil. Boil for 5 minutes, turning the pork cubes in the liquid and scraping the bottom of the skillet so that the crusty bits mix with the sauce.

5. Add the clams, mix them in well with the pork, cover the skillet tightly, and continue to cook over high heat. Lift the cover in about 7 to 8 minutes to check if the clams have opened; when they have, remove the skillet from the heat. Discard any clams that do not open.

6. Stir the ingredients well once more, empty into a serving dish, sprinkle with the chopped parsley, and serve.

Yield: 4 to 6 servings

Rumania

BUCHAREST

BUCURESTI. Westerners do not find Rumanian cuisine exceptional, and the Bucuresti is about as good a place to dine as there is in this capital. Formerly the Capsa Restaurant, it was frequented by prewar society and its pink walls, black-painted woodwork and chandeliers recall the 1930s. There are many different dining areas, and Spanish as well as Rumanian specialties are served.

The caviar at the Bucuresti is black and genuine, unlike the poisonous-looking orange stuff masquerading elsewhere in town as Manchurian caviar. One dish to try is *mititei*, meatballs made of beef, pork, and herbs and grilled over charcoal. Another dish, *sarmale*, resembles Polish *golbaki*, or rolled cabbage stuffed with meat. The Bucuresti also serves a *salmi de chevreuil*, stag stewed in a typically Balkan sauce, tomatoey and peppery. For dessert, Bucuresti makes its own hazelnut ice cream and also offers thinly sliced, sugared oranges. With your meal try Rumanian Cotnar wines, either red or white. Both come from the Moldavian region of the country and are known as the knights' wine, apparently because they were the royal drink at the fifteenth-century court.

The Bucuresti is at Calea Victoriei 36. The Natunal Theater is nearby. Meals cost up to $10 a person. The restaurant is open from noon to 5 P.M. and 9 P.M. to midnight and its phone number is 13-44-82.

—James Feron

MITITEI
Based on the recipe of the Bucuresti, Bucharest

At the Bucuresti these Rumanian meatballs are grilled over charcoal. If charcoal grilling is inconvenient, season the meatballs with charcoal powder and put them under the broiler.

1 cup beef stock (see page 95) or canned beef bouillon
1 clove garlic, minced
½ teaspoon each of black pepper, dried rosemary, marjoram, and savory
1 tablespoon baking soda
½ pound coarsely ground lean beef
¼ pound coarsely ground pork loin

1. Bring the stock to a boil in a saucepan, add the garlic, spices, and baking soda; simmer for a few minutes. Remove from heat.
2. Thoroughly mix the ground beef and pork and place the meat in a non-metallic dish. Add the seasoned stock and blend well. Refrigerate the mixture for 24 hours.
3. When you are ready to cook the meat, shape it into 4 oblong patties, about 4 inches by 1½ inches. (As hors d'oeuvres, each patty can be divided into 4 pieces, making 16 small meatballs.) Grill the patties over a charcoal fire or season them with charcoal powder and put them under the broiler.

Yield: 2 main dish servings, or 16 appetizer meatballs

SARMALE
Based on the recipe of the Bucuresti, Bucharest

At the Bucuresti the cabbage for this stuffed cabbage specialty is soured by letting it stand for two weeks in salt water. For the convenience of the home cook, a modified souring method is given in this recipe. It employs rye bread as well as salt water and cuts the standing time down to three to four days.

1 large cabbage
½ cup salt (approximately)

1 pound rye bread, sliced
¾ pound ground pork loin
6 ounces ground pork fat
½ cup beef stock (see page 95) or canned beef bouillon
1 large onion, finely chopped
2 tablespoons cooking oil
½ cup raw rice
2 teaspoons paprika
2–3 tomatoes, sliced
8 bay leaves
¼ pound sliced bacon

1. Three to 4 days before the *sarmale* will be cooked, blanch the whole cabbage by plunging it into boiling water, bringing the water to a boil again, and letting it boil for 2 to 3 minutes. Separate the cabbage into individual leaves and place the leaves in a very large nonmetallic bowl. Bring to a boil enough water to cover the cabbage leaves and add the salt. (The water should be very salty, almost too salty to taste.) Pour the boiling salt water over the cabbage leaves and let cool. When cool enough to handle, place the slices of rye bread among the leaves and press the leaves and bread down. Once or twice a day press them down again.
2. The day before the *sarmale* will be cooked, combine the ground pork, pork fat, and stock and refrigerate.
3. When the *sarmale* is to be cooked, sauté the chopped onion in the oil until golden. Add the sautéed onion to the ground pork and fat mixture; add the rice and paprika, mix well and form into about 12 thin rolls about 4 inches long.
4. Remove the cabbage leaves from the salt water. Strain and reserve the liquid. Select large leaves and wrap 1 leaf around each meat roll, tucking in the ends. Chop the remaining leaves finely.
5. Place the stuffed cabbage leaves around the edge of a large pot or pan with a cover and put the chopped cabbage in the center, cover all with a layer of sliced tomatoes, put the bay leaves on the tomatoes, and then add a layer of bacon. There should be at least 2 inches of air space above the food.
6. Add enough of the liquid in which the cabbage leaves soured to almost cover the contents of the pot. Bring to a boil, reduce heat, and simmer, covered, for about 2 hours, occasionally shaking the pot gently back and forth.
7. Ideally, once the *sarmale* is cooked it should sit at room temperature for 2 days, then be reheated and eaten.

Yield: 4 servings

Russia

LENINGRAD

HOTEL ASTORIA DINING ROOM. Unfortunately, there are few decent restaurants in Leningrad. But in the days prior to 1917 and the Bolshevik Revolution, the Hotel Astoria Dining Room was one of Russia's finest, and some of the old traditions of service and style are not quite dead. In fact, the service at the Astoria is as good as one is likely to encounter anywhere in Russia. The waitresses are efficient and polite, the table linen is clean, and a reasonable number of items on the menu are usually available (many Russian restaurants have lengthy and exciting menus, but few of the dishes are to be had). There is a Western-style orchestra at the Astoria, often a Russian chanteuse, and the atmosphere is faintly *ancien régime* and *mittel europa*.

A fine Astoria dinner might consist of a julienne served piping hot in a small metal pot (if trout julienne is available you are in luck), an excellent consommé or borsch, chicken à la kiev (extraordinarily tender and oozing with lovely sweet butter), cucumber and tomato salad, superlative black bread and butter (the bread and butter must be specifically ordered) and, for dessert, fruit or ice cream (the ice cream is almost always very good in Russian restaurants). With this meal have tea in a glass, a bit of chilled vodka to start, and possibly a bottle of Tsinindali (Georgian) red wine. Or you might want to try the very good Soviet champagne.

The Hotel Astoria is at 39 Gertzen Street. The phone number is 10-00-31. The dining room is open for lunch and dinner, and reservations are not accepted except for Saturday night and holiday evenings. There is dancing and the orchestra will very often know and play your selections if they are not more recent than two or three years old. The meal I have suggested will run about $12 to $14 a person, exclusive of vodka and wine. The waitress expects to be tipped about 15 percent. Nothing to the headwaiter or head-waitress.

—*Harrison E. Salisbury*

CHICKEN A LA KIEV
Based on the recipe of the Hotel Astoria Dining Room, Leningrad

3 large chicken breasts, skinned, boned, and halved
¾ pound (3 sticks) unsalted butter
salt
black pepper
2 eggs
2 tablespoons water
flour
fine dry bread crumbs

1. Make tiny shallow cuts into but not through the meat of each chicken breast half, trim off all fat, flatten, cover with a sheet of plastic wrap, and pound quite thin with a meat mallet.
2. Divide ½ pound (2 sticks) butter into 6 equal parts and form each into a roll about 2 inches long and ½ inch in diameter. Chill in ice water until hard.
3. Preheat the oven to 400 degrees.
4. Place a roll of butter on each chicken breast half, wrap the meat securely around it so the butter will not leak out during frying, and skewer with toothpicks.
5. Lightly beat the eggs and blend with the water.
6. Moisten the chicken breasts with water, coat with flour, dip in the beaten eggs, and roll in the bread crumbs.
7. Melt the remaining butter in a skillet and fry the chicken breasts over medium heat, turning them until they are golden brown all over. Then bake them in the oven for 5 minutes and serve. An alternate method of cooking the chicken is to fry the breasts in hot deep fat for 8 to 10 minutes and then serve.

Yield: 6 servings

MOSCOW

ARAGVI. For many years this was the only first-class restaurant in Moscow with the possible exception of the fine old dining room in the Grand Hotel (long since closed). It is still the best, although strictly speaking it is not a Russian restaurant but a Georgian restaurant specializing in the hot, spicy, and exotic foods of the Caucasus. The place is always crowded and reservations are a necessity.

As in all restaurants in Russia, the service is erratic, but the Aragvi has several excellent waiters who will even help the diner by suggesting good Georgian dishes of which he has never heard. By all means start with a selection of the hors d'oeuvres, which should include beluga caviar, warm Georgian flat bread, sweet butter (bread and butter must be specifically ordered), *satzivo iz indeka* (cold turkey in walnut sauce), *lobi kholoydne* (cold Georgian beans in a spicy sauce), and marinated mushrooms. For the main course I recommend either *shashlik po karsky* (shashlik in the style of Kars, a city in Turkey just across the border from Georgia) or *tziplyta tabakh*. The *shashlik po karsky* consists of broiled marinated lamb riblets and kidneys, and the *tziplyta tabakh* is young chicken pressed flat, fried crisp, and served with red hot garlic sauce. Have fruit or ice cream for dessert (the Aragvi's ice cream is excellent) and then some Turkish coffee.

The restaurant has a cellar of Georgian wines and good Soviet champagne. There is a Georgian band with unusual Georgian instruments, and it plays a continuous repertoire of Georgian songs. Sometimes there is a girl singer and even a Georgian sword dancer. The place is noisy and gay until the 1 A.M. closing.

The Aragvi is at 6 Gorky Street. The phone number is 29-37-62. The restaurant is open for lunch and dinner, and dinner will require a minimum of three hours. Private rooms, some with balconies overlooking the main dining room, are available. The meal I have suggested should run about $12 to $15 a person, exclusive of drinks. The waiter will expect a substantial gratuity (20 percent) and the headwaiter or maître d'hôtel should be tipped the equivalent of $5 or $10 depending on the size of the party.

—*Harrison E. Salisbury*

246

SHASHLIK PO KARSKY
Based on the recipe of the Aragvi, Moscow

At the Aragvi these skewered lamb riblets and kidneys are broiled over glowing coals and served with a hot sauce. At home they can be seasoned with charcoal powder, put in a broiler, and accompanied by an approximation of a Russian hot sauce.

1 pound lamb riblets, cut into 4 pieces
2 lamb kidneys, halved lengthwise, with center tubes and fat removed
salt
black pepper

MARINADE

1 onion, finely chopped
1 tablespoon chopped parsley
1 tablespoon lemon juice or white vinegar

HOT SAUCE

A-1 sauce
mustard
Tabasco
sugar

GARNISH

lemon slices
1 tablespoon chopped parsley
1 tablespoon chopped scallion

1. Wipe the lamb riblets and make shallow cuts across the fibers. Put the riblets and kidneys into a bowl and season with salt and pepper. Add the marinade and marinate for 2 to 3 hours.
2. Arrange the ribs and kidneys alternately on skewers and broil over charcoal, or season with charcoal powder and cook in a broiler, turning frequently, until brown.
3. To approximate the Aragvi's hot sauce, season A-1 sauce to taste with mustard, Tabasco, and a bit of sugar.
4. Remove the ribs and kidneys from the skewers and serve garnished with the lemon slices, chopped parsley, and chopped scallion. Serve the hot sauce separately.

Yield: 2 servings

Senegal

DAKAR

M'BARICK'S. Senegal used to be a French West African colony, and in the more African section of this still very French city is a Senegalese establishment called M'Barick's. Above the door is a wooden sign on which is the French equivalent of "Don't dilly-dally on the way here—you might discover the food is all gone."

Newcomers have no trouble finding M'Barick's because its open-hearth fire glowing beneath sizzling cuts of lamb sends a wonderful aroma up and down the busy street on which the restaurant is located. And Baye M'Barick, pulling himself away from an animated conversation or perhaps a card game, smiling broadly and straightening his heavily embroidered grand flowing *boubou*, greets every arrival personally whenever he is around.

Some patrons accept M'Barick's offer to select their own cuts of meat for the fire, but most move directly into the long low-ceilinged dining room with its single table stretched out some 30 feet above an array of soft Moroccan cushions. Even the most ungainly guest soon finds a way of making himself comfortable on the cushions while his fellow diners up and down the table call out or wave greetings to him. The establishment's *griot*, a musician-historian sitting near the table, will strum his 21-stringed *korah* harp, which is played with both thumbs, and either sing the diners' requests or compose a special song for the occasion.

If you let M'Barick choose your lunch or dinner, your first delight will probably be a wooden platter of sizzling lamb kebabs. This will invariably be followed by Moroccan-style *couscous* (lamb or chicken and vegetables on semolina), then a platter of grilled lamb cutlets, liver, or kidneys. A tossed salad and a selection of cheeses are also served. Dessert is your choice of fruits—mangoes, bananas, pineapple, oranges, and the like.

There is one M'Barick specialty that you cannot have unless you make arrangements ahead of time. It is the famous *tiebn diehn*, or red rice and fish, which is pronounced "chebujin" and is Senegal's most popular dish. Those in the know put their orders in a day or so in advance and M'Barick then prepares it. You have to make the arrangements in person, however, since M'Barick has no telephone. He dislikes phones, saying, "People call and make orders and then do not come. I like it when they walk in and order. Then they eat."

Very good French wines are available to grace your meal, and many of M'Barick's customers—they range from diplomats, businessmen, and civil servants to students and tourists—will share both wine and conversation with their neighbors.

The address of M'Barick's is simply Nyary Tally Street, and it is six streets north of Avenue Bourguiba. To get to M'Barick's by cab from downtown will cost between $1 and $2, and M'Barick will summon a cab for your return trip. The restaurant is open for lunch and dinner, and a full meal with wine will generally come to not much more than $5 a person.

In 1973 M'Barick opened a new and larger restaurant at La Pointe des Almadies, which is the westernmost tip of Africa. The decor here, too, is African-style with pillows, and there is an addition for dining outdoors, under the stars and near the ocean. Again, no telephone. The menu and prices are about the same as at the original M'Barick's, but the new restaurant is 12 miles outside Dakar and a taxi ride to it costs $6 or $7.

—*Thomas A. Johnson*

LAMB BROCHETTE
Based on the recipe of M'Barick's, Dakar

*This is M'Barick's most famous hors d'oeuvre, and Baye
M'Barick says: "Many good foods are easy to prepare if one
chooses the best method of preparation and is careful in his
selection of ingredients." He uses "choice cuts of the best
lamb chops and leg of lamb without fat" for his brochette
and insists on cooking it over a hardwood fire, saying
charcoal smokes too much. In place of a hardwood fire, the
home cook could use the broiler.*

1 pound choice lean lamb (chops or leg) cut into 1-inch cubes
1 pound lamb liver cut into 1-inch cubes (if unavailable, substitute calves'
    liver)
¾–1 pound Bermuda onion, cubed
½ pound lamb fat, cubed
salt
black pepper

S A U C E

1 cup white vinegar
2 Maggi bouillon cubes (or 1 tablespoon Maggi seasoning)

1. Put the ingredients on skewers—meat, onion, liver, fat/meat, onion, liver,
    fat. (The closer you pack the ingredients the rarer the results will be.)
    Season with salt and pepper.
2. Make the sauce by dissolving the cubes in the vinegar. Brush the bro-
    chettes with this sauce.
3. Place the skewers over a hot hardwood fire for about 5 minutes or in a
    preheated broiler for about 10 minutes. Turn often to brown evenly.
    Brush with sauce when the ingredients look dry. Continue broiling until
    crusty brown on the outside and pink in the center. Serve immediately.

Yield: 6 to 8 appetizer servings

Singapore

SINGAPORE

ORCHARD ROAD CARPARK. In the daytime this is, literally, a parking lot. But starting at about 6 p.m. it becomes a lively open-air gathering place where foreigners can eat out the way Asians eat out, without fear of ending up in a hospital two hours later.

Restaurants in Southeast Asia are for rich people and tourists; everyone else heads for street stalls, usually one-man or one-family wheelable carts that are actually portable restaurants. From them patrons order a bowl of soup, a dish of fried noodles, or some local concoction. Raw fish, chickens, vegetables, and other raw materials dangle in the open air from hooks on the stalls. The owners of the stalls, often old men in undershirts and shorts, fan their charcoal fires and slosh hot oil around in their woks, or cooking pans. Foreigners usually take one look and flee—and for good reason. In most Southeast Asian countries sanitation is unknown and the stalls are surrounded with flies and garbage.

Not so at the Orchard Road Carpark. Singapore is Asia's cleanest city. A cigarette butt tossed into the street can bring a fine of almost $200. The sanitation department is so strict that people say Singapore has more golf balls than flies. The carpark is spotless and flyless, and it represents the best place to really eat Asian style—that is, in the street.

About 40 different stalls set up each night—mostly Chinese, some Malay, and some Indian. There are no menus. You simply walk among them, spot interesting dishes, and ask for some. You can stand by the stall and watch the cook prepare your selection or sit down at one of the simple picnic-like tables and wait for it to come.

There are dozens of dishes to choose from—*saté* (skewered pieces of meat), fried noodles, spicy fried squid, rice dishes, curries, various eggrolls and, for the adventurous, such things as fish lip soup or fried pig snout. Each dish usually costs well under a dollar, and if you order from five or six different stalls each man will come over and collect as you get ready to leave.

The Orchard Road Carpark is close to the major hotels. It has no address more specific than "across the road from the Cold Storage Supermarket." It's open every evening from about 6 or 7 P.M. to 1 A.M. In the daytime you will find only parked cars.

—*James P. Sterba*

It is almost impossible to get recipes from "old men in undershirts and shorts" who "fan their charcoal fires and slosh oil around in their woks" while raw fish, chickens, and vegetables hang from the hooks of their wheeled, open-air, portable restaurants. But the following are recipes for three of the sort of dishes you might eat at the Orchard Road Carpark.

RICE NOODLES IN CHICKEN SOUP

1 3-pound chicken, quartered
2 quarts water
6 ounces dried white rice noodles
½ cup finely sliced shallots
oil for deep frying
1 small head lettuce, shredded
6 scallions, cut into the finest rings possible
salt
white pepper

1. Rinse chicken and put into a large pot with 2 quarts of cold water. Bring to a boil, lower flame, cover pot, and simmer for 3 to 4 hours. Lift out chicken, discard the bones and shred the meat. Return the meat to the soup. This you can do well in advance.
2. Cook the rice noodles in plenty of boiling water, uncovered, for 2 to 3 minutes. Drain the noodles, rinse in cold water, and drain again. Set aside.

3. Deep fry the shallots in oil till lightly browned. Drain on paper towels and put into a small bowl.
4. To serve: Bring soup to a boil, add lettuce and scallion rings. Boil 1 minute. Season with salt and white pepper. Divide noodles into 4 large bowls. Over the noodles ladle the hot soup with the meat and the vegetables. Sprinkle the crisp shallots on top and serve at once.

Yield: 4 servings

BEEF SATÉ

1–2 pounds flank steak or any boneless steak

MARINADE

1 cup finely chopped onions
2 teaspoons minced garlic
4 tablespoons vegetable oil
3 tablespoons curry powder
2 tablespoons smooth peanut butter
1 teaspoon hot red-chili powder
1 teaspoon lemon juice
¼ cup water
1 teaspoon sugar
salt

DIPPING SAUCE

½ marinade (see steps 2 and 3)
2 tablespoons peanut butter
juice of ½ lemon
1 tablespoon sugar
salt

1. Cut steak across the grain into long, ½-inch-wide strips.
2. Sauté onions and garlic in the oil until golden brown. Add the curry powder, peanut butter, chili powder, lemon juice, water, sugar, and salt. Mix to a smooth paste and bring to a simmer. Cool. This is the marinade.
3. In a bowl mix together the beef strips and half the marinade. Marinate for 2 hours or more. Set aside the other half of the marinade for the dipping sauce.

4. Preheat broiler or prepare a charcoal fire. Thread beef on skewers, broil until crisp and brown, turning once or twice.
5. Combine all ingredients for dipping sauce.
6. Serve the saté hot with a bowl of the dipping sauce.

<u>**Yield: 4 servings**</u>

BEEF CURRY

This curry dish is mild and quite liquid and so goes well with the large plate of rice that is part of the steady diet in Singapore.

2 tablespoons vegetable oil
1 cup chopped onions
4 cloves garlic, minced
2 pounds stewing beef, cut into bite-size chunks
3 tablespoons curry powder
4 medium potatoes, cut into 2-inch cubes
3 cups beef stock (see page 95) or canned beef bouillon or water
salt

1. In a heavy pot heat the oil and brown the onions and garlic in it. Add the beef chunks and brown them lightly.
2. Add the curry powder, potatoes, and beef stock and bring to a boil. Lower heat, cover the pot, and simmer until meat is tender, about 45 minutes.
3. Season with salt and serve over rice.

<u>**Yield: 4 servings**</u>

South Korea—see Korea

Soviet Union—see Russia

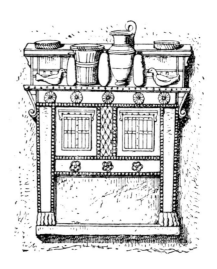

Spain

BARCELONA

TINELL. In Barcelona, chief city of Catalonia and major business center of Spain, there is a gothic quarter where the streets and buildings go back to the Middle Ages. To stroll through it is to delight the eye, and if that alone were not enough, just behind the fourteenth-century cathedral is a restaurant called Tinell, whose motto is "the refuge of the gourmet."

Tinell, which in the Catalonian tongue refers to a china cabinet or kitchen shelf, is only a decade old, but its owner, Sebastian Damunt Nicles, a white-haired cook, cooking teacher, and gastronomy buff, has made sure that it fits in with its medieval surroundings. Dark beams and woodwork, wrought-iron chandeliers, dim lighting, and a generally dim, almost scruffy interior create an ambience in harmony with the atmosphere of the gothic quarter.

The food is hearty and represents only slightly richer versions of what Catalonians have eaten for centuries in the countryside. There is a strong emphasis on game, such as hare, quail, duck, goose, and patridge, and all of it is tasty. There is also a traditional bread dish, filling and cheap enough for a peasant family, which in Tinell's version mixes bread with garlic, butter, ham, cheese, and cream and comes from the oven crusty and golden.

There is a small bar to the left of the entryway, but people who only want to drink are not served; they must also want to eat. Beyond the bar is an open kitchen which Señor Damunt surveys from his cashier's post. The restaurant seats 60 on two levels, but it is rarely crowded and one can generally enjoy a quiet meal, attentively served.

Tinell is at Calle Frenería 8–10. The phone number is 331 79-12. A meal with wine—Spanish wines are good but coarser and heavier than fine French wines—will run about $6, including tip. Lunch is served from 1 to 4 P.M., dinner from 9 to 11:45 P.M. (the cooks leave after that). Tinell is closed on Sunday and for a month in the summer.

—Henry Giniger

GOOSE WITH PEARS
Based on the recipe of Tinell, Barcelona

1 **7–9 pound goose**
salt
1 large onion
1 carrot
6 pears
1 lemon, halved
2 tablespoons cognac
1 cup chicken stock (see page 101) or canned chicken broth

1. Preheat the oven to 350 degrees.
2. Wipe the goose with a damp cloth. Remove the visible fat from inside the bird and set the fat aside for rendering. Salt the cavity of the bird and place the onion and carrot inside. Puncture the skin of the goose in several places, especially below the legs and breast, to allow fat to run off during roasting.
3. Place the goose on a rack in a shallow roasting pan and roast it about 20 minutes to the pound. A meat thermometer should register 180 degrees when the goose is done. During the cooking, fat that has dripped from the goose should be removed frequently and carefully saved. In the roasting process the goose will lose about 40 percent of its original weight.
4. About 30 minutes before the goose is done, cut the pears in halves or quarters, scoop out the cores with a spoon, and rub the cut fruit with the lemon. Put a cup of the goose fat you have been taking from the roasting pan into a baking dish and add the pears, coating them with the fat. Bake for 20 to 30 minutes, or until the pears are tender, in the same oven as the goose.
5. In a small saucepan over medium heat, reduce the cognac to half its volume and sprinkle over the pears when they are done.

6. When the goose is done, transfer it to a warm platter. Pour off and save for future use any fat still in the roasting pan. Scrape loose the goose's body juices that have solidified on the bottom of the pan and combine over low heat with the chicken stock to make a gravy *au jus*.
7. Carve the goose. Remove the baked pears from the fat. Mix the goose slices with the pears. Pour the hot gravy over all and serve.

Yield: 6 servings

NOTE: The rendered excess fat you have pulled from inside the bird and any fat left from the roasting pan after this dish has been prepared should be strained and stored in the refrigerator. Goose fat is considered a delicacy and can be used, salted, in place of butter or margarine.

MIGAS CANAS À LA PASTORA
Based on the recipe of Tinell, Barcelona

This dish of bread, ham, and cheese has a name that is somewhat difficult to translate. Migas *means crumbs, and* canas *means white hairs (possibly a reference to the thread-like strings of melted cheese but meaning more probably, in conjunction with* migas, *"old pieces of bread"). Pastora means shepherdess. At Tinell the dish is made with Serrano ham and Manchego cheese, but the home cook can substitute any ham and Monterey Jack cheese and achieve delicious results. Even Swiss cheese can be used, or any other white cheese that melts well, but the Swiss and some of the others will not give as stringy a result. At Tinell, furthermore, the dish is made* al ojo, *meaning more or less as the eye sees it as far as quantities go, so after making it once the home cook should feel no constraint whatever about changing the proportions.*

1½ tablespoons olive oil
1 clove garlic, minced
1½ teaspoons paprika
1½ cups of water
salt
½ bay leaf
pinch of dried thyme
4 cups cubed stale white bread
1 cup diced cooked ham (about ½ pound)

6 tablespoons butter
1 cup diced Manchego or Monterey Jack cheese (about ½ pound)
½ cup heavy cream

1. In a small saucepan, heat the olive oil and slowly sauté the garlic until golden. Add the paprika, water, salt, bay leaf, and thyme; stir well, cover, and boil for about 7 minutes.
2. Preheat the oven to 450 degrees or the broiler to hot.
3. Spread the bread cubes on a large dish and dribble the mixture from the saucepan over them, stirring the cubes about, so that they all absorb some liquid but do not become soggy. Use all of the mixture or as much as you need. Let the moistened bread cubes stand.
4. In a large skillet, gently sauté the ham in 2 tablespoons butter, then remove the ham temporarily from the pan. Melt the remaining 4 tablespoons butter in the pan, add the moistened bread, and sauté, turning once with a spatula, so the bread becomes golden all over. Return the ham to the pan and mix it thoroughly with the bread. Add the cheese cubes and mix them in.
5. Spoon the bread, ham, and cheese mixture into an ovenproof serving dish, pour in the heavy cream, and place the dish in the oven or under the broiler until the cheese melts and the top of the mixture is golden brown.

Yield: 3 to 4 servings

MADRID

LA TRAINERA. The best thing Madrid has to offer, gastronomically speaking, is seafood, and of all the good fish restaurants in Spain's capital, La Trainera is probably the best. It's unpretentious, perhaps too unpretentious. One eats on polished wooden tables without tablecloths and this contributes to the noise of the place. Another noise factor is the full house at lunch and dinner, not only at the tables but along the long bar where one can have a drink and taste the shrimp, cockles, and other delicacies. Fishing nets, anchors, oars, and wooden beams give La Trainera the feeling of a modest fishing inn along some coast. But its location, on a small residential and business street, is decidedly middle class/upper class and so is its clientele. Nearby is Calle Serrano with its elegant shops and not far off are Retiro Park and one of the world's great art museums, the Prado.

The secret of La Trainera's success is the freshness of its seafood. The restaurant's owners are in the commercial fishing and wholesale fish distribution business, so much of what La Trainera offers comes from its own boats, so to speak. Fish, king crab, lobsters, oysters, prawns, and crayfish are flown in daily from the Atlantic coast and the Mediterranean, and because of the restaurant's large clientele and the big volume of home delivery orders, the highly perishable food never stays around long enough to perish.

La Trainera is at Lagasca 60. The phone number is 226 11-81. A meal for two, including wine and tip, can run from $15 to $30 (the king crab and lobster are expensive). The restaurant is open from 1:30 to 3:30 P.M. and 9:30 P.M. to around midnight.

—Henry Giniger

KING CRAB XANGURU
Based on the recipe of La Trainera, Madrid

TOMATO PASTE

1 medium tomato, chopped
¼ cup chopped onion
1 tablespoon olive oil

1 cup minced onion
2–3 tablespoons olive oil
1 clove garlic, minced
1 leek (white part only), minced
1 bay leaf
¾ pound cooked king crab meat chunks (if fresh crabmeat is unavailable, substitute frozen)
1 tablespoon dry white wine
1 tablespoon dry sherry
1 tablespoon cognac

1. To make the tomato paste, sauté the tomato and chopped onion in a tablespoon of olive oil until the onion is translucent. Force through a sieve and simmer for 10 minutes. Set aside.
2. Place the cup of minced onion in a pan with 2–3 tablespoons of olive oil and sauté a few minutes. Add the garlic, leek, and bay leaf and sauté until the onion is golden.
3. Add the crabmeat, mix thoroughly with the ingredients in the pan, and sauté a few minutes until the crabmeat is heated through. Remove the bay leaf.
4. Combine the wine, sherry, and cognac in a small saucepan. Heat the mixture briefly until its volume is reduced by half. Pour over the crabmeat.
5. Pour the tomato paste (there should be about ¼ of a cup) over the crabmeat, mix well, and serve.

Yield: 2 servings

Sweden

STOCKHOLM

KÄLLAREN AURORA. A very good place for genuine Swedish dishes in this handsome capital city of Sweden is the Källaren Aurora. It occupies the first floor and cellar of a charming seventeenth-century house with stepped gables and decorative masonry. The twin entrance doors of beautifully painted wood are framed by carved stone architraves. Inside, to the left, is a cozy bar with a fine beamed ceiling that, prior to restoration, was hidden for two centuries. Downstairs, in the cellar, are vaulted dining rooms of old red brick. The tables are covered with white linen tablecloths and on each is a thick white candle.

With the candlelight playing on the old bricks, you can dine from the regular menu on the likes of marinated salmon, roast elk, or reindeer fillet. And if you give the Aurora's young chef, Staffan Enander, a few day's notice, he will prepare special dishes for you, including his ptarmigan soup. This is made by browning ptarmigans in butter with leeks, carrots, celery, crushed juniper berries, and thyme, flaming the ptarmigans with cognac, dousing them with dry white wine, cooking them in veal broth with sliced artichoke, removing them from the broth, reducing the broth to half its volume, straining the broth and bringing it back to full volume by adding heated heavy cream, then adding fresh goose liver, sweet brandy, and lemon juice and, just before serving, stirring in whipped cream and strips of ptarmigan breast that have been steeped in cognac. It is not recommended for dieters or teetotalers.

The most popular dish at the Aurora is the charcoal-grilled *gravad lax*, or marinated salmon, a house specialty. It is served with dill and a sweet mustard sauce and can be ordered à la carte as a main dish or eaten the way I enjoy it, which is as part of the restaurant's three-course Queen's Dinner. The second course is fillets of reindeer with a husky brown hunter's sauce, peeled baked potato, string beans, half a canned pear, fried parsley, and a glob of chestnut paste topped with a maraschino cherry. For dessert there is ice cream flavored with Swedish punch and ginger, topped with mocha, and served in a delightful porcelain pot.

The Queen's Dinner, at around $10, is the most expensive one on the menu, but it is a real feast. For slightly less you can have a dinner of toast with roe of bleak and shrimp, for instance, followed by roast elk with baked potato and salad, and so on. Other popular items are salmon pâté, herring, lobster, pepper steak, and roquefort steak flambé. Individual dishes à la carte range from about $4 for the *gravad lax* to $7 or more for elk fillet or the roquefort steak. There is a rich assortment of fine wines at reasonable prices.

If you haven't taken in the sights of the Old Town section of Stockholm before your meal, be sure to do so afterwards. From the Aurora's steps you look right across the square to the House of the Nobility, a premier tourist attraction, and are only a brief stroll from the Royal Palace, the thirteenth-century Storkyrkan, which is Stockholm's oldest church, an unusual postal museum, and any number of historic old buildings and quaint new boutiques.

The Källaren Aurora is at 11 Munkbron. The phone number is 21-93-59. It is open Monday through Saturday from 11:30 A.M. to midnight. Closed Sunday.

—Richard J. Litell

SALMON PÂTÉ AURORA
Based on the recipe of Källaren Aurora, Stockholm

PÂTÉ

¼ **pound smoked salmon**
¼ **pound fresh salmon**
1 **ounce chicken breast meat**
2 **egg yolks**
¼ **cup heavy cream**
pinch of salt
pinch of cayenne
dash of dry sherry
dash of cognac

SAUCE

2 tablespoons finely chopped onion
white wine vinegar
dry white wine
12 tablespoons (1½ sticks) unsalted butter, softened
dry English mustard
cayenne
salt

GARNISH

4 slices smoked salmon

1. Put the smoked salmon, fresh salmon, and chicken through a grinder until finely ground, or blend in a blender.
2. Preheat the oven to 425 degrees.
3. Lightly stir the egg yolks into the cream, season with salt, cayenne, sherry, and cognac. Mix into the ground salmon and chicken.
4. Spoon the mixture into a large buttered pan, forming 4 oval patties, and bake for 8 to 10 minutes. Place the patties on a serving dish and garnish each with a slice of smoked salmon. At the Källaren Aurora each salmon slice is shaped to form a rose.
5. While the patties are baking, prepare the sauce as follows: Place the finely chopped onion in a small saucepan, add enough white wine vinegar to cover and cook until all the vinegar dissipates and the pan is dry. Then add enough dry white wine to cover and cook again until the pan is dry. Beat in the butter over low heat, a little at a time, with a wire whisk or a spoon. Season to taste with the dry mustard, cayenne, and salt.
6. Serve the sauce separately with the patties.

Yield: 4 appetizer servings

Switzerland

GENEVA

A L'OLIVIER DE PROVENCE. In a city with a wealth of restaurants, A l'Olivier de Provence is often my choice. The *carré d'agneau* (rack of lamb) breaded, herbed, and served with a white wine sauce, the *scampi provençal*, and other specialties of the French chef, Albert Guanter, recall the sunny, aromatić countryside of southern France with its olive trees, which inspired the restaurant's name.

Also going for this fine dining place is its location—in the heart of Carouge, a suburb. Although Carouge is only ten minutes by car from downtown Geneva, it has retained a personality all its own from the days when it lived beyond Swiss rule under the flag of the Kingdom of Sardinia.

The round-trip by taxi from downtown Geneva costs about $5, but a real bargain is to be had by riding the fast No. 12 trolley on the city's only surviving streetcar line. The uniform fare of 80 centimes (less than 30 cents) for one hour of public transport, including transfers and backtracking, puts Carouge within easy reach of any starting point.

The trolley stop at the Place du Marché is only two blocks from A l'Olivier de Provence. This square and the Place du Temple, a block before the stop, with their flower-decorated fountains and facing buildings in the style of another day, typify the gracious air that still clings to Carouge. A stroll around the two squares and along adjoining streets reveals unpretentious antique shops and art galleries, while the Protestant church that gives the Place du Temple its name is noted for its wood sculptures.

A l'Olivier de Provence's low-ceilinged, tastefully decorated dining rooms are in keeping with its setting and cuisine. So is the attentive care of its efficient staff. The restaurant is at 13 Rue Jacques Dalphin in Carouge. A completely satisfying three-course meal for two, with a bottle of Brouilly, excellent even though one of the more modestly priced offerings on the impressive wine list, should come to about $30, including coffee and the 15 percent service charge. For reservations phone 42-04-50. Lunch and dinner are served daily except Sunday, when A l'Olivier de Provence is closed, and Monday, when it opens for dinner only.

—*Victor Lusinchi*

SCAMPI PROVENÇAL
Based on the recipe of A l'Olivier de Provence, Geneva

CREAMED BUTTER

4 tablespoons butter
1 rounded tablespoon Dijon-type prepared mustard
salt
black pepper
1 tablespoon minced shallots
6 finely chopped pitted green olives
1 tablespoon chopped parsley
2 anchovy fillets, chopped
1 tablespoon chopped sour pickle
Provençal herbs to taste (pinch each dried thyme, powdered sage, dried rosemary)
3–4 drops worcestershire sauce (optional)

1 pound large shrimp, shelled and deveined
flour
2–3 tablespoons olive oil
¼ cup dry white wine
1 small tomato, peeled, seeded and chopped

1. Let the butter soften and then cream in the mustard. Add salt and pepper to taste. Add the remainder of the creamed butter ingredients and mix.
2. Salt and pepper the shrimp and coat them with flour.
3. Sauté the shrimp in the olive oil until they are brightly colored. Add the wine and tomato and simmer for 3 to 4 minutes.
4. Place the shrimp and pan juices in a serving dish, add the creamed butter and serve.

Yield: 2 servings

MONTREUX

MONTREUX PALACE HOTEL RESTAURANT. Edward VII and Lillie Langtry dined here. So did Russian princes and princesses in the days when those honorifics meant something. And so now does Vladimir Nabokov, the Russian-born American author of *Lolita*, who resides in the hotel, a wonderful, rambling, late-Victorian pile that has an unexampled view of Lac Léman, vulgarly known as Lake Geneva.

The restaurant, like the hotel in which it is situated, is elegant with just the right amount of fading grace. The ample room looks out upon the lake. The tables are far enough apart for unstrained conversation, the silverware gleams, the napery is crisp, the candelabra are cut glass, and the wine goblets reflective of the light.

The cuisine is continental, which is to say mostly French. I've seen a wurst ordered and served—to the visible distress of the waiter. And pastas, too, although the servitor in this case was less disapproving. Some of the best dishes are fish, the celebrated pike from Lac Léman, which can be broiled, baked, or poached and served with butter and lemon or a variety of sauces.

Chicken in any form is also estimable, as are the veal selections. Less rewarding is the beef, which tends to be grainy and arrives more medium than rare. The béarnaise sauce, however, is beyond praise. My advice is to skip the fondues, Swiss to the bottom of the cheese pot but out of place in a restaurant that evokes the grand duke in even the most democratic of its patrons. For dessert the *mousse au chocolat* is out of this world.

The Montreux Palace's cellar is extensive. I myself am tepid about Swiss vintages as being nutty in flavor. The French, Austrian, German, and Italian wines are all that you'd expect.

Jacket and tie are required for men. Pants-suited women are admitted, but no miniskirts, no see-through tops. These, the management feels, might offend the understatedly elegant women and their husbands redolent of wealth who make up the bulk of the restaurant's year-round clientele.

The Montreux Palace Hotel is in the center of Montreux, which is on the so-called Swiss Riviera. The restaurant is open for lunch and dinner all year and it isn't cheap. Count on $10 or more per person for lunch, $15 or more for dinner, wines extra. It's best to book a table in advance. Telephone 61-32-31.

—*Alden Whitman*

Taiwan—see China,
Republic of

Tanzania

DAR ES SALAAM

THE PALM BEACH. Looking out at a white beach and the Indian Ocean from the shade of coconut palms, this restaurant is a relaxed amalgam of the faded East African colonial past and Tanzania's pride of independence. A terrace leads through curving open Victorian verandas to the bar-lounge with its English dart board, and the unpretentious dining room where ceiling fans twirl leisurely. Crisp linens, tropical flowers, and spice dispensers adorn each table. The Swahili greeting, "Jambo," brings a pleased response from the staff.

Dar es Salaam (the "Abode of Peace" in Arabic), with its population of more than 300,000 Africans, Asians, and Europeans, has a cosmopolitan cuisine that includes curries, Chinese dishes and, lately, even pizzas, milk shakes, and ice cream. At the Palm Beach the specialty is seafood, with shrimp and giant Indian Ocean lobster topping the list. There is also chicken, steak, and various traditional spicy concoctions of fish, fowl, meat, rice, beans, vegetables, and fruits. Some special African dishes may have to be ordered in advance, such as the Palm Beach's *supu ya ndizi*, or banana soup, which is made with chicken, green bananas or plantains, tomatoes, celery, shredded coconut, and a variety of seasonings and spices.

No one ever hurries at the Palm Beach. In this establishment there is preserved the pleasant custom of ordering food while enjoying drinks and then having the waiter call you to your table when the meal is ready to be served. The restaurant is near Dar es Salaam's "Embassy Row" and its patrons include representatives of countries as diverse as the People's Republic of China, North Korea, Sweden, and the Netherlands. The place is also patronized by locals, including gatherings of whole African and Asian families, and by many of the growing number of tourists who are discovering the quiet charm of Dar es Salaam. Even those patrons on a short stay seem to come back often, and so the restaurant's clientele is always varied, which doubtless adds to its popularity. But the food and the Bantu hospitality clearly remain the premier attractions.

The Palm Beach is on the Upanga Road, five minutes' drive from the city center. The telephone number is 22931. The place is open every day for lunch from noon to 3 P.M. and for dinner from 6 to 10 P.M. An average three-course meal, which might include half an Indian Ocean lobster as an entrée, should run around $6, excluding drinks and tip. Beer, at about 50 cents a quart bottle, is the popular beverage; imported whiskies and gins, usually at not more than $1 a drink, are available; wine choice is minimal. A 10 percent tip is standard, but 15 percent will get you hearty thanks and extra attention when you return.

—*Brendan Jones*

WALI NA SAMAKI
Based on the recipe of the Palm Beach, Dar es Salaam

*Wali na samaki, or rice with fish, is a staple menu item in
Tanzania, a sort of East African equivalent of meatballs and
spaghetti. For full authenticity it should be made with even
more pepper than this recipe calls for, but Western
palates would probably rebel. However, the pepper can be
adjusted up or down to suit one's taste. The best
accompaniment is cold beer.*

4–5 large tomatoes, sliced
2 large green peppers, sliced
2 medium onions, chopped
2 cups water
juice and finely chopped peel of 1 lemon
½–1 tablespoon crushed red pepper
1 tablespoon salt
1 tablespoon black pepper
cooking oil
2 bay leaves
4–5 pounds red snapper, halibut, or other flaky fish, cut into 4-ounce pieces
1 cup flour
4 cups raw rice

1. Cook the tomatoes, green peppers, and onions in a saucepan with the water, lemon juice, lemon peel, red pepper, ½ tablespoon salt, ½ tablespoon black pepper, ½ cup oil, and bay leaves for 25 minutes or until well cooked.
2. Rub the fish with the remaining salt and pepper, dip the fish in the flour, and fry on both sides in ½-inch hot oil until lightly brown.
3. Cook the rice according to package directions.
4. To serve, dish generous beds of rice onto a large platter or separate large plates, place pieces of fish on top, and cover with the vegetable sauce. (Remove bay leaves from sauce before serving.)

Yield: 6 to 8 servings

SUPU YA NDIZI
Based on the recipe of the Palm Beach, Dar es Salaam

Supu ya ndizi is *"banana soup," spicy-hot and hearty, and cold beer goes well with it.*

1 5–pound chicken, cut into serving pieces, or 5 pounds chicken parts
2 quarts water
5 green bananas or plantains, quartered
4 large tomatoes, thickly sliced
3 cups chopped celery
1 cup shredded coconut
1 tablespoon curry powder
½–1 tablespoon crushed red pepper
1 tablespoon salt
1 teaspoon black pepper
8 tablespoons (1 stick) butter
1 clove garlic, crushed

1. Place the chicken and water in a large pot, bring to a boil and simmer 5 minutes.
2. Add the bananas, tomatoes and all the rest of the ingredients. Bring gradually to a boil and let simmer for 30 minutes, or until the chicken is well cooked.

Yield: 6 to 8 servings

TANZANIAN FRUIT MEDLEY

*Not from the Palm Beach or any other Dar es Salaam
restaurant is this extra added attraction, which was sent along
by Brendan Jones with the following note: "Here is one
devised by a friend. Although not traditional, this dessert
combines some of Tanzania's most typical food favorites—
coconut, honey, pineapple, and cashew nuts. It is especially
satisfying after a very spicy main dish of fish or meat. The
proportions may be varied to taste."*

1 cup ½-inch pineapple cubes (preferably fresh; if canned, rinse off syrup)
2 heaping tablespoons grated coconut
1 heaping tablespoon chopped cashew nuts
4 tablespoons light cream
1 tablespoon honey
3 tablespoons banana liqueur or white rum

1. Combine the pineapple, coconut, and cashew nuts in a bowl.
2. Add the cream, honey, and liqueur or rum. Mix well. Let stand an hour
   or two to allow the flavors to blend before serving. Serve moderately
   chilled if desired.

Yield: 2 servings

THE WHITE ELEPHANT

*Here is another of Brendan Jones's bonuses, this time in the
alcoholic beverage line. His note said: "The following has
become a popular refreshment with the East African safari set.
Otherwise it is not very African, since most Africans would
be quite puzzled by a white elephant either in a literal or
figurative form."*

1 cup milk
6 ounces white rum
2 ounces white crème de cacao
½ cup shredded coconut

4 teaspoons sugar
1 cup shaved ice

1. Put all the ingredients into the container of an electric blender. Blend well.
2. Serve straight from the blender or strain first if less coconut is preferred. Repeat as necessary.

Yield: 4 servings

Turkey
ANKARA

ATATÜRK ORMAN CIFTLIGI MERKEZ LOKANTASI. This eating place—the Atatürk Forest Farm Restaurant—is perhaps the only one in the world that was founded by the founder of a state. When Kemal Atatürk, the father of modern Turkey, made Ankara the capital of the country in 1923, he set out to transform what was then a remote, dusty little Anatolian town into the handsome modern city it is today. One of the things he did was to have trees planted, creating a green belt, and in it he set up a farm that he hoped would serve as a model for rural Turkey. As part of the farm he established a restaurant to cater not only to the farm workers but also to the politicians and bureaucrats who suddenly found themselves in a town with insufficient facilities to accommodate them.

Today the Atatürk Forest Farm Restaurant still manages to preserve some of the atmosphere of the early days of the capital, and its food, all from the farm, remains of high quality. The place is spacious and reservations are never necessary. It is about six miles from town, there is a railroad station nearby and in the old days people used to make a real trip of going to the farm. At that time it was possible to see Atatürk himself seated at a table next to that of a group of farm workers eating and paying with lunch vouchers. Atatürk would ask about the workers' welfare, personally concern himself with the quality of the food, and even join in the folk dancing on days when he felt jolly.

Now the patrons are a mixture of civil servants, high-ranking military officers, businessmen, and occasional diplomats. Few woman are present, except on weekends when whole families have a go at the celebrated *kuzu dolma* (lamb stuffed with spicy rice). On weekends also one can see mistresses being treated to *raki* (anise-flavored brandy) and *meze* (hors d'oeuvres) by businessmen seated carefully in out-of-the-way corners with their backs turned to possible acquaintances.

The restaurant is most popular in the summer months, when patrons can sit outside in the garden, and for those who like quiet and dislike strong lighting, lunch is a better bet here than dinner. Besides the *kuzu dolma*, other noted specialties are *tandir kebabi* (baked leg of tender young lamb) and the *pilic izgara* (grilled chicken), the latter owing its tastiness not to any oriental sauce but to the quality of the chicks raised on the farm. There are several other dishes to choose from and the maître d'hôtel will advise about the dish of the day. Drinks include beer, a mixture of the farm's own fruit juices, and Turkish wines, including the farm's own. Meat dishes in which vegetables predominate start at under a dollar. Meat dishes in which the meat is the main attraction are mostly in the $2 range. Wines run from $1 to $3 a bottle and desserts are under a dollar.

A newcomer to Turkish cuisine could not go wrong if he ordered *kuzu dolma* or *tandir kebabi* with salad and rosé wine or beer. When in season, strawberries or raspberries with powdered sugar, cream, or ice cream are delicious because they come freshly gathered. In winter, for those with a sweet tooth, Turkish pastry desserts are a "must." After lunch the weight-conscious can stroll in the Atatürk Zoo, only a few yards away, or examine the botanical gardens opposite the restaurant, where during working hours any plant one fancies can be purchased. Coming back to the city there are fine views of Ankara with its hills, concrete buildings, shanty towns, and historic citadel silhouetted against the sky.

The Forest Farm Restaurant has no address other than Atatürk Orman Ciftligi Merkez Lokantasi, and if you are driving you can reach it by taking the highway to Istanbul (there are signs to the farm). By cab the ride each way is about $2.50. There are also very frequent trains and the fare is mere small change. The phone number of the restaurant is 13-17-50 and it is open every day from noon to 3 P.M. and 6 to 11 P.M. A meal with meat dish, salad, vegetables, dessert, Turkish coffee, and a bottle of good wine, with 15 percent tax and 10 percent service charge included, will rarely come to as much as $7 a person.

—*M. A. Kislali*

BAKED LEG OF LAMB WITH PILAV
Based on the recipe of the Atatürk Forest Farm Restaurant, Ankara

*Chef Nizamettin Bozok makes this dish with a leg of very
tender young lamb that he cooks, with no seasoning or
basting, in a special brick oven heated with coals. The
home cook can substitute an ordinary oven, but the lamb
must be young and tender. The pilav is made separately and
can be served with other meat dishes and poultry.*

1 7–8 pound leg of tender young lamb
salt
black pepper

1. Preheat the oven to 425 degrees.
2. Wipe the lamb dry and put it in a shallow pan in the oven. Cook it at the rate of 15 minutes to the pound. Add no seasoning, fat, or liquid.
3. The meat is cooked when it can easily be separated from the bone. When it is cooked, baste it with its own pan juices, season it with salt and pepper, and serve it with pilav and roast potatoes.

PILAV

1 tablespoon slivered blanched almonds (about 9 almonds)
1 tablespoon chopped pistachio nuts
1 tablespoon golden raisins
6 tablespoons butter
3 cups raw rice
5 cups hot water
1 teaspoon salt
black pepper

1. In a large heavy saucepan, sauté the almonds, pistachio nuts, and raisins in the butter until lightly browned.
2. Add the rice and sauté for a few minutes, stirring constantly; take care that the nuts do not burn.
3. Add the hot water and salt. Stir once more and bring to a boil. Cover and cook slowly over medium heat, checking periodically, until enough of the liquid has been absorbed so that you can see the rice through the bubbles of liquid. Turn the heat very low and keep covered until all the liquid is absorbed and the rice is cooked. Stir once more, very lightly, in order not to break the rice grains. Put back the lid and let stand for 10 minutes before serving. Serve with lots of freshly ground pepper.

Yield: 6 servings

ISTANBUL

KONYALEZZET LOKANTASI, known as Konyali. Whenever a stranger asks where to find really good traditional Turkish food in this great old city that stands astride Europe and Asia, Turks will tell him about Konyali, which is opposite Istanbul's European-side railroad station at Sirkeci. And the Turks don't have to be from Istanbul to know that Konyali's food is good. The restaurant enjoys a wide reputation for traditional dishes properly prepared, with the right ingredients and tasting exactly as they should.

If you want to enjoy a typical Turkish lunch or dinner, make sure the meal includes a vegetable dish, preferably something with eggplant. You will wonder at all the shapes and tastes this vegetable can take on in the hands of a skilled Turkish cook. *Pilav* (rice) or *börek* (a kind of puff pastry) are also "musts." Then there are the meat dishes like the inevitable and delicious shish kebab (charcoal-broiled skewered pieces of lamb), *döner kebab* (leg of lamb roasted on an upright spit), and *kagit kebab* (ground meat and vegetables baked in paper or aluminum foil). Among desserts, the most famous is *baklava* (strudel-like pastry filled with ground nuts and drenched with syrup).

No alcoholic beverages are served at Konyali, not even beer. "My grandfather, Haci Baba Doganbey, was anti-alcohol on principle," says Nurettin, the present owner. "He told us never to serve it, not even beer. Today we figure we actually make more money that way. Drinkers sit longer than nondrinkers and maybe eat less. With nondrinkers we get a faster turnover and so more customers per meal." In place of beer Konyali serves *ayran* (a mixture of yogurt and water), fruit juices, and soft drinks.

Grandfather Haci Baba established the restaurant in 1879, almost a hundred years ago, because he saw people arriving at the railroad station hungry and unable to buy even a piece of bread or a sweet. He first called his place Lezzet Lokantasi, meaning roughly a restaurant serving delightful food, then Konyalezzet Lokantasi, prefixing it with the name of Konya, the city of the Whirling Dervishes. This is still its legal name, but people coming to Istanbul would ask for the restaurant of the man from Konya—that is, Konyali Lokantasi—and Konyali it soon became in popular usage. Haci Baba's son Mustafa took over the restaurant and enlarged it, and today his son Nurettin, who is about 50 years old, says, "Insallah [if God wishes] my teen-age son Mehmet will be the fourth generation to run the family business."

These days Konyali, now occupying four rooms on two floors, is a haven of comfort and cleanliness in an area full of shoddy shops and eating places in the heart of Sirkeci, which is bordered by warehouses and heavily trafficked all day long by trucks and cars rushing from the European highway to cross the Galata Bridge over the Golden Horn. The interior of the restaurant is simple, warm, and in good taste, with wood-paneled walls, tan leather chairs, yellow tablecloths, modern ceiling lamps, and a shiny Italian espresso machine. Konyali's own bakery in the basement turns out fresh rolls, breads, and pastries, some of which are sold at retail. Konyali also sells box lunches to travelers boarding the Orient Express and other trains at the Sirkeci Station.

Nurettin got the idea for box lunches for travelers because he provided the basket lunches for the film companies making the movies *Topkapi* and *From Russia With Love*. At the Topkapi Museum he saw that tourists had to stand for two hours to get into the small restaurants in the area or go without food, so in 1969 he suggested establishing a branch of Konyali on the Topkapi grounds. Today it serves, outdoors on the terrace as well as inside, about 600 to 800 people at a single sitting, and it is open from 8 A.M. to 5 P.M. every day except Thursday, when it and the museum are closed. Because of its setting, the Konyali at Topkapi is much more spectacular than the Konyali in Sirkeci, but it is also much more touristy (85 percent of its customers are tourists). The prices run about the same in the two restaurants, but the one at Topkapi serves beer and its choice of food is much more limited because of its big tour-group clientele. Its address is simply Konyali-Topkapi and its phone number is 26-27-27.

At the Konyali in Sirkeci, which I prefer to its Topkapi offspring, perhaps only 40 percent of the thousand or so persons served daily are foreigners, and the impressive framed guest lists begin with Kemal Atatürk, the father of modern Turkey, who lunched there in 1924. The place opens for breakfast at 7:30 A.M. and stays open until 9 P.M. There is a staff of more than 100, including 20 cooks. Shish kebab or *döner kebab* is about a dollar. A soup, vegetable, or dessert will run from under 50 cents to something less than a dollar, depending on choice. There are also standard international dishes like beefsteak, filet mignon, and beef stroganoff (all under $2). It's more fun to stick to the Turkish cuisine. The address is just Konyali-Sirkeci and the phone number is 27-02-02 or 27-03-03 or 27-04-04.

—M. A. *Kislali*

EGGPLANT PUREE
Based on the recipe of Konyalezzet Lokantasi, Istanbul

This eggplant puree can be served piping hot in place of
mashed potatoes with any meat dish. It goes especially well
with goulash-type dishes.

4 pounds eggplant
4 tablespoons lemon juice
2 tablespoons butter
1 tablespoon flour
1 cup milk
3 tablespoons grated cheese (parmesan and mild cheddar, mixed)
salt
black pepper

1. Place the eggplants in a 450-degree oven (or place them one by one over a strong flame) until all the skin is charred and the inside is soft when pricked with a fork. Turn as necessary. Peel the skin off each eggplant.
2. Cut all the eggplants into pieces and put them through an electric blender until a smooth puree is formed. Or dice the eggplants and mash them to a puree in a large bowl by hand.
3. In a large saucepan, place the eggplant puree, 4 tablespoons lemon juice (approximately the juice of 1 lemon), and 1 tablespoon butter. Beat, with a wooden spoon, over low heat.
4. In a separate, small saucepan, melt the remaining tablespoon butter. Blend in the flour and cook briefly, without letting the flour brown.
5. Add the butter-flour blend to the eggplant puree. Continue cooking and beating. While beating, slowly add the milk. The consistency should now be like soft mashed potatoes. Stir in the grated cheese. Add salt and pepper to taste and serve.

Yield: 6 servings

United Arab Republic–
see Egypt

USSR – see Russia

Venezuela

CARACAS

TONY'S 65. The inhabitants of Caracas often refer to their modern city as a southern suburb of Miami Beach. It is a fast money city, at least for those who have money, and many in the capital of oil-rich Venezuela do. So many, in fact, that Caracas boasts dozens of first-rate restaurants—all serving European and North American dishes. Anyone searching for Venezuelan dishes in these restaurants would have about the same chance of finding them as he would in New York.

If truth be told, monied Venezuelans and members of the large foreign community in Caracas don't eat *pabellon* in public. That typical Venezuelan plate of fried shredded meat, rice, and black beans, usually served with an *arepa* (a hot, dry corn muffin), is too closely associated with the poverty and hard times that prevailed before the beginning of the oil boom in World War II.

When a Venezuelan of means dines out he will go, like as not, to a restaurant like Tony's 65 with its air of elegance. At each meal there are four large copper pots on rolling carts that contain the four featured main courses. One will undoubtedly be roast beef. As the maître d' lifts the lid off another, he will disclose a fish dish, perhaps lobster, trout, or Dover sole. Chances are the two other gleaming kettles will contain an exciting poultry preparation and a specialty such as roast suckling pig. In addition, there are numerous international dishes that can be ordered from a long menu, as well as starters like smoked trout or salmon, caviar, and other delicacies.

Getting to Tony's 65 is part of the joy of eating there, for there is no sign or other indication of its existence on Avenida Francisco de Miranda in the Centro Comercial Lido in the fashionable East End, or Sabana Grande, section of Caracas. But most hotel cab drivers and others not connected with the hotels know which unmarked door to drive up to, day or night. They have to know because in Caracas there are few street numbers.

Tony Grande, the owner-host, usually escorts his guests to their tables, whether they be tourists or, more likely, persons in top government or business circles. The restaurant is open for lunch and dinner, and because Caracas is not an inexpensive city a lunch with a cocktail can quite easily run to $10 a person. Dinner costs about 20 percent more. Unlike the host and staff, guests need not wear formal dress but should be in jacket and tie because money, though plentiful in Caracas, is still largely new and those who have it are expected to show they have it. During dinner a pianist helps drown out the sound of new money. Reservations are recommended. Phone 325-759 or 324-774.

—*H. J. Maidenberg*

West Germany—
see Germany

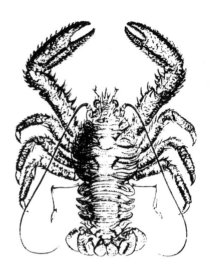

Yugoslavia

BELGRADE

IMA DANA. In this capital city of Yugoslavia a cluster of fine restaurants can be found in the old bohemian district of Skadarlija, which has been restored and closed to motor traffic. Each has a prewar Serbian atmosphere, but Ima Dana is best for diners who like excellent food, candlelight, fresh flowers, polite young waiters who speak English, and ballad singing soft enough to permit conversation in a normal voice.

Ima Dana is in a one-story building that once was the home of Milorad Gavrilovic, a theater director. The dining rooms have old ceramic stoves, hanging lamps, and portraits of Serbian notables. The decor is predominantly blue and yellow. No member of the staff is older than 30, one reason Ima Dana is popular with young intellectuals.

Although the restaurant opened just a few years ago, it has already won numerous gold medals at competitions. Diners usually begin with the hors d'oeuvres, which are brought to the table on a cart. Among the best of them are the stuffed eggs, sweet peppers stuffed with white cheese, and Serbian beans. Main courses include international as well as Serbian dishes, with the emphasis on grilled meats. A favorite is steak Skadarlija style, which is actually veal cutlet with grilled cheese on top.

The special pride of Ima Dana's director, Ratko Uljarevic, is *bosanski lonac* (Bosnian Pot), a sort of stew cooked for hours in a sealed vessel. It must be ordered at least half a day in advance. Also good is the lamb with scallions and spinach, served with yogurt on top, and the stuffed cabbage.

Ima Dana is at Skadarska 38, a few blocks from the Opera. The phone number is 334-422. An average bill for two diners, with hors d'oeuvres, main course, a bottle of wine, salad, and coffee, runs about $10 to $12, including the 10 percent service charge. Ima Dana is open seven days a week from 11 A.M. to 2 A.M. in the summer months and 11 A.M. to around midnight the rest of the year.

—*Raymond H. Anderson*

BOSANSKI LONAC
Based on the recipe of Ima Dana, Belgrade

This is a Bosnian stew, cooked in the oven in a sealed vessel.

2¼ pounds mixed pork, beef, and lamb, cubed
¾ pound potatoes, peeled and cubed
1 cup sliced cabbage
½ pound small white onions
¾ cup sliced leek (white part only)
1 cup diced carrots
2 heads garlic, peeled
1 cup diced celery
½ cup dry white wine
½ pound cherry tomatoes
¾ cup lard
paprika
black pepper
3 sprigs parsley

1. Preheat the oven to 350 degrees.
2. Combine all the ingredients in an earthenware pot or other ovenproof dish with a cover. Seal with 2 layers of heavy-duty aluminum foil and put on the cover.
3. Cook in the preheated oven for 3 to 4 hours.
4. To serve, take the pot to the table and remove the lid and foil before the diners, releasing all the appetizing aromas.

Yield: 4 servings

LAMB WITH SCALLIONS AND SPINACH
Based on the recipe of Ima Dana, Belgrade

1½ pounds lamb (preferably from a lean leg of lamb)
½ cup flour
1 tablespoon salt
3 tablespoons lard or oil
1 cup chopped scallions
2 cups water
2 tablespoons tomato paste
black pepper
2 pounds spinach
4 tablespoons plain yogurt

1. Cut the lamb into pieces about 2 inches by 1 inch. Rinse in cold water and dry well.
2. Put the flour and the salt into a paper bag. Put in the lamb pieces and shake the bag well. Remove the pieces, gently shake off the excess flour, and place the pieces individually on a plate.
3. Brown the lamb on all sides in 2 tablespoons lard or oil. At the same time, in a separate skillet, gently sauté the scallions in the remaining tablespoon lard or oil for 5 minutes, until tender and transluscent. Add the scallions to the lamb and sauté them together for a few minutes.
4. Add the water, tomato paste, and pepper to the lamb mixture. Stir thoroughly and let simmer, covered, for 40 minutes.
5. Wash the spinach leaves thoroughly, pick off stalks, and drain well. Add to the lamb mixture, pressing the leaves into the liquid. When the mixture begins to simmer again, cook it, uncovered, for 10 more minutes. The spinach should be almost tender; test by tasting.
6. Just before serving, spoon yogurt on top.

Yield: 4 servings

DUBROVNIK

RIBLJI RESTORAN. This lovely old walled city beside the clear blue Adriatic was for centuries a thriving mercantile republic and center of Dalmatian literature and culture. Today, because of its medieval architecture and other charms, Dubrovnik is one of Yugoslavia's prime tourist attractions, and the traveler's checks of as many as 40,000 foreign visitors at a time are an important part of the city's economic sustenance.

Dubrovnik has many fine restaurants, including some in luxury hotels outside its massive walls, but the special character of the city is perceived only within the walls, and it is there that hungry travelers will find the Riblji Restoran, a fine seafood place with a cheerful Adriatic ambience and a decor of fish nets, boat lights, and other maritime gear. Everything within the walls is a stone's throw, or at most a few hundred yards, from the restaurant.

The menu features lobster, shrimp, scallops, oysters, and a wide variety of fish. The fish that gourmets here praise most highly is called *zubatac*, and the way they like it is grilled over charcoal. Also good are the restaurant's lobster salad, which is boiled lobster meat atop a mixture of boiled carrots, potatoes, green peas, mayonnaise, and pickles, and the shrimp à la Riblji Restoran, which are batter fried and served with rice and a thin piquant mayonnaise sauce.

The Riblji Restoran is at Siroka 1, just off the shop-lined Stradun. The phone number is 275-89. An average bill for one person, with wine and tip, should run to about $5 or $6. The place is open seven days a week from before noon to 2 A.M.

—*Raymond H. Anderson*

LOBSTER SALAD
Based on the recipe of Riblji Restoran, Dubrovnik

1 3½–4 pound lobster
1 pound carrots
1 pound potatoes
1 pound shelled green peas
2 cucumber pickles, finely sliced
1½ cups mayonnaise (recipe below)
parsley for garnish
salt
black pepper

1. Insert a sharp knife between the lobster's body and tail shells, severing the spinal cord and killing it. Plunge the lobster, head first, into boiling water and cook until it is bright red, about 20 minutes. Remove it from the water, drain, and cool. Remove the meat from the shell and claws and cut into small pieces. Set aside the tail part of the shell for decoration.
2. Meanwhile, boil the vegetables separately until they are just tender. Cut the carrots and potatoes into small cubes. When all the vegetables are cool, mix them with the finely sliced pickles.
3. Bind the vegetable and pickle mixture together with the mayonnaise. Season to taste with salt and pepper.
4. Heap the vegetable salad on a large plate. Place the lobster pieces on top, decorate the dish with small sections of the lobster tail shell, and garnish with parsley.

Yield: 4 servings

MAYONNAISE

2 large egg yolks
½ teaspoon Dijon-type mustard
½ teaspoon sugar
1 teaspoon salt
white pepper
a few drops of lemon juice
2 tablespoons white wine vinegar
1 cup best French olive oil

1. To insure success all ingredients should be at room temperature. One can use a bowl and wooden spoon, whisk, egg beater, or an electric blender.
2. Put the egg yolks in the bowl with the mustard, sugar, salt, pepper, lemon juice, and 1 teaspoon of wine vinegar. Beat until the mixture thickens.
3. Add 2 tablespoons of olive oil, 2 drops at a time, beating constantly until the mixture is the consistency of heavy cream. Continue adding the oil, and as the sauce thickens, the oil can be added in a thin stream. When completed, the mayonnaise should be stiff enough to hold its shape and show the marks of a whisk or spoon. It is now ready for use.

Yield: 1½ cups

NOTE: If the mayonnaise starts to separate, you are adding the oil too quickly. However, it is easy to save. Begin again with 1 egg yolk, and instead of using oil steadily add the separated mayonnaise, beating all the time.

A NOTE ABOUT FOOD SOURCES

Specialty foods of all sorts are becoming increasingly available in the United States, if not at every crossroads store and corner grocery, then at least in big city department stores. Every reader must surely know one of these, but if not, Bloomingdale's, Lexington Ave. and 59th St., New York, N.Y. 10022, Macy's, Herald Sq., New York, N.Y. 10001, Marshall Field, 111 N. State St., Chicago, Ill. 60602, and City of Paris by Liberty House, Union Sq., San Francisco, Cal., 94119 can stand as prime examples. Their delicacies shops carry a vast assortment of gourmet items—tins of chanterelle and morel mushrooms, fresh green peppercorns in cans, truffles, artichoke bottoms, Chinese, Japanese, and Indonesian foods—the list is seemingly endless. And one of the nice things about these and most other department stores is that they fill mail orders, which means that you can live in the proverbial Podunk and still get your *pâté de fois gras*.

For specialty meats and game, including venison, bison, and pheasant, try J. Ottomanelli & Sons, 1155 First Avenue, New York 10021, or the Maryland Market, 412 Amsterdam Avenue, New York 10024. Both will ship meats in dry ice.

Throughout the country there are many stores specializing in the foods of a particular country or region. Some will fill mail orders, some won't, and some will fill them sometimes and not other times, depending on the size of the order and their mood on a particular day. Take your chances. A few are listed below:

CHINESE

Kam Shing Company, 2246 South Wentworth Street, Chicago, Ill. 60640

Wing Fat Company, 35 Mott Street, New York, N.Y. 10013

Wing Woh Lung Company, 50 Mott Street, New York, N.Y. 10013

Shing Chong & Company, 800 Grant Avenue, San Francisco, Cal. 94108

JAPANESE

Katagiri & Company, 224 East 59th Street, New York, N.Y. 10022

Japanese Foodland, 2620 Broadway, New York, N.Y. 10025

Japan Mart, Inc., 239 West 105th Street, New York, N.Y. 10025

PHILIPPINE

Filipinas International, Ltd., 528 Ninth Avenue, New York, N.Y. 10018

Filipino Lou, 533 Ninth Avenue, New York, N.Y. 10018

SPANISH AND LATÍN AMERICAN

Casa Moneo, 210 West 14th Street, New York, N.Y. 10011

MISCELLANEOUS SPECIALTIES (Spices, Italian Foods, Asian Foods, etc.)

Trinacria Importing Company, 415 Third Avenue, New York, N.Y. 10016

Index of Restaurants

Index of Recipes

LEE FOSTER has worked for *The New York Times* virtually all his adult life, coming to the paper straight from wartime service as a lieutenant in the Navy. He has been interested in food and travel as long as he can remember, and his first article in *The Times* was a column on the editorial page about such things as a seventeenth-century British naval punch for 6,000 that was mixed outdoors in a fountain and ladled out by a lad in a rowboat. His second article was about apples, his third, salads. He also wrote editorials for the paper, edited foreign news for eight years, was a contributor to *The Columbia Encyclopedia* and an editor of *The Times* Byline Books on international affairs. He subsequently became Associate Editor of *The Times* Book Division and later Editor-in-Chief of *The New York Times Encyclopedic Almanac*. Currently he is Assistant Travel Editor of *The Times* and happily involved with what are still his two favorite subjects—travel and food.

LESLIE FOSTER has had a commitment to the culinary arts ever since her marriage to the editor of this book twenty years ago, and she has prepared dishes from most of the world's cuisines in her own kitchen. Her professional career in urban affairs has been intertwined with food, too. She has evaluated school lunch programs, prepared a federal report on the nutritional needs of the elderly, analyzed employment projects in the food-service field and most recently completed a survey of the restaurant industry in New York City.

MAY WONG TRENT is the author of *80 Precious Chinese Recipes* and *Oriental Barbecues*. She served as a consultant on Time/Life's *Chinese Cooking*, and contributed the Chinese recipes to Pearl Buck's *Oriental Cookbook*. She teaches cooking in New York and demonstrates it throughout the country. Mrs. Trent, who was born and brought up in Hong Kong and attended the university there, studied cooking at the London Cordon Bleu. She is married to an American and now makes her home in Manhattan.

MOLLIE E. C. WEBSTER was born and educated in England, holds a diploma from the London Cordon Bleu and continued her cooking studies with James Beard and at the China Institute. An interviewer on British television before coming to the United States, she subsequently worked at Time/Life books, where she helped produce several volumes in the Foods of the World series. Married and living in New York, she contributes to *Gourmet* magazine and is currently at work on a book about England that will include both local history and recipes.